T0373426

DUMBARTON OAKS
MEDIEVAL LIBRARY

Jan M. Ziolkowski, General Editor

POETIC WORKS

BERNARDUS SILVESTRIS

DOML 38

Poetic Works

Bernardus Silvestris

Edited and Translated by

WINTHROP WETHERBEE

DUMBARTON OAKS
MEDIEVAL LIBRARY

Harvard University Press
CAMBRIDGE, MASSACHUSETTS
LONDON, ENGLAND
2015

Printed in the United States of America

Library of Congress Cataloging-in-Publication Data
Bernard Silvestris, active 1136, author.
Poetic works / Bernardus Silvestris ; edited and translated by Winthrop Wetherbee.
pages cm—(Dumbarton Oaks medieval library ; 38)
ISBN 978-0-674-74378-6 (alk. paper)
I. Wetherbee, Winthrop, 1938– II. Bernard Silvestris, active 1136. Poems. English. 2015. III. Bernard Silvestris, active 1136. Poems. 2015. IV. Title. V. Series: Dumbarton Oaks medieval library ; 38.
PA8275.B25A2 2015
871′.03—dc23 2014032673

Contents

Introduction

Little is known about the life of Bernardus Silvestris beyond his devotion to Tours. The city is recalled affectionately in the *Cosmographia,* and a nephew inherited Bernardus's house there.[1] His *Cosmographia* contains a handsome compliment to Pope Eugenius III, and a gloss declares that the work was read "in his presence in Gaul,"[2] presumably during the pope's visit to France in 1147. A manuscript of the *Mathematicus* has been dated between 1145 and 1153, and a brief *epitaphium Bernardi Silvestris* is tentatively dated around 1160.[3]

Bernardus's writings define a figure remarkably representative of the scholastic culture of his place and time, the student of scholars who were pioneers in philosophy and science, and a renowned teacher of *dictamen* and the art of poetry. His versatility is clearly seen in his masterpiece, the *Cosmographia,* a synthesis of important intellectual movements of the early twelfth century and a foundational text for later Latin and vernacular literature.

1. Twelfth-Century Intellectual Culture

France in Bernardus's lifetime was an expanding, affluent, and relatively peaceful society. Governance was increasingly administered on the basis of written law and required men trained in the verbal arts as administrators. Schools, and particularly cathedral schools in urban centers, assumed a new importance. Clerical literacy had been an important aim of the Gregorian reform movement, and the schools had long played an important role in court culture, but in the later eleventh century education began to take new forms; traditional models and authorities were challenged by a new emphasis on reasoned argumentation, the resolution of conflicts between authorities, skill in disputation. This development largely reflects the availability of new paths to advancement, and certain schools were fiercely criticized for offering careerists a superficial education in the verbal arts.[4] But the new openness of the scholastic environment was an attractive force in itself. The scope of the traditional liberal arts curriculum was enlarged by newly available texts, many of them translated from Arabic sources in southern Italy and Spain, and a newly investigative approach to the traditional disciplines.

That the liberal arts were the gateway to wisdom had been dogma since the Carolingian period, but the arts now became the basis for an intellectual project, a "scientific humanism," which sought to restore the knowledge lost by mankind through the Fall.[5] Essential to this reconstruction was an understanding of the laws of nature, the organization of the universe, and the divine purpose of a creation in which mankind occupied the central position.[6] This movement is commonly associated with the cathedral school at Chartres, where a number of the leaders of this movement were teachers. Chartres seems clearly to have been a center of the new learning,[7] but it was also a stronghold of traditional pedagogical values. The *Metalogicon* of John of Salisbury (1159) describes the program of study at Chartres as grounded in the *cohaerentia artium,* a synthesis of the verbal arts, or *trivium* (grammar, dialectic, and rhetoric), and the sciences, or *quadrivium* (arithmetic, music, geometry, and astronomy).[8] Its aim, as expressed by Thierry, chancellor of Chartres and almost certainly one of Bernardus's teachers, was to lead students to "the coherent understanding of the true nature of existence."[9]

For Thierry, and for William of Conches, another of Bernardus's probable mentors, such understanding was largely a matter of decoding the cosmology of Plato's *Timaeus,* read in the partial translation of Calcidius and augmented by his commentary.[10] The *Timaeus* teaches that the soul is "somehow akin to the stars and the sky," in a universe that is a living being, shaped by a creator god in conformity with an ideal model.[11] To the extent that Plato's cosmic exemplar and world soul are divine attributes, this god is brought into intimate contact with his handiwork. From the *Timaeus,* says William of Conches (ca. 1085–after 1154), we not only attain "perfect understanding of philosophy," but "when divine power and wisdom and goodness are seen in the creation of things, we fear one so powerful, venerate one so wise, love one so benevolent."[12]

By his own account William was a lover of Plato,[13] but over the course of his long career, he became increasingly concerned with the character of the elements and natural process. His final work, the *Dragmaticon,* makes clear the unique power of God, who by his word alone created the elements and from them heaven and earth; but thereafter, by the assent of the divine will,[14] the work of generation is delegated to created powers. The interaction of the fiery stars with the other elements produces living creatures,[15] and ongoing life is sustained by a power that has effectively absorbed the cosmic function of the world soul, and which William now calls *natura,* "a certain force implanted in things producing similar from similar."[16]

Thierry, in his *Treatise on the Work of the Six Days,* proposes to interpret the Genesis cosmogony *secundum phyisicam,* and places a similar emphasis on the autonomy of natural forces. Once God has created matter, the fiery celestial sphere—all-encompassing and hence incapable of locomotion, but volatile and hence incapable of remaining still—begins its rotation, and its heat and light act on the other elements.[17] Each of its full rotations constitutes a day of the Mosaic narrative, and when these have run their course, ongoing life in the universe is sustained by "seminal causes" implanted in the elements, which become in effect a closed system. The focus on natural process is particularly striking in the work of a scholar like Thierry, most of whose writings deal with questions raised by the *opuscula sacra* of Boethius and reveal the influence of works such as the *Asclepius,* a late-antique translation of a Greek hermetic work that offered twelfth-century scholars a concise, Neoplatonized version of Aristotelian and Stoic physics.[18] The same concern with causality has been seen in Thierry's commentary on Cicero's *De inventione,* reflecting the coherence of his view of knowledge and his commitment to discovering "the truth of those things that exist, those things that are unchanging."[19] In William's case the new emphasis is largely due to an awareness of Arab medicine, as transmitted in the translations of Constantine the African. Both of these influences appear clearly in the *Cosmographia,* which gives expression to the full range of the thought of his mentors, beginning in the mind of God and ending with a careful account of human physiology.

The defining framework for the thought of both scholars, as for Bernardus in the *Cosmographia,* remained the *Timaeus,* which had rich implications for literature as well as for philosophy and science. Plato's cosmogony is avowedly a "likely story," a myth; the creation it describes is the work of a ποιητής, a maker of myths.[20] Plato's "gods" are heavenly bodies distinct from the Olympian gods. They were fused allegorically by Hellenistic writers, and the *Timaeus* largely defined the scope of serious mythography for late antiquity and the Middle Ages, but Plato's mythic cosmology had an importance of its own.[21] The dialogue is continually cited in Macrobius's commentary on the *Somnium Scipionis,* an authoritative source for the cosmology in terms of which ancient literature was read,[22] and a brilliant poetic distillation of the Timaean cosmology is the centerpiece of Boethius's *Consolation of Philosophy.* The *Timaeus* and its tradition profoundly influenced the twelfth century's conception of classical poetry, and it offered a distinctive conception of myth and its function: the myths of the poets could harbor deep meaning, but a writer gifted with originality and vision, a Bernardus Silvestris, could, like Plato, create myths of his own.

2. Bernardus as Teacher

In the mid-twelfth century, scholars like William and Thierry, scholars in the tradition idealized by John of Salisbury's almost mythical portrayal of Bernard of Chartres,[23] who could deploy a curriculum based on the *cohaerentia artium* to study man and the universe scientifically, were becoming obsolescent. A more rigorous division among the branches of learning was emerging, in which grammar and the study of ancient *auctores* would play a restricted role.

Bernardus's career reflects this transition. Tours, where he apparently spent his teaching career,[24] had been a center of literary culture since the time of Alcuin. From 1125 to 1133 its archbishop was Hildebert of Lavardin (ca. 1056–1133), the finest Latin poet of the early twelfth century,[25] and from the mid-century the city was an important center for the teaching of *dictamen,*[26] or composition. Bernardus was renowned as a teacher of this art, and Matthew of Vendôme proudly recalls having learned *dictamen* from "Master Silvestris, gem of learning, pride of the schools."[27] The *Flores rhetorici,* the earliest known French treatise on *dictamen,* may well be by Bernardus and suggests the likely character of his teaching.[28] It follows Italian models, but is largely devoted to metaphor, and prescribes a complex, allusive style reflecting the traditional emphasis of French schools on the study of classical authors and the writing of Latin poetry.[29] Bernardus was traditionally credited with a masterly treatise on *dictamen,* but the *ars dictaminis* attributed to him by its modern editor is certainly not his,[30] and the modest *Flores rhetorici* seems unlikely to have enjoyed such renown. The masterwork in question is probably the *Cosmographia,* exemplary rather than prescriptive of excellence in composition, as attested by the rich allusions in the widely influential *Poetria nova* of Geoffrey of Vinsauf (ca. 1210) and the reverence of Gervase of Melkley, for whom the *Cosmographia* is the illustration *par excellence* of the art of poetry.[31]

3. The *Cosmographia*

The dignity of man and the meaning of the natural order with which man's nature has profound affinities assume aesthetic form in Bernardus's *Cosmographia.* Its ultimate model is the *Timaeus,* but it is deeply indebted to the tradition of the *prosimetrum,* represented most meaningfully by two great allegories of spiritual pilgrimage, the *De nuptiis Philologiae et Mercurii* of Martianus Capella and Boethius's *Consolation.*

For Bernardus, the allegory of the *De nuptiis,* the marriage that frames Martianus's presentation of the liberal arts, was a serious exercise in Neoplatonist philosophy. Mercury's marriage with Philology gives a transcendent significance to the union of learning with eloquence: as Jove's messenger, Mercury is an aspect of the divine mind, *ο νοῦς sacer,* as well as Jove's "genius" or angel.[32] Philology, in preparation for her ascent to the palace of Jove, is visited by the Muses, who reveal to her the true, divinely illumined meaning of the liberal arts, and through her marriage the human mind will attain a visionary understanding of the presence of the divine in all things.

The prose of the *De nuptiis,* as Bernardus recognized, reflects the movement of the narrative through the universe. There is a somber power in the description of Mercury's long wandering, through abandoned shrines where oracle and augury have been silenced, before coming to an idealized Delphi, where Apollo greets him with a dazzling prophecy of his marriage and its implications.[33] The vivid response of the physical universe as Apollo and Mercury ascend to heaven, a passage that culminates in their respective transformations to sun and planet, elicits correspondingly exuberant prose; and a ritual solemnity informs Philology's prayer when, arrived at the "vast fields of light" of the empyrean, she wonders at the hidden power by which the whole universe is moved and prays to "the truth which exists by virtue of powers beyond existence."[34] All of these moments have their counterparts in the *Cosmographia.*

The *Consolation of Philosophy* is set in a prison cell rather than in the universe at large, but the imagery of cosmic order is central to the dialogue. The Prisoner recalls a time when Philosophy had made his life conform to "the pattern of the ordered heavens," and when his inner darkness is dispelled, he looks to heaven and recovers self-awareness.[35] Philosophy's cosmological hymns, offering the hope of an integrating vision and further enlightenment, are audible at many points in the *Cosmographia,* but audible too is a darker note, telling of the constant struggle required to achieve liberation from the ties, fears, and confusions of life in the world.

Deeply indebted to these *auctores,* the *Cosmographia* remains a radically original work, like the *Timaeus* itself. Its *personae* are not partners in a Boethian dialogue, and their roles are more complex than those of Martianus's elaborate pantheon.[36] They are cosmic principles engaged in continuous, dynamic interaction, a creative process that issues in what Silverstein aptly calls a "fabulous cosmogony."

4. *Megacosmus.* Cosmogony and Cosmology

The *Cosmographia* opens with the appeal of *Natura* to *Noys,* the divine wisdom, on behalf of unformed matter, called both *Silva* and *Hyle.* Noys responds by separating and ordering the elements, creating the forms of a universe and its creatures, and producing *Endelechia,* the informing spirit of physical life.

It is clear that Noys partakes of godhead. Nature calls her *deus orta deo;* brought forth by primal Being "of itself, a second self," she is "one in nature with God and not distinct in substance." But she specifies her role as "the knowledge and judgment of the divine will *in the disposition of created things,*" a subordinate office exclusively engaged with the created universe.[37] And Noys is susceptible to something like emotion: Nature observes a certain sadness in her, and Noys confesses herself concerned about the disorderly state of her domain.[38]

Nature's very presence is startling, for "nature" at this stage can hardly amount to more than the innate desire of Hyle for form.[39] As the "blessed fertility" of the womb of Noys, born like Noys herself, of the primal Being, Nature exists before time, but her role, like her name, is in effect a future participle, a fruitfulness yet to issue into existence. But her strikingly human voice is fully formed and arouses Noys to creative action.

Nature will later be defined astrologically, as "elementing" Nature, "sovereign principle" of cosmic life,[40] adapting the elements to their natural activity and ensuring the continuous reproduction of creatures. In *Microcosmus* 11 she is assigned to join the human soul and body created by Urania and Physis, and her ongoing function will be the informing of bodies with souls transmitted from above. As such she is recognizably the "mother of generation," to whom the natural world joyfully responds when she descends to earth in

Microcosmus 9. But she learns her identity only over time. As Bernardus emphasizes repeatedly, the universe is pervaded by knowledge, and Nature acquires this knowledge, through the discourses of Noys and Urania and through her own observation, as she ascends and descends through the spheres.[41]

Matter, *Silva* or *Hyle,*[42] is necessarily limited to a passive role in the cosmic drama, but its importance is made clear. It is on behalf of Silva that Nature first appeals to Noys, and the refinement of Silva is the principal concern of the cosmogony of *Megacosmus* 2. The vivid celebration of the life of the universe in *Megacosmus* 4 reminds us that the all-encompassing life of Silva, what Bernardus calls "the spirit of an eternal vitality," is present also in the universe born of Silva: the creatures that come to be and pass away are manifestations of a larger, constant life. As Urania declares, drawing a lesson for Nature from their tour of the universe, "form flows away, the essence of the thing remains; the power of death destroys nothing, but only disunites united parts."

But Silva poses fundamental problems, inherited from the *Timaeus.* Plato did not assume an omnipotent creator-God capable of producing matter out of nothing. His Demiurge begins its work with an existing medium, a "receptacle" suffused with a chaos of elemental qualities.[43] Creation is "the triumph of reasonable persuasion over necessity," necessity denoting the condition of the ungoverned elements.[44]

A preexistent, discordant matter presents the danger of a dualist view of the universe, and both Thierry and William of Conches avoid any such suggestion in describing material creation.[45] But the first words of the *Cosmographia* are *conge-*

ries informis (formless, chaotic mass), and Bernardus makes clear that matter harbors perverse tendencies, a *malignitas* that will remain latent in creation, a threat to unstable mankind. This idea is derived largely from Calcidius, who offers several interpretations,[46] and also credits Silva with an aptitude and desire for form, so that as the formative qualities of the elements become fully realized, it lends itself "willingly" to their refining influence.[47]

Having brought the elemental properties into a cooperative relation, and created the physical elements, Noys next produces Endelechia, who corresponds to the World Soul of the *Timaeus.* But Bernardus first devotes a long paragraph to Noys herself, defining her as in effect the mind of God, an understanding that encompasses the intelligible universe, where all history and the forms of all life are preconceived. She is the origin of "life and light," a dynamic role made clear by the echoing of this phrase as Endelechia, "the life and light of creation," emerges, like the biblical Wisdom, "by a sort of emanation."[48]

Abelard, William of Conches, and Thierry of Chartres had seen in Plato's World Soul an adumbration of the Holy Spirit.[49] Bernardus calls Endelechia "soul," though her fiery energy *(fomes vivificus)* sustains only physical life, and the souls she imparts are accidental forms. In emphasizing her divine origin Bernardus anticipates the depiction of cosmic life in *Megacosmus* 4, which stresses the intimate involvement of divine powers, Noys and the *Usia primaeva* itself, as well as Nature and Endelechia, in the life of the material universe.

The infusion of Endelechia's vital energy initiates the final stage of cosmic creation in *Megacosmus* 2: the procession of created life "unfolds" from the womb of Silva, as the *ordo fatalis* "unfolds" from all-embracing Providence in Boethius's classic account.[50] The process is represented panoramically in *Megacosmus* 3, where wide-ranging surveys of geography and vividly detailed catalogs of trees, plants, and animals supplement traditional cosmological and astronomical material.

What Boethius calls Fate becomes in *Megacosmus* 4 the manifold operation of Nature, Endelechia, and the serial law, *Imarmene,* which ensures the continuity of birth and death in the world.[51] Bernardus makes plain that the ultimate source of cosmic life is the wisdom of a single supreme divinity, the *Usia primaeva,* but the further stages of the process are described in astrological terms, as the heavens are informed with the "knowledge" they will transmit to the sublunar world through a series of secondary causes.

Bernardus's astrology has been seen to reflect the influence of the *Greater Introduction to Astrology (Introductorium maius)* of Abu Ma'shar,[52] which provided a scientific rationale for astrology, drawing on Aristotelian physics and cosmology to explain how celestial motion and divine disposition effect generation and corruption in the terrestrial world.[53] Such ideas are clearly at work in *Megacosmus* 4, where Nature is identified with the firmament and the stars, which "adapt the elements to their natural activity," but a source at least equally important is the *Asclepius,* which, like the *Cosmographia* itself, discusses hierarchy and continuity in the universe, the principles of created life, and the position of man, within the cosmic system and in his relation to the divine. It affirms divine transcendence but places a marked Stoic emphasis on the immanence of the divine, a God whose beneficent influence is expressed largely in astrological terms.

All creatures, says Bernardus, derive "the causes and nature" of their subsistence from the heavens, as if from "a life-giving god." Noys is the source of a *ratio* that becomes an "ethereal fire," the creative principle of Stoic physics;[54] Endelechia is in effect this energy personified, the ethereal *fomes,* which the planets draw from the celestial sphere and transmit to the lower world, to generate the life that the earth then sustains. All of this is expressed concisely in the *Asclepius.* There too the heavens are "a sensible god," governor of all bodily existence;[55] fire descends from above with vivifying power, while what emanates from the earth below is nurturing; soul and matter, embraced by Nature, are "agitated" to produce the infinite variety of species.[56]

Matter (Hyle) "comes first," Bernardus tells us, followed by "elementing" Nature, who draws from Hyle the "simple" or "pure" elements that, in themselves unchanging, generate the baser physical elements, or *elementata.* "The spirit of an eternal vitality" has informed Hyle from the beginning and ensures that the material components of universal life respond to the formative influences that descend from above. It makes the universe as a whole an animal, informed by knowledge, responsive to the guidance of soul.

In creating a Noys who is "one in nature with God" and at the same time active in the physical life of the universe, Bernardus comes as close as possible to drawing God himself into play, and he complements this bold invention with a Silva who is palpably real, utterly distinct from the scarcely existent preelemental matter of William and Thierry. Virtually every sentence of *Megacosmus* 4 aims to express continuity and immanence.

The final factor in the cosmic process is time, "the moving image of eternity,"[57] which ensures that the universe is as nearly as possible "eternized" in emulation of its divine model. Bernardus's discussion of time is in effect a meditation. Time and all that it contains are born from eternity and resolved again into eternity, and were it not for the necessity of movement, time would be identical with eternity.

5. *Microcosmus*

After Noys has celebrated her creation in prose and verse, Nature is instructed to seek Urania and Physis, who will assist her in creating Man. She first ascends to the firmament, where Urania studies the stars, then descends with Urania to earth, where Physis dwells in paradisal Gramision, imagining humankind as if in a dream.

After long wandering, Nature is guided to Urania by a venerable "Usiarch," whose office is to "delineate and give shape to things," conforming them to "whatever likeness the motion of the heavens imparts." His role combines a Platonist view of form with the astrological view that differentiation among creatures is caused by the revolution of the heavens.[58] Urania too is both Platonist and astrologer, and her role is defined in religious terms.[59] She knows Nature's mission "by divine insight." Their "sacred" mission requires divine favor, and a vivid description of the dwelling of Tugaton, the supreme divinity,[60] frames their prayer.

Urania will impart wisdom to the human soul by guiding

it through the heavens, as in the *Timaeus,* to learn "the nature of the universe and the laws of destiny."[61] Once encased in a fleshly body it will lose this awareness, but Man can recover it through the arts and philosophy and, as Noys will later declare, realize his true role as "ruler and high priest" of the universe.[62]

Urania's anthem of greeting ends by declaring Nature the guide whom it is always right to follow. Though the Nature we have seen seems uncertain of her path and role, the lines are prophetic: Man will realize his dignity and destiny by understanding Nature as the ordering presence in the universe she informs. Nature first appears as a goddess in the *Cosmographia,*[63] and Urania's words anticipate the Nature whom Alan of Lille will celebrate as "leader, source, life, light, splendor, beauty, form, universal law."[64]

As the goddesses descend they encounter Psyche, the human soul, in the circle of the Sun. Martianus had called Psyche "daughter of Endelechia and the Sun," and the "fiery beams" that she gathers from the Sun also recall Martianus, describing the gifts with which Psyche has been endowed by the gods. These include Vulcan's bestowal of *igniculi,* fiery beams of "unquenchable perennity," lest she be "shrouded in dark night."[65] For Carolingian glossators this gift was *ingenium* (apprehension and imagination), the means, according to Eriugena, whereby the soul preserves some memory of its original dignity and vision.[66] The Psyche of the *Cosmographia* is preparing herself to be the vessel of the knowledge that Urania will impart.

As the goddesses enter the atmosphere, Urania delivers a second poetic address, which includes a stern vision of the soul, bound to body and menaced by the tyranny of the flesh, followed by thoughts on death, its power over physical life, and the finally illusory nature of that power. Death is reduced to a moment in the larger, ongoing existence of a universe that enjoys perpetual life. The "vitalizing spark" of life imparted to every creature by Endelechia is given back at death, but the "spirit of Silva" lives on, and matter will realize itself in ever new forms.[67]

Though our initial vision of Gramision, home of Physis and her two daughters, recalls the Eden of *Megacosmus* 3, Physis is shown pondering the disruptions that affect the constitution of animals, "the shifting influence of mutability," and probing the curative properties of the elements. She deploys learning of a new, practical kind, combining an expert knowledge of physical properties with an astrological understanding of the elemental composition of things, and her preoccupation suggests the challenges man will face in his natural environment.

The central role Physis will play in the concluding chapters of *Microcosmus* is further defined by the Book of Memory, bestowed by Noys to aid her in her work. The Mirror of Providence, given to Urania, shows creation issuing from the divine mind, and Nature's gift, the Table of Fate, reveals truth as manifest in the temporal order. The Book of Memory does not engage the higher realm, but records intellectual work directly concerned with the largely mysterious workings of elemental nature. It will enable Man in some measure to regulate his own nature, adapting it to principles empirically deduced and experimentally mastered, a process of trial and error that Physis herself undergoes in fashioning the human body. But it must at the same time be grounded in natural philosophy in the larger sense, drawing on a knowledge of causes and principles that cannot be gained from observation alone.

As the creation of Man goes forward, only the work of Physis is described,[68] and *Microcosmus* 13 emphasizes its difficulty, contrasting the divine ordering of Hyle with the inability of Physis to follow the divine pattern. Frustrated by inferior materials, Physis works empirically, experiencing shame, doubt, frustration, and anger, but in the end she replicates the creative process of the *Megacosmus,* disciplining the elements and shaping Man on the model of the greater universe, a creative effort that combines practical knowledge with poetic and philosophical vision.[69]

The effort this has required is concealed in the clinical anatomy of the concluding poem, but it is recalled by the somber final lines, on the ceaseless warfare of human generation against the threat of annihilation. The experience of Physis illustrates the resourcefulness that will be essential to survival and well being in a universe where, whatever his spiritual destiny, Man's physical existence is a brief and minor event.[70]

Bernardus's emphasis on Physis reflects the shifting intellectual currents of his time. The detailed account of the physics of creation reflects a newly practical emphasis in the study of the natural world, which cannot be reconciled easily or completely with an idealist or hierarchical view of the relation of the universe to God. Theology and natural science are becoming as Urania and Physis, and the waning of the older, "Chartrian" Platonist vision is suggested by the role of Nature, who seems a faltering presence in the metaphysical realm of Noys and Urania but receives an orgasmic welcome in Gramision.

6. The Religious Significance of the *Cosmographia*

The question of orthodoxy seems not to have troubled Pope Eugenius, or the Cistercians who summoned him to France, when the *Cosmographia* was read in his presence, but it has provoked debate in modern times. Gilson declared it an essentially orthodox commentary on Genesis;[71] Curtius saw only a "pagan Humanism" that omitted "everything Christian except for a few ultimate essentials."[72]

For Gilson, Bernardus's Noys was plainly the Word, second person of the Trinity. But Noys is clearly feminine, and for Curtius this was sufficient to invalidate Gilson's reading.[73] A way out of this impasse was shown by Silverstein, who suggested viewing Noys as "a separate fabulous construction," a "figurative representative" of the Word.[74]

Silverstein's careful words nicely define the literary mode of the *Cosmographia,* a type of allegory that, for Bernardus and his mentors, was classically exemplified by the *Timaeus.* Plato's "likely story" treats the known world as the image of a higher world that can be represented only in this imaginary way: *Sensilis hic mundus, mundi melioris imago,* in the words of Noys. For Abelard and William of Conches a representation of this kind was an *involucrum* or *integumentum,* a veil or covering of language that conceals, but figuratively represents, an underlying truth,[75] and played a role in the work of secular *auctores* close to that of allegory in biblical texts.[76]

The license that enables Abelard to read theological meaning into Plato's cosmology is close to that which produces the *personae* of the *Cosmographia,* none of whom can be assigned a precise theological definition. Noys is not the divine Wisdom, but represents the role of Wisdom in creation and is subject to the divine will in all that she does.[77] Endelechia, Nature, Urania, and Physis express this will as they inform and order the universe. The true God dwells beyond, *extramundanus,* and his "threefold majesty" can be approached only in prayer.[78] When Bernardus speaks of a realm of "pure and uncontaminated light" and adds that this is the abode of God *summi et superessentialis* ("if you give credence to theological arguments"),[79] it is not the existence of such a realm that he is questioning but the attempt to define it in orthodox terms. Whenever his *fabula* approaches the realm of the truly divine, he avoids precise definition: what might seem a straightforward reference to the threefold majesty *(trinae maiestati)* of the Trinity is prefaced by *cuidam;* the viewers, Nature, and Urania recognize this supreme power but do not possess full knowledge of its nature.

The roles and work of Bernardus's goddesses can also be compared to the magnificent Christian Neoplatonist system of Eriugena, in which creation is a sequence of manifestations of the divine:

> When [God] first descends from the superessentiality of his own nature, in which he may be said not to "be," he is created by himself in the primordial causes, and becomes the principle of all essence, all life, all intelligence, and all those things which gnostic theory considers in their primordial causes.

In God's "creation of himself" we may see the genesis of the "goddesses" of the *Cosmographia.* Noys can be seen as God in his role as "principle of all essence," the exemplary cause of creation in its dynamic aspect; her children, Endelechia, Urania, Nature, and Physis, are the primordial causes of created life. It would perhaps be overinterpreting to relate the desire of Silva for a new birth to the impulse that informs material creation in Eriugena's vast scheme of emanation and return, but similarities of language and idea suggest that Bernardus was at least aware of this aspect of Eriugena's system.[80]

A broader problem is the tendency of any Platonist system to detemporalize the order of things and deemphasize the pivotal events of sacred history. When man, the microcosm, falls prey to his lower nature, salvation, what Hugh of St. Victor calls the *opus restaurationis,* consists in a renewal of participation in the cosmic harmony and a rediscovery of the divine likeness within—in effect the destiny promised by Urania and Noys. The unfolding of sacred history becomes hard to trace, and Jolivet can complain that the *Cosmographia* presents Christ as just one in a chain of heroes, his baptism one in a series of events involving rivers.[81]

The relation of sacred to cosmic history is further complicated by Bernardus's apparent acceptance of astrological determinism. Bernardus was certainly not the author or translator of the *Experimentarius,* a work designed to enable the user to determine *sortes* or make predictions, prompted by the stars, but a preface has been attributed to him that includes a brief, lucid statement of the value of an understanding of the influence of the planets and constellations on the world below: "God permits mortals, seriously and sensibly inquiring about future or distant events, to discover many things through careful consideration of these constellations."[82] Astrology was emerging as an important branch of study in the mid-twelfth century: celestial influence is vividly defined in *Megacosmus* 4, and the connection of medicine with astrology is an important concern for Physis. But Bernardus nowhere defines the relation between fate as revealed in the stars and human freedom. The difficulties of the human condition are made plain, but they are balanced by affirmations of man's power to determine his destiny for himself.

In *Megacosmus* 3 the panorama of human history foretold in the stars concludes with a couplet on the birth of Christ, which, appended to a survey of pagan history, can seem to be subsumed to the continuum of fated events.[83] But the language of Bernardus's couplet can also be read as countering the determinist emphasis of what has gone before, emphasizing a new, authentic manifestation of God, an orientative power superior to those that have driven the violent course of secular history.[84] And as Albertus Magnus will observe, commenting on Abu Ma'shar's account of the astral prophecy of Christ, Christ himself caused his miraculous birth to be foretold in this way.[85]

7. The *Cosmographia* as Literature

The *Cosmographia* represents an attempt to engage the classical tradition as Bernardus understood that tradition. Its broadest and deepest debt is to the tradition of philosophical allegory, the *Timaeus,* the *Somnium Scipionis,* the *prosimetra* of Martianus and Boethius, and the commentaries on these works, but Bernardus is also fully aware of classical Latin poetry. Nature's opening appeal is informed by a range of poetic voices. It clearly recalls Ovid's description of the *rudis indigestaque moles* from which the world emerged, and the *De raptu Proserpinae* of Claudian, where Jupiter reports the complaints of Nature at the harsh life that denies fulfillment to man's divine gifts.[86] There are echoes of the great prayer of Boethius's Philosophy for stability and illumination. But there are less elevated notes as well:

> What does it avail Silva, mother of all, that her birth preceded all others, if she is deprived of light, abounds only in darkness, cut off from her fulfillment?—if, finally, in this wretched condition, her countenance is such as to frighten her very creator?

The very humanness of this challenge, its restrained but audible irony, is augmented by the theological absurdity of the final reproach. The sense of wrong and the hint of self-righteousness, which recall the *Heroides,* are balanced elsewhere in Nature's appeal by echoes of the *Ars amatoria,* where the disarming of a coy mistress is compared to the imposition of order on the *confusa moles* of the primordial chaos.[87]

I have said that Bernardus's career marks a transition in the activity of the schools, and this transition is perhaps reflected in the remark of Gervase of Melkley that the author of the *Cosmographia* is "a nightingale in verse, a parrot in prose."[88] To Gervase, at a distance of some seventy years, Bernardus's double commitment, as a Platonist-cosmologist in the tradition of William and Thierry and as a teacher of poetry and *dictamen,* may have been hard to understand. Prose passages studded with technical terminology and heavy with verbatim quotations from difficult late-antique *auctores* might well seem parroted and pedantic.

But the interplay of poetry and prose achieves remarkable effects: the cascading hexameters of Nature's opening appeal are answered by the more solemn rhythms of prose, where vivid description is interspersed with meditation; the panorama of cosmic life that follows in *Megacosmus* 3 is then glossed by a richly reiterative prose celebration of the forces that underlie and sustain this life.[89] The prose is remarkably versatile and keeps us constantly aware of what is at stake in Bernardus's narrative, as in this description of chaotic Hyle:

> Erat Hyle Naturae vultus antiquissimus, generationis uterus indefessus, formarum prima subiectio, materia corporum, substantiae fundamentum. Ea siquidem capacitas, nec terminis nec limitibus circumscripta, tantos sinus tantamque a principio continentiam explicavit, quantam rerum universitas exposcebat.
>
> Hyle was Nature's most ancient manifestation, the inexhaustible womb of generation, the primal ground of bodily form, the matter of bodies, the foundation of substantive existence. From the beginning this capaciousness, confined by no boundaries or limits, unfolded such vast recesses and such scope for growth as the totality of creatures demanded.

The vast thing being described is chaos, but before exploring it we are given this prefatory sentence in which every word emphasizes the rich capacity of Hyle, the fecundity that will give rise to the *rerum universitas.* What follows is the most densely technical portion of the chapter, as the elemental properties are distinguished and aligned, but this leads to an almost lyric account of the elements, newly freed, coming forth to assume their cosmic roles. Bernardus then pauses to reflect on Noys, a solemn litany of the attributes of divine wisdom followed by the intricate account of Endelechia, whose shape and substance can be perceived only intellectually. In such passages there is a beauty that the poetry cannot convey.

The long poem in which created life emerges from the womb of Silva is a display of creative energy that seems increasingly to assume a life of its own. Bernardus describes the heaven of the fixed stars, and the events they cryptically unfold, largely in terms of writing and signification,[90] summarized in a concluding couplet that by its gracefulness reminds us that the writing is that of Bernardus as well as of God:

> Sic opifex, ut in ante queant ventura videri
> saecula, sidereis significata modis.

> Thus the Creator works, that ages to come may be beheld in advance, signified in starry forms.

There is a definite pattern to this astrological catalog. Prototypes of wisdom, beauty, strength are coupled with examples of vanity and treachery. Chivalry and *clergie* are balanced: learned Greece is paired with warlike Rome, Plato with Achilles, Ulysses with Hercules.

As the account of creation descends to earth, a sense of spontaneity emerges: the traits of the various creatures are drawn seemingly at random from mythology, folklore, ancient science, and sheer whimsy. The catalogs show little attention to chronology or geography but tend to conclude with details that bring western and sometimes northern Europe into play. That the catalog of rivers ends with the Loire, shimmering as it flows past Bernardus's native Tours, may be no more than charming *pietas.* But this is preceded by a couplet on the Seine, and the warlike land that has produced the lines of Pippin and Charles. A survey of mountains devoted almost entirely to Greece and the Middle East ends with a couplet on the Alps and, apparently, the Pyrenees, followed by two couplets on the barrenness and danger of mountain terrain. A deft couplet concludes the catalog of "groves" with the strange names of three French forests. These passages seem to hint at something undomesticated in northern Europe: French soil that spawns warriors, as it were, by nature, set against the sanctity of St. Martin; forests very different from the poetic and scholarly groves of the classical past; mountain terrain as hostile as Dante's *selva oscura.* It is as if Bernardus were calling attention to the new and peculiar difficulties of his project in its cultural aspect.

Sic enim cohaeserunt principia principibus. This might be the motto of *Megacosmus* 4. As Frank Bezner has well shown, the chapter is concerned, not just to define but to *demonstrate* the interconnection and collaboration of the powers responsible for creating and sustaining the universe, the *Usia Prima,* as well as the spirit of Silva.[91] Repeatedly, and in richly varied language, Bernardus traces the process by which divine power informs the natural world, then provides a vivid summation:

> For just as the sensible Universe participates in the flawlessness of its flawless model, and waxes beautiful by its beauty, so by its eternal exemplar it is made to endure eternally.

Integrascit . . . pulchrescit . . . aeternatur. It is as if new language were being formed to express each stage in the evolving perfection of the new universe.

In the *Microcosmus,* Nature becomes a questing figure. Though Urania will assure her of the glorious destiny of humanity, her only glimpse of her human progeny is the grim vignette of the unborn souls clustered about the house of Cancer. The obvious model for Nature's travels is the opening book of Martianus's *De nuptiis,* where Mercury, after long wandering, is greeted at last by Apollo's prophecy.[92] But we may also think of Virgil, and Aeneas's encounter with Anchises, whose prophecy is to the history of Rome as Urania's proud assertion of human destiny to the prophecy in Nature's Table of Fate and the ceaseless labor that will be the lot of the *genii* of human generation.

The comparison with Virgil is not far-fetched; the *Aeneid* was readily associated in twelfth-century scholarship with the great allegories of intellectual pilgrimage, and the commentary on the *De nuptiis* attributed to Bernardus makes the connection explicitly. Martianus takes Virgil as his model. For just as Aeneas is led through the underworld to meet Anchises, so Mercury traverses the universe to the court of Jove. So also in the *Consolation* Boethius ascends through false goods to the supreme good, guided by Philosophy. Thus, says the commentators, "these three figural structures express virtually the same thing."[93]

The identification becomes all the more plausible when Aeneas's meeting with his father produces Anchises's concise Stoic account of the cosmic order, lines quoted again and again in twelfth-century cosmological writings:

> A spirit within nourishes heaven and earth and the watery tracts, the shining globe of the moon and the Titanian orb. Mind, infused through each part, stirs the whole mass, and mixes with the vast body.[94]

To view the *Cosmographia* in this context is to see how, by the standard of its place and time, it can be seen as epic. The experience of Bernardus's Nature anticipates that of man, whose fulfillment of his destiny will depend on his attaining the knowledge of cosmic and ideal reality essential to understanding himself. But as Aeneas must return from Elysium to a world of conflict, the human spirit must enter the prison of the body and live out a more uncertain destiny. The shield of Aeneas will be inscribed with the future history of Roman violence, and Nature will behold a long chain of fate and history in the Table of Fate; the conflict between order and violence in which human history will consist, already foretold in the stars, will end in an Age of Iron.

8. The *Mathematicus*

The *Mathematicus* is based on the fourth of a series of *Declamationes* falsely attributed to Quintilian. The declamation was a school exercise in which students were trained in rhetoric by debating on fictional topics, usually framed as legal cases, though the situations are often such as to make resolution in legal terms extremely difficult. The *Mathematicus* and the related poems in this volume, though their ancient sources are readily identifiable, develop their *causae* well beyond the point at which they could plausibly provide roles for novice debaters, emphasizing "the open-endedness of the cases, their intractable, if sometimes implausible, paradoxes."[95]

The hero of the ancient *Mathematicus* is a Roman military hero who has lived his life knowing of an astrologer's prophecy that he will kill his father. The declamation is a speech before the Senate that explains his desire to avoid the fate foretold for him by committing suicide.

Bernardus reduces this speech to less than a quarter of the whole and develops a family drama around it. A Roman noblewoman, happy save in being childless, learns from an astrologer that she will bear a son who will be a great hero but will kill his father. The child is born, and the mother disobeys her husband's command that he be destroyed at birth; he is raised by foster parents, and though named Patricida, he is ignorant of the astrologer's prophecy and embarks on a glorious military career. When he rescues the king of Rome and his army from the Carthaginians, he himself is made king. Eventually the mother reveals her disobedience to her husband, and the couple report the prophecy to Patricida, who meets his father for the first time. The hero resolves to defy the fates by taking his own life, and in a long oration persuades the Roman people to grant an unspecified request, which he then reveals as permission to commit suicide. In the final lines Patricida lays aside his robes of office and declares himself free to choose his destiny.

The poem's opening reflection that "even fortunate people always find some grounds for complaint" recalls Boethius's Philosophy, rebuking the Prisoner for complaining that his happiness is not complete.[96] It quietly introduces a tragic narrative that is set in motion by the inability of the childless couple to accept this flaw in their happiness as what Boethius calls the *humanorum conditio bonorum.*[97] It also shows the narrator markedly detached from his story; he neither expresses sympathy for the protagonists nor passes judgment on them, and he reveals no clear attitude toward the prophecy that looms over them. He can declare at one moment that the gods are conspiring with fate to ensure Patricida's victory over the Carthaginians, only to seemingly contradict himself by explaining the hero's triumph as due to "blind chance" and capricious Fortune.[98]

The *Mathematicus* preserves the extreme fatalism of its source. The astrologer's prediction to the mother of Patricida that her son will kill his father is emphatic:

> So it will be, rest assured; the will of Jove is set. There is no ambiguity in what I have prophesied. The fates, the gods, the stars promise you this; and what the stars, the fates, the gods promise is unalterable.

The parents remain noble but powerless in the face of what they see as inevitable. Rome itself seems equally at the mercy of the hero's fated progress. Unconcerned with historical accuracy,[99] Bernardus has created a mock-imperial city: its description is muscle-bound with the vocabulary of Roman civic institutions and the pomp and circumstance proper to them, but dignity is undercut by the Romans' haplessness when invaded by Carthage, their abrupt and absolute submission to Patricida as legislator and protector, and the futility of their elaborate attempts to dissuade him from his declared intention to end his life.

All of this is set in perspective by Patricida himself. In youth he had been the companion of philosophers and achieved perfect knowledge of the liberal arts. As he ponders the astrologer's prophecy, cosmic vision asserts itself in the face of the perceived injustice of fate, and we are allowed to see beyond the world these powers control:

> Why is our mind so closely akin to the heavenly stars, if it must suffer the grim necessity of harsh Lachesis? In vain do we possess a portion of divine understanding, if our reason is unable to provide for itself. God made the elements and the fiery stars such that man would not be subjected to the stars; instead he is endowed with the greater resource of pure intelligence, that he may confront opposing evil.

We have moved in an instant from fatalism to the vision of Urania, and it is in the language of Urania that Patricida announces his decision to take his own life:

> My mind, secure in its merit, does not fear to go forth from the dark confines of the blind body; once departed from the flesh it will journey to the high heavens, to be restored to the place of its star.

But the very confidence with which Patricida proclaims his destiny, repeatedly asserting his purity of spirit and loftiness of mind, together with an acute awareness of how the sin of parricide would stain his reputation, may make us question his motives. An Oedipus empowered to withstand his patricidal fate, he seems clearly committed to suicide but thinks and speaks almost exclusively of suicide as a means of preserving his personal integrity,[100] and we may wonder if this integrity is finally his religion, more important to him than the life of his father or the common good.[101]

A second issue is the significance to be given to suicide itself. Patricida can cite Seneca in support of his resolve, but at least equally authoritative is Macrobius's long discussion of suicide, based on the rebuke of Aemilius Paulus, father of Scipio, to his son's desire to end his earthly life and join his ancestors in the higher world.[102] Regarding death, Macrobius enjoins strict obedience to the laws of nature and the will of the gods. The soul is defiled and cut off from light when it is expelled from the body by force[103] but can become dead to the world by freeing itself from lust and passion. The very yearning for freedom through suicide is itself a passion and a snare. Macrobius's arguments clearly resonate with the exhortations of Urania and Noys in the *Cosmographia.*

But the poem ends without providing a clear perspective on Patricida's position. The narrator remains silent, and in the final lines, what is emphasized is freedom:

> I quickly lay aside my royal robes, quickly cease to be your king—my own man, set free *(liber et explicitus)* to pursue my goal.

How to evaluate this conclusion? The play on *liber* and *explicit* in the final line seems to indicate the poem's completion, its ending at once a conclusion and a release.[104] Whether it is a resolution is matter for debate. For Steinen the poem is complete but unfinished, "because there existed no possible ending."[105] Dronke finds the conclusion satisfying, in that Patricida establishes, "not so much his freedom to commit suicide as, more fundamentally, his freedom to choose."[106] Godman suggests that in divesting himself of kingship Patricida is perhaps performing an act of *parricidium,* a symbolic slaying of the *pater urbis* or *pater patriae.*[107] The fact remains that Patricida devotes thirty lines to his intention to commit suicide by the sword, and that is all we know.

9. Minor Poems

The *Mathematicus* is the most substantial and complex of the surviving twelfth-century poems based on ancient declamations, or *controversiae.* The two shorter poems included here, tentatively attributed to Bernardus because they are similar exercises and appear in two manuscripts as satellites of the *Mathematicus,* deal with simpler, if no less implausible situations, but discover substance and the complexity of moral choice in what were originally little more than tests of rhetorical ingenuity.

De gemellis is based on the eighth of the *Declamations* of pseudo-Quintilian. Twin boys suffer from what doctors declare to be the same disease. The case is considered hopeless by all doctors but one, who promises to cure one of the twins if he can examine the internal organs of the other. With the father's permission he dissects one twin, diagnoses the disease, and cures the other. The mother accuses the father of maltreatment, and the *declamatio* consists of the speech of her attorney before the court.

The *De gemellis* resembles the *Mathematicus* in structure. Most of the poem is devoted to the background of the crisis, and the dispute itself is given only twenty lines. Like Patricida, the twins are perfect works of Nature. The disease, like the curse of patricide in the *Mathematicus,* seems to offer no choice: the doctors have an authority like that of the astrologer in the *Mathematicus,* who knows the "hidden causes" and "inner depths of Nature."[108] The father, deferring to the doctors' authority, is placed in very much the same position as Patricida and his parents by the difficult moral choice he is forced to make.[109] It is perhaps to set off this difficulty by contrast that the wife is made to challenge the authority of the doctors, wholly ignoring the nature of the case.

In the *controversia* on which *De paupere ingrato* is based,[110] a man whose wife, children, and possessions had been destroyed by fire, and who had himself been shipwrecked, hangs himself, but a passerby cuts the noose, only to be sued by the man he has saved. The *controversia* takes place in court and consists of the words of the two men, to each other and to the judge. The rescuer urges the would-be suicide to live in hope of better fortune, claiming to have acted only out of pity. The other insists that the rescuer be punished but that he himself receive the harsher sentence of death.

In *De paupere ingrato* there is none of the vigorous dialogue that brings Seneca's litigants to life. The rescuer is also a benefactor, but that is all we know about him, and of the other we know only that he is poor. We learn from the opening couplet that poverty is "harsh enough, more than enough" on its victims. When the rescuer, after supporting the poor man for several months, considers that he has done "enough" for him (17), life apparently offers no further hope of "enough," and death remains his only solace; hence the bitter question with which the poem ends. Seneca's unique and hardly credible series of misfortunes has become a social condition.

10. Fortunae

Bernardus was highly praised and widely imitated in the twelfth-century schools;[111] the *Cosmographia* was "la sommet de l'ambition créatrice," the masterwork which provided the fullest expression of the capacities of poetry.[112] But while Bernardus can fairly be said to have inaugurated a tradition that leads directly forward to the *Rose* of Jean de Meun and Dante's *Commedia,* this great contribution was realized almost entirely through the response of Alan of Lille to the *Cosmographia.* In Alan's *De planctu Naturae,* a *prosimetrum* charged with allusions to Bernardus's masterpiece, the goddess Nature reveals that her authority in human life has been compromised, and the story she tells amounts to the realization of the potential for disruption in the microcosmic world that exists as a persistent undertone in the *Cosmographia.* The *Anticlaudianus,* Alan's masterpiece, is in effect a super-Bernardus: the flawed life of humankind under Nature's governance is redeemed by the creation of a New Man, perfect in understanding and pure in spirit.

Both of Alan's works survive in well over a hundred manuscripts. The *De planctu Naturae* became a standard text for the teaching of rhetoric, and the *Anticlaudianus,* with the *Al-*

exandreis of Walter of Chatillon, was accorded the dignity of a classic, equipped with extensive glosses, and translated and imitated in several languages. Bernardus enjoyed no such fame. Though the *Cosmographia,* too, became a school text, it evidently circulated far less widely after the early thirteenth century, perhaps because its allegory was less straightforwardly didactic than those of Alan. The *Cosmographia* is quoted by Gervase of Tilbury[113] and by Vincent of Beauvais,[114] a manuscript of the work was owned by Richard de Fournival,[115] and two female figures in a creation scene in the Ainwick Bestiary have been identified by the editor as Bernardus's Noys and Natura.[116]

But what might be called Bernardus's last stand as a major literary figure occurs in the *Bataille des sept ars* of Henri d'Andeli, which allegorizes the state of the schools of central France toward the mid-thirteenth century as the outcome of a battle between the forces of Logic and the traditional humanist curriculum. At one point Grammar and the Authors, hard pressed, summon a rear guard that includes Martianus Capella, "Anticlaudien," and "Bernard Silvestris, who knew all the languages of the sciences and the arts."[117] But Grammar—and with her the scholastic milieu in which Bernardus had been an honored figure—is defeated and Logic holds sway.

Thereafter Bernardus becomes hard to trace. Toward the end of the thirteenth century Hugh of Trimberg, in his *Registrum multorum auctorum,* discusses Alan, Walter, and Bernardus's student Matthew of Vendôme, but not Bernardus himself. Attempts to determine Bernardus's influence on vernacular literature have yielded mixed results. Pollman sees the *Cosmographia* as having significantly influenced the

Perceval of Chrétien de Troyes.[118] Jaeger finds in the poetry of Gottfried von Strassburg the pervasive influence of the French cathedral schools and points to suggestive correspondences between his *Tristan* and the *Cosmographia.*[119] Several critics have seen the influence of Bernardus in the poetry of Frauenlob.[120]

A manuscript of the *Cosmographia* survives written in the hand of Boccacio, who cites *Megacosmus* and *Microcosmus* in his *Esposizioni* of Dante's *Inferno.*[121] But Boccaccio does not make use of the *Cosmographia* in his own literary works, and this is the case for later medieval vernacular literature in general. The work of Alan is a basic ingredient in the literary culture of Dante, Jean de Meun, Guillaume de Machaut, and Chaucer, but it is hard to detect the presence of Bernardus.[122]

The *Cosmographia* was not edited until 1876. The *Mathematicus* appeared in print in 1708, but its authorship was established only in 1895, by the edition of Hauréau. And it was not until 1948 that the lucid study of Theodore Silverstein provided the first clear assessment of the intellectual and literary character of the *Cosmographia.*

Like many admirers I felt an *amor de lonh* for Bernardus before actually reading him, through Helen Waddell's *The Wandering Scholars* and C. S. Lewis's *The Allegory of Love.* Theirs are true appreciations, and I hope that in deploying the heavy weapons of annotation and commentary I have not done violence to the qualities they saw so clearly. I am grateful to Peter Dronke, who knows the *Cosmographia* as well as anyone, for graciously permitting me to use his edition as the basis for my own, and to the editors of the St. Ottilien edition of the *Mathematicus* for a similar kindness; to Nigel Palmer, for a copy of his fine article on plant names in the *Cosmographia;* to Charles Burnett, for copies of critical essays unavailable in North America; and to Robert Ziomkowski, for making available his copy of Vernet's study and edition of the *Cosmographia* and for reading carefully through my translations to my great profit. In translating the *Cosmographia* I have gratefully incorporated corrections to my earlier translation by Peter Dronke, Bengt Löfstedt, and Christine Ratkowitsch. I have also had the versions of Michel Lemoine and Enzo Maccagnolo at my elbow, and I regret that I cannot share my new attempt with those fine scholars. Deirdre Stone's translation has helped me with the *Mathematicus.* I am also grateful for the fine work of Robert Edwards on the *Mathematicus* and its satellites. Danuta Shanzer, Julian Yolles, and John Magee have been through my texts and translations with great care, and the book is much the better for their attentiveness. My greatest debt is to Paul Piehler, who opened the twelfth century to me fifty years ago.

Notes

1 Vernet, "Bernardus Silvestris," 168.

2 Oxford, Bodleian Library, MS Laud misc. 515, f. 188v; Dronke, ed. *Cosm.,* 1–2; Haye, *Päpste und Poeten,* 167–69. The couplet on Eugenius appears in all manuscripts of the *Cosmographia* known to me, suggest-

ing that the work was completed close to the time of the pope's visit to France.

3 Angers, Bibliothèque Municipale, MS 303, f. 127v: *Non Bernardus obit, sed abit; non interit, immo / incipit; hospes erat, amodo civis erit* ("Bernardus has not died, but departed; he has not perished, indeed he is beginning; he was a sojourner, now he will be a citizen"); Wollin, "Epitaphium," 369–82.

4 Ferruolo, *Origins of the University,* 47–183.

5 Southern, *Scholastic Humanism,* 1:22–35.

6 Chenu, *La théologie,* 19–51; Speer, *Entdeckte Natur,* 1–18, 289–306.

7 Dronke "New Approaches"; Burnett, "Contents and Affiliation"; Giacone, "Masters, Books and Library."

8 *Metalogicon* 1.24.

9 *Prologus in Heptateuchon,* ed. Jeauneau, 174. On Thierry's teaching career and the likely role of the *Heptateuchon* at Chartres, Ward, "Date of the Commentary," 238–47.

10 Both translation and commentary end at *Timaeus* 53C.

11 Burkert, *Greek Religion,* 199, 327–28.

12 *Glosae super Platonem,* 60.

13 *Glosae super Platonem,* 119: *nos Platonem diligentes.*

14 *Dragmaticon* 3.4.6.

15 *Dragmaticon* 3.4.1–4.

16 *Dragmaticon* 1.7.3–4; *Glosae super Platonem* 37. Compare Thierry, *Abbreviatio Monacensis* 1.4, ed. Häring, 442; John of Salisbury, *Metalogicon* 1.8.

17 *Tractatus* 5–15, ed. Häring, *Commentaries,* 557–61; Dronke, "Thierry of Chartres," 374–84.

18 Lucentini, "L'*Asclepius* ermetico"; "Il corpo e l'anima," 226–28; Dronke, *Spell of Calcidius,* 123–26.

19 Copeland, "Thierry of Chartres," 94–95.

20 Brisson, "Discours comme univers," 209–211; *Plato the Myth Maker,* 40–43; Bourgain, "La conception de la poésie," 166–68.

21 John Whittaker, "Plutarch, Platonism and Christianity," 57, observes that throughout late antiquity the *Timaeus* was "not only the most frequently read dialogue of Plato, but in general the most influential work of a philosophical nature."

22 Jeauneau, "Macrobe," 16–19.

23 *Metalogicon* 1.24, 3.4, 4.35.

24 Tentative evidence for Bernardus's teaching career is discussed by Poole, "The Masters of the Schools," 327–42.

25 That Bernardus was influenced by Hildebert is suggested by Dronke, ed. *Cosm.*, 7, and strenuously denied by Godman, "Ambiguity," 588–91, 642–43.

26 On Tours and *dictamen,* see Köhn, "Schulbildung und Trivium," 278–79; Southern, *Scholastic Humanism,* 2:182–84; Camargo, "Twelfth-Century Treatise," 163–69. Kauntze, *Authority and Imitation,* 15-49, provides an excellent view of the literary culture of twelfth-century Tours.

27 *Epistulae* 1.3.69–70; *Opera* 2, 90.

28 Camargo, "Twelfth-Century Treatise," 165–66.

29 Camargo, *Medieval Rhetorics,* 2; Witt, "Arts of Letter-Writing," 73–75.

30 Brini Savorelli, "Il 'Dictamen.'" The actual author was Bernard of Bologna: Klaes, "Die 'Summa' des Magister Bernardus."

31 Kelly, *Arts of Poetry,* 57–65; Woods, *Classroom Commentaries,* 47–48; Tilliette, *Des mots à la parole,* 56–63. Geoffrey's debt is well expressed by Woods, *Classroom Commentaries,* 266: his view of the generative qualities of language "had its origin in the great works of twelfth-century Platonism . . . His pedagogical focus . . . balances the more pessimistic, philosophically driven cosmic visions of flux in the works of writers like Bernardus Silvestris . . ."

Gervase de Melkley, *Ars poetica* (1215–16), ed. Gräbener, 1, declares that Matthew of Vendôme presents the art of poetry "fully," Geoffrey of Vinsauf "more fully," and "most fully Bernardus Silvestris," whom he cites more frequently than any other author.

32 *De nuptiis* 1.92.6; See Cristante, ed. *De nuptiis,* 239–40; Gersh, *Middle Platonism,* 2:603–5.

33 *De nuptiis* 1.9–22; Ratkowitsch, *Die Cosmographia,* 88–89.

34 *De nuptiis* 1.9–10 ; 1.27–29, 2.200–206.

35 *Consolatio* 1.metr.3, pr.4.4: *hausi caelum et mentem recepi.* In *Micr.* 4, Urania's greeting to Nature is cast in the meter of *Cons.* 1.metr.3, inviting us to compare her revelation with the renewal of the Prisoner's vision.

36 Bezner, *Vela Veritatis,* 430; Asper, *"Silva Parens,"* 132–33.

37 See Jolivet, "Les principes féminins," 273; Bezner, *Vela Veritatis,* 445–47.

38 *Meg.* 1.1.57, 2.2; Whitman, *Allegory,* 230–32.

39 Newman, *God and the Goddesses,* 59–60.

40 Gregory, *Platonismo medievale,* 138.

41 Stock, *Myth and Science,* 66, 164–67; Whitman, *Allegory,* 238. As Pabst notes, *Prosimetrum,* 448, Nature is always present, and we see creation through her eyes.

42 For Calcidius, 123, 268, and Servius, *ad Aen.* 1.314, *silva* is a synonym for Greek ὕλη.

43 *Tim.* 30A, 52D–53B. Translation for quotations from the *Timaeus* is that of Cornford, *Plato's Cosmology.*

44 *Timaeus* 53B.

45 Thierry asserts that matter, created by God at the beginning of time, was chaotic only insofar as the elements were not at first differentiated: "confusion" preceded distinction as sound precedes voice or genus precedes species. (*Tractatus* 24, ed. Häring, *Commentaries,* 563–64.) William claims that matter was created as a stable body from which were immediately produced the four elements; the primal confusion or agitation never existed, but might have existed, absent the creator's controlling power. (*Philosophia* 1.11.35–39; *Glosae super Platonem* 50–51; *Dragmaticon* 1.7.)

46 *Meg.* 2.2n.

47 Calcidius, 269–70, on Plato's account of matter responding to persuasion (*Timaeus* 48A); and 286–87, on the desire of matter for form according to Aristotle, *Phys.* 1.9.192a.

48 Wisdom 7:25.

49 Bezner, *Vela Veritatis,* 106–13, 150–62; Gregory, *Anima mundi,* 123–52; Dronke, "L'amor che move," 410–17; *Spell of Calcidius,* 121–29; Luscombe, *School of Abelard,* 123–27.

50 *Consolation* 4.pr.6.10.

51 On *Imarmene,* Thierry, *Glosae* on Boethius, *De Trin.* 2, 21; *Commentaries,* ed. Häring, 273.

52 See Lemay, *Abu Ma'shar,* 258–84.

53 On the importance of the *Introductorium,* Burnett, "Scientific Speculations," 173–74.

54 On the importance of this concept, and of Stoic physics generally, for twelfth-century cosmologists, Lapidge, "The Stoic Inheritance."

55 *Asclepius* 3.

56 *Asclepius* 2.

57 *Timaeus* 37CD.

58 *Asclepius* 34–35; *Meg.* 2.7.

59 Godman, "Search for Urania," 76–80, rightly dismisses the astrological readings of Urania by Lemay, *Abu Ma'shar,* 277, and Stock, *Myth and Science,* 16, 166. But astrology is evidently one source of Urania's power to foreknow man's destiny: "for it is not permitted to the stars to lie" (*Micr.* 4.52).

60 Tugaton is τὸ ἀγαθόν, the Good.

61 *Timaeus* 41E.

62 *Micr.* 10.50.

63 "Dronke, "Natura and Personification, 16–24; Newman, *God and the Goddesses,* 52. Pabst, *Prosimetrum,* 454n362, offers qualified agreement.

64 *De planctu Naturae* 7.6–8.

65 *De nuptiis* 1.7.

66 *Annotationes,* ed. Lutz, 13; ed. Ramelli, 110–11.

67 With *Micr.* 8.43–46 compare Macrobius, *In Somn. Scip.* 2.12.13, 15.

68 Finckh, *Minor Mundus Homo,* 131–33.

69 Gersh, *Concord in Discourse,* 271–73.

70 On the conclusion of the *Cosmographia,* Finckh, *Minor Mundus Homo,* 148–55.

71 Gilson, "La cosmogonie," 8. Silverstein surveys responses to the *Cosmographia* from the early nineteenth century forward, "Fabulous Cosmogony," 92–93.

72 Curtius, *European Literature,* 112.

73 Gilson, "La cosmogonie," 12–14; Curtius, *European Literature,* 112–13n21; Newman, *God and the Goddesses,* 36–39, 64–65.

74 Silverstein, "Fabulous Cosmogony," 93, 110.

75 Jeauneau, "L'usage de la notion *d'integumentum*"; Dronke, *Fabula,* 13–78. The *Aeneid* commentary defines *integumentum* as "a type of demonstration that wraps a truth to be understood within a fabulous narrative" (*Commentum,* ed. Jones and Jones, 3). On the history of the term, Dronke, *Fabula,* 48n2; on the history of *involucrum,* 56n2.

76 Gregory, "Abélard et Platon," 39–44.

77 In *Meg.* 2.1 Noys declares herself a function of the divine will; she acts only "as I am bidden by the harmonious expression of that will."

78 *Micr.* 5.3–4.

79 *Micr.* 5.1.

80 See *Periphyseon* 3.681CD, on the creation of primal matter and its relation to the divine wisdom; Whitman, *Allegory,* 151–53, 156–59 (on the concept of matter in the *Periphyseon*); 250–51.

81 Jolivet, "L'univers de Bernard Silvestre," 67.

82 Brini Savorelli, ed. *Experimentarius,* 316–17; Burnett, *"Experimentarius,"* 123.

83 Stock, *Myth and Science,* 132–33; Curtius, *European Literature,* 109–10.

84 Pfeiffer, *Contemplatio Caeli,* 269–71.

85 Albert, *Speculum Astronomiae* 12, ed. Zambelli, 252–57.

86 *De raptu* 3.33–45. Jove has ended the Golden Age, but Ceres has not yet granted mankind the knowledge of agriculture. On the significance of Claudian's cosmic mythology for the *Cosmographia,* Ratkowitsch, "Die Gewebe in Claudians Epos," 38–40.

87 *Ars Am.* 2.467–70; Silverstein, "Fabulous Cosmogony," 99n39.

88 *Ars poetica,* ed. Gräbener, 1. But more than a third of the examples of style Gervase draws from the *Cosmographia* come from the prose chapters. Janson, *Prose Rhythm,* 75, 113, observes that almost every prose sentence in the *Cosmographia* ends with some form of the *cursus,* most often the *cursus velox.*

89 Dronke, *Verse with Prose,* 46.

90 Lomperis, "Play of the Text," 54–55.

91 Bezner, *Vela Veritatis,* 448–61.

92 *De nuptiis* 1.9–22; Ratkowitsch, *Die Cosmographia,* 88–89.

93 *Commentary,* ed. Westra, 47.114–20.

94 *Aen.* 6.724–27.

95 Edwards, "Poetic Invention," 185.

96 Boethius, *Cons.* 2.pr.4.11–12, cited by Godman, *Silent Masters,* 246.

97 Ratkowitsch, "Astrologie und Selbstmord," 186–88.

98 *Math.* 147–52, 175–76.

99 Bertini, "Tragedie latine," 163n21.

100 See especially *Math.* 625–32, 781–92.

101 D'Alessandro, ed. *Math.,* 33–34, and Godman, "Ambiguity," 627, *Silent Masters,* 259, point to the Stoic character of Patricida's reflections. Ratkowitsch, "Astrologie und Selbstmord," 207–8, notes his lack of altruism.

102 Macrobius, *In Somn. Scip.* 1.13; Cicero, *Somn. Scip.* 4.3–5.

103 See Edwards, "Poetic Invention," 189–90, commenting on lines 781–88.

104 Wetherbee, *Platonism and Poetry,* 157. The poem ends here in all but one of the full manuscript versions. The twenty-six additional lines in Kraków, Biblioteka Jagiellonska, MS theol. oct. 94, add nothing meaningful, and can hardly be by Bernardus. That the poem is incomplete is argued by Ratkowitsch, "Astrologie und Selbstmord," 183–84, 224–27.

105 Steinen, "Sujets d'inspiration," 378.

106 Dronke, *Fabula,* 137.

107 Godman, "Ambiguity," 635–38, *Silent Masters,* 266–67; D'Alessandro, ed. *Math.,* 33.

108 *De gemellis* 45–46; *Math.* 41.

109 Edwards, "Poetic Invention," 208–9.

110 Seneca the Elder, *Controversiae* 5.1.

111 Dronke, ed. *Cosm.,* 7–13, surveys the evidence.

112 Bourgain, "Le tournant littéraire," 311. See above, n. 31.

113 Gervase quotes *Meg.* 3 in *Otia* 1.5 and 3.45, acknowledging "the distinguished versifier and philosopher Bernardus Silvester."

114 *Speculum Doctrinale* 4.124, 4.156, 5.65, 5.108; *Speculum Historiale* 3.44; *Speculum naturale* 31.49. Passages of six lines or less from different parts of the *Cosmographia* are combined without regard for context, suggesting that they were not drawn directly from Bernardus's text.

115 *Biblionomia,* Paris, MS Univ. I.II.1, f. 19r (no. 107).

116 Millar, *Thirteenth-Century Bestiary,* 17. The Bestiary is now MS 100 of the J. Paul Getty Museum. The image (fol. 5v) may be viewed on the museum website. I am grateful to Professor Sarah Kay of New York University for this reference.

117 *Bataille des vii ars,* 328–30.

118 Pollman, *Chrétien de Troyes,* 106–8, 142–45, *Das Epos,* 87–88.

119 Jaeger, *Medieval Humanism,* 52–54, 153–55.

120 Steinmetz, *Liebe als universales Prinzip,* 126–33; Huber, *Aufnahme und Verarbeitung,* 159–66; Krayer, *Frauenlob,* 100–104, 113, regards most traces of Bernardus as mediated by Alan of Lille.

121 Florence, Biblioteca Medicea MS Laurentiana XXXIII 31; *Esposizioni sopra la Comedia di Dante* 2.2.30–31.

122 Zingesser, "Genesis of Poetry," sees the Natura of Bernardus as the model for the Nature of Machaut's general Prologue to his work. A gloss in several manuscripts of Chaucer's *Canterbury Tales* quotes *Meg.* 3.39–44 as the source of *Man of Law's Tale,* 197–203.

COSMOGRAPHIA

Summa Operis

In huius operis primo libro, qui *Megacosmus,* id est maior Mundus, dicitur, Natura ad Noym, id est Dei Providentiam, de primae materiae confusione conquerens inducitur, et ut Mundus pulchrius poliatur humiliter implorat. Noys igitur, eius mota precibus, ei libenter annuit, et ita quattuor elementa ab invicem disiungit. Novem hierarchias Angelorum in caelo ponit, stellas in firmamento ponit, signa duodecim facit, per Zodiacum orbes septem planetarum currere facit, quattuor cardinales ventos sibi invicem opponit. Sequitur genesis animantium et terrae situs medius. Postea montes famosi describuntur, sequitur proprietas animalium, deinde famosi fluvii, sequitur proprietas arborum, postea species odoratae, deinde genera leguminum, proprietas aristarum, virtus herbarum, genera natatilium; sequitur genus aerivagum. Postea unde sit vita animantibus disseritur. In primo itaque libro ornatus elementorum describitur.

2. In secundo libro, qui *Microcosmus* dicitur, id est minor mundus vocatur, Noys Naturam alloquitur et demum facta expolitione gloriatur, et in operis sui completionem se

Summary

In the first book of this work, which is called *Megacosmus,* or the greater universe, Nature is shown complaining to Noys, or Divine Providence, about the confused state of primal matter, and pleading humbly that the Universe be more beautifully wrought. Noys, moved by her prayers, willingly assents, and accordingly separates the four elements from one another. She sets the nine hierarchies of Angels in heaven, sets the stars in the firmament, creates the twelve signs, causes the orbits of the seven planets to pass through the Zodiac, sets the four cardinal winds in mutual opposition. Then follow the creation of living creatures and the central placement of earth. After this famous mountains are described, then follow the properties of animals, then famous rivers. Then follow the characteristics of trees, then the varieties of scents and spices, next the kinds of vegetables, the characteristics of grains, and then the powers of herbs, the kinds of swimming creatures; then follows the race of birds. Then the source of life in animate creatures is discussed. Thus in the first book is described the ordered disposition of the elements.

2. In the second book, which is called *Microcosmus,* or the lesser universe, Noys speaks to Nature, glories in the beautification now achieved, and promises to create Man as the

hominem plasmaturam profitetur. Iubet itaque ut Uraniam, quae siderum est regina, et Physim, quae rerum omnium est peritissima, sollicite perquirat. Natura protinus iubenti obsequitur, et per caelestes circulos Uraniam quaeritans eam sideribus inhiantem reperit. Eiusque itineris causa praecognita, itineris se et operis comitem Urania pollicetur. Ambae igitur surgunt, planetarumque circulis excursis eorumque potentiis pernotatis, tandem quodam terrae fluentis gremio inter odoramina aromatum Physim cum duabus filiabus, Theorica et Practica, residentem inveniunt, et quid veniant exponunt. Subito Noys affuit, suoque eis velle ostenso ternas speculationes tribus assignando tribuit et ad hominis plasmationem eas accelerat. Physis itaque de quattuor elementorum reliquiis hominem format, et a capite incipiens, membratim operando, in pedibus opus suum feliciter consummat.

completion of her work. Accordingly she orders Nature to search carefully for Urania, who is queen of the stars, and Physis, who has deep knowledge of all created things. Nature obeys her instructress at once, and searching for Urania through all the celestial spheres, finds her gazing in wonder at the stars. The cause of Nature's journey being already known to her, Urania promises to join her, in her journey and in her task. And so the two set out, and when the circles of the planets have been traversed, and their several influences duly noted, they at last discover Physis, dwelling in the bosom of the flourishing earth amid the odors of spices, with her two daughters, Theory and Practice, and they explain why they have come. Suddenly Noys is present there, and having made her will known to them she assigns to the three kinds of scientific knowledge, and urges them to the formation of Man. And so Physis forms Man out of the remainder of the four elements, and beginning with the head, and working limb by limb, completes her work appropriately with the feet.

Dedicatio

Terrico veris sententiarum titulis doctori famosissimo, Bernardus Silvestris opus suum.

Aliquamdiu, fateor, sensu mecum secretiore quaesivi utrum opusculum meum in amicas aures traderem, aut non expectato judice penitus abolerem. Siquidem de Mundo, de universitate tractatus sua natura difficilis, sed et sensu tardiore conpositus, sicut aures sic oculos arguti iudicis reformidat.

Verum sensus vester benevolus, simplicem sed devotam vobis paginam inspecturus, erexit audaciam, animos impulit, fiduciam roboravit. Consilium tamen fuit, ut perfecta minus pagina nomen sui tacuisset auctoris, adeo usque vestro suscepisset iudicio vel egrediendi sententiam vel latendi. Viderit ergo discretio vestra si prodire palam, si venire debeat in commune. Si interim vestro praesentetur aspectui, iudicio correptionique transmittitur, non favori.

Duret in longum valeatque vita vestra.

Dedication

To Thierry, doctor most renowned for true eminence in learning, Bernardus Silvestris offers his work.

For some time, I confess, I have been debating with my inner self, whether I should submit my little work for a friendly hearing or destroy it utterly without waiting for judgment. For since a treatise on the Universe, on the whole of creation is difficult by its very nature, and this the composition of a dull wit as well, it shrinks from being heard or scrutinized by a perceptive judge.

To be sure, your kindly willingness to look over a piece of writing lacking in art, but dedicated to you, has aroused my boldness, quickened my spirits, and strengthened my confidence. Yet I have decided that my imperfect piece of writing should not declare the name of its author until such time as it had received from your judgment the verdict of publication or suppression. Your discernment, then, will decide whether it should come forth openly and become generally known. If meanwhile it is presented for your consideration, it is submitted for judgment and correction, not for approval.

May your life be long and flourishing.

INCIPIT MEGACOSMUS
BERNARDI SILVESTRIS

Megacosmus 1

Congeries informis adhuc, cum Silva teneret,
sub veteri confusa globo primordia rerum,
visa Deo Natura queri, Mentemque profundam
compellasse Noym: "Vitae viventis imago,
prima, Noys, Deus, orta Deo, substantia veri,
consilii tenor aeterni, mihi vera Minerva:
Si sensu fortasse meo maiora capesso—
mollius excudi Silvam, positoque veterno,
posse superduci melioris imagine formae—
huic operi nisi consentis, concepta relinquo.
"Nempe Deus, cuius summe natura benigna est,
larga, nec invidiae miseros sensura tumultus,
in melius, quantum patitur substantia rerum,
cuncta refert, operique suo non derogat auctor.
Non igitur livere potes, sed pondus ineptum
perfecto reddes consummatoque decori,
consilii si rite tui secreta recordor.
"Silva rigens, informe chaos, concretio pugnax,
discolor usiae vultus, sibi dissona massa,
turbida temperiem, formam rudis, hispida cultum
optat, et a veteri cupiens exire tumultu
artifices numeros et musica vincla requirit.

HERE BEGINS THE *MEGACOSMUS* OF BERNARD SILVESTRIS

Megacosmus 1

When Silva, still a formless pile, held the first beginnings of things mixed confusedly in its ancient mass, Nature appeared, complaining to God, and challenging Noys, his unfathomable Mind: "O Noys, image of unfailing life, firstborn of God, yourself God, essential truth, issue of eternal deliberation, my true Minerva: If perhaps I grasp at things beyond my understanding—that Silva, her ancient lethargy cast aside, may be made more malleable, and be vested with the likeness of a nobler form—if you do not consent to this task, I abandon my conceptions.

"Surely God, whose nature is supremely benevolent, generous, and untouched by the wretched agitations of envy, wills the melioration of all things, so far as their materiality will allow; the author does not disparage his work. Thus you cannot be jealous, but will bestow upon the unwieldy mass a full and perfect beauty, if I recall rightly the hidden ways of your deliberation.

"Silva, an unyielding, formless chaos, a hostile coalescence, the motley aspect of substance, a mass discordant with itself, longs in her turbulence for a tempering power; in her crudity for form; in her rankness for cultivation; yearning to emerge from her ancient confusion, she demands formative number and bonds of harmony.

Ut quid ab aeterno primae fundamina causae
ingenitae lites germanaque bella fatigant,
quando fluit refluitque sibi contraria moles,
fortuitis elementa modis incerta feruntur,
distrahiturque globus raptatibus inconsultis?
Quid prodest quod cuncta suo praecesserit ortu
Silva parens, si lucis eget, si noctis abundat,
perfecto decisa suo—si denique possit
auctorem terrere suo male condita vultu?

"Ante pedes assistit Hyle cum prole suorum,
invidiam factura tibi, quod cana capillos
informi squalore suum deduxerat aevum.
Rursus et ecce cupit res antiquissima nasci
ortu Silva novo, circumscribique figuris.

"Debetur nonnullus honos et gratia Silvae,
quae genetiva tenet, gremio diffusa capaci.
Has inter veluti cunas infantia Mundi
vagit et ad speciem vestiri cultius orat.
Has lacrimas tener orbis habet, nutricis ut ipse
discedat gremio, Silvamque relinquat alumnam.
Adsistunt elementa tibi poscentia formas,
munus et officium, propriis accomoda causis,
affectantque locos ad quos vel sponte feruntur,
consensu deducta suo: levis ignis in altum,
terra gravis pessum, medio tenus humor et aer.
Ut quid enim permixta trahit confusus acervus?
Stare suum Silvae est vertigine circumferri
vorticibusque vagis iterum confundier in se,
sed neque pax nec amor, nec lex, nec cognitus ordo.
Omnibus his quia Silva caret, vix nomine vero

Why then do inborn conflicts and wars among kindred properties assail foundations established from eternity by the first cause, when the mass ebbs and flows, at odds with itself, when hapless elements are borne about at random, and the whole body is rent by sudden agitations? What does it avail Silva, mother of all, that her birth preceded all others, if she is deprived of light, abounds only in darkness, cut off from her fulfillment—if, finally, in this wretched condition, her countenance is such as to frighten her very creator?

"Hyle, with her progeny, presents herself at your feet, to express to you her resentment that, though grown white-headed, she has lived out her age in formless squalor. Behold, Silva, oldest of things, yearns to be born again, and to be defined in her new birth by forms.

"No small honor and favor are owed to Silva, who contains the forces of generation diffused throughout her vast womb. Here, as if in its cradle, the infant Universe squalls, and cries to be clothed with a finer appearance. The tender world is in tears, longing to come forth from the bosom of its nurse and leave fostering Silva. The elements come before you, demanding forms, qualities, and functions appropriate to their causal roles, and seek those stations to which they are almost spontaneously borne, drawn by a common sympathy: lively fire to the height, heavy earth downward, moisture and air abroad through the middle region. Why then does this chaotic mass draw them confusedly together? Silva's state is one of being whirled about in flux, then thrown back confusedly into herself by random eddies; peace, love, law, and order are unknown to her. Because she is lacking in all these Silva may hardly be assigned her true

divinum censetur opus, sed lubrica caecae
machina Fortunae, melioribus orba patronis.
"Pace tua, Noys alma, loquar: pulcherrima cum sis,
informi nudaque tibi regnatur in aula
regnum, Silva, tuum; vetus et gravis ipsa videris.
Ut quid ab aeterno comitata Carentia Silvam?
Ornatu specieque superveniente recedat!
Adde manum, rescinde globum, partesque resigna
et distingue locis; melius distincta placebunt.
Pigra move, moderare vagis, ascribe figuram,
adde iubar: fateatur opus quis fecerit auctor!
"Pro Mundo Natura rogo. Satis est, nihil opto,
si rerum Mundique suum natale videbo.
Sed quid ego tibi plura? Pudet docuisse Minervam."

Megacosmus 2

Hactenus haec, cum ad loquentem oculos vultu Noys sustulit blandiore, et quasi mentis penetralibus foras evocato colloquio: "Vere," inquit, "et tu, Natura, uteri mei beata fecunditas, nec degeneras nec desciscis origine, quae, filia Providentiae, Mundo et rebus non desinis providere. Porro Noys ego, Dei ratio profundius exquisita, quam utique de se, alteram se, Usia Prima genuit, non in tempore sed ex eo

title as the work of God; rather she appears a giddy contrivance of blind Fortune, an orphan with no better guardian.

"By your leave, kind Noys, I must speak: supremely beautiful though you are, Silva, your dominion, is ruled in an ugly and barren court; you yourself seem old and sad. Why has Privation been the companion of Silva from eternity? Let it depart, through the imposition of order and form! Apply your hand, divide the mass, show forth its components and set them in their stations; they will appear more pleasing when thus disposed. Quicken what is inert, control what moves at random, impose shape and bestow splendor: let the work declare the author who has made it!

"It is for the Universe that I, Nature, appeal. It is enough, I seek no more, if I may behold the birth of the Universe and its creatures. But what more can I say to you? I blush to have given lessons to Minerva."

Megacosmus 2

Nature said no more; then Noys, her countenance brightening, raised her eyes to the speaker, and, in speech that seemed summoned forth from the inner chambers of her mind, replied: "Truly, O Nature, blessed fruitfulness of my womb, you neither dishonor nor fall away from your high origin; daughter of Providence as you are, your concern for the Universe and its creatures is unceasing. But I am Noys, the deeply considered reason of God, whom Primal Being brought forth of itself, a second self, not in time, but out of

quo consistit aeterno. Noys ego, scientia et arbitraria divinae voluntatis ad dispositionem rerum, quemadmodum de consensu eius accipio, sic meae administrationis officia circumduco. Inconsulto enim Deo, priusquam de composito sententia proferatur, rebus ad essentiam frustra maturius festinatur. Sua rerum nativitas divina prior celebratur in Mente; secunda vero est quae sequitur actione. Quod igitur de Mundi molitione sanctis ac beatis affectibus et consilio conceperas altiore ad efficientiam non potuit evocari praesentem, adusque terminum supernis legibus institutum. Rigida et inevincibili necessitate nodisque perplexioribus fuerat illigatum, ne quem Mundo desideras cultus et facies praesentius contigisset. Nunc ergo, quia tempestive moves et promoves, causisque ad ordinem concurrentibus, tuis desideriis deservitur.

2. "Siquidem Hyle ancipiti quadam est conditione, inter bonum malumque disposita, sed praeponderante malitia eius, vergit inclinatior ad consensum. Silvestris, video, obsolescere demutarique malignitas non poterit ad perfectum; abundantior enim, et, nativis erecta potentiis, quibus insedit sedibus, facile non recedit. Verum ego, quo non operi, quo non meis officiat disciplinis, malum Silvae pro parte plurima Silvaeque grossitiem elimabo. Moles porro tumultuaria, quam de confusione conceptus motus exagitat inquietus, ea ad ordinatos temperatae discursionis limites pace quam meditor refigetur. Silvae formam molior, de cuius

that eternal state in which it abides unmoved. I, Noys, am the knowledge and judgment of the divine will in the disposition of created things; as I am bidden by the harmonious expression of that will I conduct the operations over which I preside. For God's will has not been ascertained, and until his judgment concerning creation is brought forth, it is futile to hasten created life toward substantial existence prematurely. The nativity of creation is celebrated first in the divine mind; the enactment which ensues is secondary. Thus what you had conceived, by sacred and blessed instincts and deep deliberation, concerning the construction of the Universe could not be brought to present realization until the term established by divine law. It had been determined by unbending and invincible necessity and indissoluble bonds that the cultivation and adornment which you desire for the Universe might take place no earlier. Now, because you urge and press forward at the proper time, and causes concur in the movement to order, your desires are therefore served.

2. "Now Hyle exists in an ambiguous state, placed between good and evil, but since her evil tendency preponderates, she is more readily inclined to acquiesce to it. I recognize that this rough perversity cannot be made to disappear, or be completely transformed; for it is too abundant and, being sustained by the native properties of the matter in which it has established itself, does not readily give way. However, so that it may not impede my work or resist my ordering, I will refine away the greater part of the evil and grossness of Silva. Then the teeming mass, now violently assailed by a restless motion born of confusion, will be reduced to controlled movement within definite limits by that peace which I have in mind. I am fashioning a form for Silva,

florente consortio nec ultra poterit vultibus incompositis displicere. Usiae pepigi: reformabitur in melius. Amicitiam Mundo, morem gesserim elementis. Pertaesum mihi est Carentiam rerum initium exstitisse. Succedet species et Carentiam semoverit a subiecto. Opus igitur promissionis aggredior, quia qui tardior est cruciat expectantem. Et te, Natura, quia callida es ingenio et ad ipsum votis aspiras, sociam comitemque operis non dedignor."

3. Occupatis ad vocem animis, Natura stabat attentior; quae enim de optatis eius texebatur oratio delicias fecerat audiendi. Cumque jam sentiat quod desiderat exoratum, tam mente quam vultu gratiosa summittitur Providentiae, genibus advoluta.

4. Erat Hyle Naturae vultus antiquissimus, generationis uterus indefessus, formarum prima subiectio, materia corporum, substantiae fundamentum. Ea siquidem capacitas, nec terminis nec limitibus circumscripta, tantos sinus tantamque a principio continentiam explicavit, quantam rerum universitas exposcebat. Quodque variae et multiplices aeternitatis suae materiam subiectum obeunt qualitates rerum, non turbari non potuit id quod ab omni natura tam multiformiter pulsaretur. Stabilitatem bonumque tranquillitatis excussit frequens nec intercisa frequentatio naturarum; egredientium numerus ingredientibus locum pandit.

in flourishing union with which she can no longer cause displeasure by her ill-ordered appearance. I have determined for primal substance. It will be refashioned in a better condition. Would that I had instilled amity in the Universe and regularity in the elements: It has disgusted me that Privation should have been the initial state of creation. But form will take possession, and remove this Privation from subject matter. Accordingly I will begin the promised work, for one who acts too slowly torments the one who waits. And since you, Nature, are innately artful, and aid the work with your prayers, I will not scorn to accept you as ally and companion in my task."

3. Nature stood alert, her mind intent upon the voice; for this speech wrought out of things she had hoped for was delightful to hear. And when she understood that what she had desired was granted, she bowed low before Providence, grateful in mind and countenance alike, and threw herself at her feet.

4. Hyle was Nature's most ancient manifestation, the inexhaustible womb of generation, the primal ground of bodily form, the matter of bodies, the foundation of substantive existence. From the beginning this capaciousness, confined by no boundaries or limits, unfolded such vast recesses and such scope for growth as the totality of creatures demanded. And since the diverse and manifold qualities of creatures crowded in upon matter, that which was their eternal foundation could not help being thrown into confusion, when it was assailed by all natural existence in so many forms. The dense and uninterrupted crowding together of natures dispelled stability and peaceful repose; departing multitudes afforded space for more to enter.

Irrequieta est, nec potuit Hyle meminisse quando vel nascentium formis vel occidentium refluxionibus intermissius adiretur. Illud igitur inconsistens et convertibile huius et illius conditionis, qualitatis et formae, cum propriae descriptionis iudicium non expectet, elabitur incognitum, vultus vicarios alternando; et id quod figurarum omnium susceptione convertitur, nullius suae formae signaculo specialiter insignitur.

5. Verum quoquo pacto frenata est licentia discursandi, ut elementorum firmioribus inniteretur substantiis, eisque quaternis velut radicibus inhaereret materies inquieta. Unde Silva multo tutius porrigi dilatarique se patitur, vel essentiis vel qualitatibus vel quantitatibus infinitis. Quemadmodum quidem ad conceptus rerum publicos parturitionesque praegnabilis est et fecunda, non secus et ad malum indifferens est natura. Inest enim seminario quaedam malignitatis antiquior nota, quae prima causae suae fundamina facile non relinquat. In illa quidem congerie repugnantia sibi semina, glacialibus flammida, velocibus pigra, contrariis motibus occurrendo, subiecti sui materiam vel substantiam differebant.

6. Ad id ergo debita melioratione curandum divina Providentia circumspexit, animo sensum contulit, ingenium

Hyle knew no rest, and could not remember when she was less continually engaged with the forms of nascent creatures or the flowing back of dying ones. Since matter, unstable and liable to change from one state of quality and form to another, might not hope to be assigned an identity proper to itself, it remained elusive and unnamed, shifting among borrowed shapes; and that which was altered by the assumption of all shapes was not specially stamped with the seal of a single form of its own.

5. Yet this freedom to move at random was restrained by a certain agreement, in that the restless material was sustained by the more stable substantiality of the elements, and clung to these as if to four roots. Thus Silva might much more safely allow herself to be drawn out and expanded in an infinity of substances, qualities, or quantities. But just as her nature was fertile and prolific in conceiving and giving birth to all creatures in common, it was no less impartial with respect to evil. For there was infused in her seedbed from of old the taint of a certain malign tendency which would not readily abandon the primal basis of its existence. The seeds of things, warring with one another in the chaotic mass, fiery particles with icy, sluggish with volatile, drove apart the material or substantial qualities of their common subject matter by the clash of their contradictory tendencies.

6. Accordingly divine Providence, to remedy this condition by the required transformation, surveyed the situation, mustered her faculties, and summoned up her power of in-

evocavit. Cumque discors adunatio, globus absonus iugum detractantium sic posita principia viderentur, permixtis sejunctione, confusis ordine, informibus expolitione consuluit; leges indidit, licentiam refrenavit. Rudes ut erant, indisciplinatas reluctantesque materias exaequavit potentiis, coniunxit medietatibus, numeris illigavit. Ex consultis igitur Providentiae secretioribus, foederantis amicitiae ligaminibus interiectis, silvestris asperitas facilitate duritiam demutavit, litemque ingenitam retulit in consensum.

7. Antiqui et primarii rigore generis expugnato, in quos ductus Providentia voluit materiae secuta est tractabilis aptitudo. Cumque quam fert Silva grossitiem elimatius expurgassset, ad aeternas introspiciens notiones, germana et proximante similitudine rerum species reformavit. Hyle, caecitatis sub veterno quae iacuerat obvoluta, vultus vestivit alios idearum signaculis circumscripta. Mater igitur generum, ubi praegnationis gremium et ad parturiendum sinus fecunditatis exsolvit, ex ea et in ea factus est suus ortus essentiis, sua nativitas elementis.

8. De confuso, de turbido prius egreditur vis ignita, et nativas derepente tenebras flammis vibrantibus interrumpit. Secuta est terra, non ea levitate, non ea luce spectabilis, sed refixior et corpulentiae grossioris, ut quae rerum fetus ex se

vention. And since the state of the first principles appeared as a discordant union, a hostile mass of things rejecting the yoke, she decided to proceed by separating mixed natures, giving order to their confusion, and refining their unformed condition; she imposed law and restrained their unruliness. Rough though they were, she effected a balance of powers among her undisciplined and recalcitrant materials, joined them with means, and bound them by numerical proportion. When through the inner deliberations of Providence the bonds of a reconciling concord were interposed, the rough and harsh strain in matter changed its obstinacy to agreement, and submitted its innate conflict to a reconciliation.

7. Once this rigidity of ancient and primordial lineage had been overcome, an adaptability took its place in the material, capable of being drawn into such channels as Providence willed. And when Noys had more carefully refined away that coarseness which Silva harbors, reflecting inwardly upon eternal ideas, she fashioned the species of created life in intimate and close resemblance to these. Hyle, who had lain shrouded in her ancient state of darkness, assumed a different aspect when given shape by visible images of the ideal. When the mother of kinds opened forth the fullness of her generative power, the womb of her fecundity to the production of life, there straightway took place, from this source and within it, the origin of the created essences, the birth of the elements.

8. From the confusion and turbulence the power of fire emerged first, and instantly cut through the primeval darkness with vibrant flame. Earth came next, distinguished by no such lightness or radiance, but more stable, and of a more concrete corporeity, as she who would produce from herself

gigneret, earundem refluxiones finito circuitu susceptura. Prodit liquentis aquae clara substantia, cuius plana ac lubrica superficies figuras reddit aemulas, umbrarum incursibus lacessita. Tractus aerius subinfertur, levis quidem et convertibilis: nunc consentire tenebris, nunc suscepto lumine resplendere, calore et frigore nunc rigescere, nunc dissolvi. Eorum singulo occupato domicilio, ad quod consensu materiae inclinatius ferebatur, sedit tellus, ignis emicuit, aer, aqua, medioximi substiterunt.

9. Nodus ille tenorque medius intercessit, de cuius dono pacifico limitaria sibi elementa amicas insumerent et complacitas proportiones. Instituti iuncturas operis ignis forsitan, excandentior et levior, exturbasset, nisi aqua, nisi aer foederata germanitate iuratisque auxiliis obstitissent. Siccum contra stetit humecto, levitatem ponderatio praepedivit. Aquis terra contiguis genuino reflorescit ex arido, et spiritu sustentatur aerio, ne corpulentis ponderata substantiis fine legitimo plus descendat. Sic neque licuit diversorum generum differentiis eo in opere differentiam importare, ubi differentiae convenirent. Controversus igitur et discors numerus repugnantium, armis velut depositis, ad pacificam ingressus est unitatem.

10. Ad delibati primitias operis oculos coeperat circumferre. Bona vidit omnia quae fecisset, Deique aspectibus placitura: quippe quibus ex politione species; tenor esset ex

a progeny of creatures, and receive them flowing back when their earthly round was finished. Forth came the clear substance of liquid water, whose level and shimmering surface gives back rival images when disturbed by the intrusion of shadows. The region of the air was interposed, light and subject to change; now giving itself to darkness, now gleaming at the infusion of light, now growing crisp with frost, now languid with heat. When each of these bodies had taken up the abode to which it was most readily drawn by material affinity, the earth remained stable, fire darted upward, and air and water assumed intermediate positions.

9. That bond and mediating continuity interceded under whose peacemaking influence the elements, while separated from one another, might adopt amicable and mutually agreeable proportions. Fire, hotter and more volatile than the others, would perhaps have disrupted the linkages of the established order had not air and water, allied by their kindred properties, pledged their support to resist it. Dry stood forth against moist, gravity restrained lightness. The earth, inherently arid, began to flourish through contact with the waters, and was sustained by the infusion of air, lest it sink below its ordained position, weighed down by corporeal substance. Thus discrepancies among these differing materials were not allowed to introduce discrepancy in the total scheme, where discrepancies were reconciled. Thus the contentious and discordant group of quarrelers, as though laying aside their arms, entered into a condition of peaceful unity.

10. Noys began to review the first fruits of the work she had begun. She saw that all that she had made was good, and would be pleasing in the sight of God: for there now existed

ligamine; ex materia firmitas, ex partibus plenitudo. Plenum etenim et consummatum necesse erat compositum componentia reformarent, ubi plena et consummata perfectione tota per potentiam, tota per essentiam, ignis, terra ceteraeque materiae convenissent. De quorum materiali continentia brevis et quantalibet particula si citra operis sortem relinqueretur extraria, ex eo turbam noxamque posset incurrere Mundi molitio mox futura, cum peregrinis ut erat promptum viribus extrinsecus temptaretur.

11. Inde est, ut imbecilla hominum natio, quia ex totis integraliter non substiterit elementis, exteriorum semper accidentium incurrentiam reformidet. Si enim calor naturalem calorem extraneus interpellat, pax turbatur interior, et tranquilla quae fuerat erigitur qualitas ad nocendum. Cautum est igitur altiori consilio, ut cum causis suis succidatur et pereat quicquid possit in tempore vel ingenium Mundi laedere vel turbare substantiam vel illius officere disciplinae.

12. Necessariis circa materiam desecutis, ubi elementorum structura stetit ad solidum, ad gratiam species, ad miraculum internexus, de Silva ad genituram Animae ingenium transportavit.

13. Erat fons luminis, seminarium vitae, bonum bonitatis divinae, plenitudo scientiae quae Mens Altissimi nominatur.

forms through the refinement of matter; continuity through its bonding; from the material had come stability, from its diverse components plenitude. And indeed it was inevitable that the components should form a full and consummate whole, since fire, earth and the other materials had contributed all their power and substance to its full and consummate completion. But if a single particle, however small, were left out of the synthesis of these materials and what was allotted to the work were to fall short, the imminent creation of the Universe might thereby incur disruption and damage, since it would manifestly have been attacked from without by foreign forces.

11. Hence it is that the feeble race of men, because they do not subsist through a perfect fusion of the elements, are in constant fear of incurring external accidents. For if heat from without intrudes on our natural heat, our inner peace is disrupted, and a quality that had been at rest becomes aroused to destructive activity. Therefore provision was made through deliberation on high that whatsoever in the temporal order might violate the scheme of the Universe, confuse its substance, or interfere with its orderly operation should be cut off with its causes and destroyed.

12. When these traces of necessity with regard to matter had been eliminated, when the framework of the elements was firmly established, its appearance beautiful and its coherence miraculous, Noys turned her intelligence from Silva to the production of a Soul.

13. Noys was the fountain of light, seedbed of life, a good born of the divine goodness, that fullness of knowledge which is called the Mind of the Most High. This Noys, then,

Ea igitur Noys summi et exsuperantissimi est Dei intellectus, et ex eius divinitate nata est Natura; in qua vitae viventis imagines, notiones aeternae, mundus intelligibilis, rerum cognitio praefinita. Erat igitur videre velut in tersiore speculo quicquid generationi, quicquid operi Dei secretior destinaret affectus. Illic in genere, in specie, in individuali singularitate conscripta, quicquid Hyle, quicquid Mundus, quicquid parturiunt elementa. Illic exarata supremi digito dispositoris textus temporis, fatalis series, dispositio saeculorum. Illic lacrimae pauperum, fortunaeque regum, illic potentia militaris, illic philosophorum felicior disciplina, illic quicquid angelus, quicquid ratio conprehendit humana, illic quicquid caelum sua conplectitur curvatura. Quod igitur tale est, illud aeternitati contiguum, idem natura cum Deo nec substantia est disparatum.

14. Huiuscemodi igitur sive vitae sive lucis origine, vita iubarque rerum, Endelichia, quadam velut emanatione defluxit. Comparuit igitur exporrectae magnitudinis globus, terminatae quidem continentiae, sed quam non oculis, verum solo pervideas intellectu. Eius admodum clara substantia liquentis fluidique fontis imaginem praeferebat, inspectorem suum qualitatis ambiguo praeconfundens, cum plerumque aeri, plerumque caelo cognatior videretur. Quis enim tuto definivit essentiam quae consonantiis, quae se numeris emoveret? Cum igitur quodam quasi praestigio veram imaginem fraudaret, non erat in manibus inspectantis

is the intellect of supreme and all-powerful God, and Nature is born of her divinity; in Noys are the images of unfailing life, the eternal ideas, the intelligible universe, predetermined knowledge of things. There, then, as if in a clearer glass, could be seen all that a secret disposition destined to come to be, to become a work of God. There were enrolled, in genus, in species, in individual uniqueness, whatever Hyle, the Universe, the elements labor to bring forth. There, inscribed by the finger of the supreme arbiter, were the fabric of time, the chain of destiny, the disposition of the ages. There were the tears of the poor and the fortunes of kings, the soldier's strength and the happier discipline of the philosophers, all that angels, all that human reason comprehends, all that heaven encircles with its curving dome. What exists in such a way is closely joined to the eternal, one in nature with God and not distinct in substance.

14. From such a source, then, whether of life or of light, there issued forth by a sort of emanation the life and light of creation, Endelechia. She had the appearance of a sphere, of extended magnitude yet of fixed dimensions, but such as one might not perceive with the eyes, but only by intellect. Her utterly pure substance presented the appearance of a clear and freely flowing fountain, confounding the viewer by its uncertain quality, since it seemed so closely akin to the atmosphere, and at the same time to heaven. For who has defined with certainty that essence which exerts itself by means of harmony, of number? Since, then, one was deceived as if by a kind of magic as to its true aspect, it was beyond the reach of scrutiny to tell how this vitalizing

unde fomes ille vivificus sic maneat ut perire non possit, cum speciatim singulis totus et integer refundatur.

15. Haec igitur Endelichia, propinquis et contiguis ad Noym natalibus oriunda, Mundum Silva matre progenitum ne maritum sponsa gloriosior imparem recusaret, cuiusdam foederis pactiones Providentia procuravit, quibus silvestris caelestisque natura congruo per congruos numeros modulamine convenirent. Quod enim spontanea obtusitati subtilitas non accedit, applicatior numerus in virtute conplexionis medius intercessit, qui corpus animamque quasi quodam glutino copulisque coniugibus illigavit. Ergo moribus ad gratiam immutatis cum alteri in altero conplaceret, consensus amicitiam peperit, amicitia fidem, quod hactenus approbatur.

16. Pulsationibus et molestiis aegritudinem quas patitur plerumque Mundus indoluit, quotiens vel de calore pyrosis vel de humore nimio cataclysmus cursum Naturae solitum perturbavit. Ad id Endelichia totius celeritatis auxilio occurrit, et resarcire citius sedes quas incolit elaborat. Fide quidem hospitii reservata, cum expugnatore tabernaculi sui non participat nec consentit.

17. Ubi igitur Animae Mundique de consensu mutuo societas intervenit, vivendi Mundus nactus originem, quod de spiritus infusione susceperat mox de toto reportavit ad singula, eo vitae vel vegetationis genere cui pro captu proprio

spark should so endure that it might not be extinguished, since it was given back, whole and undiminished, by each individual creature.

15. Now in her birth this Endelechia is closely and intimately related to Noys. Lest so glorious a bride should protest that the Universe spawned by mother Silva was an unworthy husband, Providence arranged the terms of a special compact, whereby the rough and the celestial nature might arrive at an agreeable harmony by way of agreeable proportions. For since what is light and freely moving does not readily accord with solidity, a more adaptable mean proportion interceded to effect their connection, and fastened body to soul as if with a kind of glue and bonds of marriage. Thus when their behavior had been transformed to favor, and each took pleasure in the other, agreement gave birth to amity, and amity to trust, a condition which is observed to this day.

16. The Universe grieved continually over the poundings and troubling afflictions it suffered whenever an irruption of fire or an inundation due to an excess of moisture disturbed the accustomed course of nature. Endelechia hastened to address this problem with swift assistance, and strove to restore quickly the dwelling she inhabits. While the rites of hospitality are maintained, she neither joins with nor suffers any assailant of her tabernacle.

17. When an alliance had thus come about by mutual agreement of Soul and Universe, the Universe, now possessed of the power to produce life, quickly transmitted what it had received through the infusion of spirit from the total structure to individual creatures, by the type of vitality or vegetation for which they were best adapted by their

fuerant aptiora. Aethera aethereis, pura puris conveniunt. Nimirum consentaneum Natura fidelius amplexatur: cum caelo, cum sideribus Endelichiae vis et germanitas invenitur, unde plena totaque nec descisa potentiis ad comfortanda caelestia supera regione consistit, verum in inferioribus virtus eius degenerat. Quippe imbecillitas corporum tarditatem inportat, quo se minus talem exerat qualis est per naturam.

18. Itaque viventis Animae beneficio comfortata, de nutricis Silvae gremio se rerum series explicavit.

Megacosmus 3

Ergo sideribus levis aether, sidera caelo,
caelum secessit aere, terra freto.

In caelo divina manus caelique ministris
omne creaturae primitiavit opus:
caeli forma teres, essentia purior ignis,
motus circuitus, numina, turba deum.

Dico deos quorum ante Deum praesentia servit,
quos tenet in vero lumine vera dies.
Pacis enim locus aethereae, totoque tumultu
aeris exceptus, sepositusque sibi,
separat arcanas sedes. Super, immo superne,
extramundanus creditur esse Deus.

particular capacities. The ether befits ethereal creatures, pure is mated with pure. Nature, to be sure, embraced more closely what was consonant with her. The true virtue and affinity of Endelechia is inherently with the heavens and the stars, so that in the supernal realm her power to sustain celestial life endures wholly undiminished, while in the lower world its efficacy declines. This weakening accounts for the sluggishness of bodily existence, wherein Endelechia appears less powerful than she is in her true nature.

18. And now, sustained by the gift of vivifying Soul, the ordered progression of created life unfolded from the nurturing womb of Silva.

Megacosmus 3

Thus the subtle ether grew separate from the stars, the stars from the firmament, the heavens from the atmosphere, the earth from the waters.

In heaven and in the heavenly powers the hand of God produced the first fruits of the entire work of creation: the rounded form of the celestial sphere, its essence a purer fire, circular motion, heavenly powers, the host of the gods.

I call "gods" those beings whose presence is attendant upon God, those whom true day retains in its true light. For a region of ethereal calm, exempt from all the tumult of the atmosphere, secluded unto itself, sets apart their secret dwelling places. Belief holds that God exists far above, indeed above all, beyond the limits of the universe.

Ad sensum perfecta, Cherub propiusque magisque
cernit in arcanis consiliisque Dei.
Quam secus ardescit Seraphin, sed civibus illis
et Deus est ardor, et sacer ardor amor.
Pura Throni legio, quibus insidet ille profundus
spiritus et sensus, mensque profunda Noys.
Officio decorata suo cognomina servit
iure Potestatis turba iubere potens.
Spiritibus quibus ipse facit Dominatio nomen
subditur ordo, sua conditione minor;
sed quamvis minor a superis, in subdita Princeps
agmina disposuit et sua iussa facit.
Virtutes, sacer ordo, facit miracula rerum,
cum propriae causas commoditatis habent.
Caelestis pars militiae, numerosus ad astra,
Angelus obsequitur sub Michaele suo.
Angelus inferior gradus est; ordire priores,
in hierarchias concidet ordo novem.

Terrenis excepta super, substantia caeli,
ut melior, cultu sic meliore fuit;
scribit enim caelum stellis, totumque figurat
quod de fatali lege venire potest.
Praesignat qualique modo qualique tenore
omnia sidereus saecula motus agat.
Praeiacet in stellis series quam longior aetas
explicet et spatiis temporis ordo suis.
Sceptra Phoronei, fratrum discordia Thebae,
flammae Phaethontis, Deucalionis aquae.
In stellis Codri paupertas, copia Croesi,
incestus Paridis Hippolytique pudor.

Perfect in understanding, the Cherub discerns most closely and fully the hidden deliberations of God. How different is the burning desire of the Seraphim, but God is the desire of these subjects too, and their desire is a sacred love. The Thrones are that pure host in whom resides the profound spirit and understanding, the profound mind of Noys. That throng mighty in command by right of Power bear a name that is the emblem of their office. To those spirits whose special Dominion provides their name is subordinated an order inferior in condition; but although of lesser rank than those above, the Prince governs subordinate ranks, and issues commands of his own. The sacred order of Virtues creates miracles, for they possess the principles of their own function. The Angels, a portion of the heavenly army as numerous as the stars, serve obediently under their Michael. The lowest grade is that of the Angels. Align those above: ordering will divide them into nine hierarchies.

Far beyond earthly existence, the substance of the heavens, being finer, was distinguished by a finer ornamentation; for Noys inscribes heaven with stars, and prefigures all that can come to pass through decree of fate. She foretells through signs in what manner and along what path the influence of the stars impels all temporal existence. That sequence of events which long ages and the measured course of time will unfold appears first in the stars. There are the scepter of Phoroneus, the conflict of the brothers at Thebes, the flames of Phaethon, Deucalion's flood. Among the stars are Codrus's poverty, Croesus's wealth, the unchastity of Paris, Hippolytus's modesty. Among the stars are the

In stellis Priami species, audacia Turni,
sensus Ulixeus, Herculeusque vigor.
In stellis pugil est Pollux, et navita Tiphys,
et Cicero rhetor, et geometra Thales.
In stellis lepidum dictat Maro, Milo figurat,
Fulgurat in Latia nobilitate Nero;
astra notat Persis, Aegyptus parturit artes,
Graecia docta legit, proelia Roma gerit.
In causas rerum sentit Plato, pugnat Achilles,
et praelarga Titi dextera spargit opes.
Exemplar speciemque Dei virguncula Christum
parturit, et verum saecula numen habent.
Munificens deitas Eugenium commodat orbi,
donat et in solo munere cuncta semel.
Sic opifex, ut in ante queant ventura videri
saecula, sidereis significata modis.

Figit utrosque polos, circumvolubile caelum
flectit; et aeternum volvere stare fuit.
Quinque parallelis medium circumligat orbem:
hinc extrema rigent, hinc mediata calent.
Temperat ergo duas algoribus extremarum
et medii Solis collaterante via.
Dividit in quadras caelum cingente coluro,
sed neuter plenus ad sua puncta redit.
Signiferumque locat: tendit deductior austrum,
sidereos brevior frigida plaustra boves.
Obliquatur item quae vicinantibus astris
undique confectum Lactea nomen habet.

grandeur of Priam, the boldness of Turnus, Odyssean cleverness and Herculean strength. Among the stars are the boxer Pollux, Tiphys the helmsman, Cicero the orator, and the geometer Thales. Among the stars Virgil composes with grace, Milo creates forms, Nero glitters in Latian pomp; Persia charts the heavenly bodies, Egypt gives birth to the arts, learned Greece gathers knowledge, Rome wages war. Plato intuits the principles of existence, Achilles fights, and the generous hand of Titus pours forth riches. A tender virgin gives birth to Christ, at once the idea and the living form of God, and earth possesses true divinity. Divine munificence bestows Eugene upon the world, and grants all things at once in this sole gift. Thus the Creator works, that ages to come may be beheld in advance, signified in starry forms.

Noys fixes the two poles, and sets the firmament in circular motion; and this revolution was its eternal state. With five parallel zones she encircles our middle orb: of these the extremes are frozen and the central portion fiery hot. Therefore she creates two zones tempered by the coldness of the extremes, and on the other side by the Sun's course across the central region. She divides the firmament into quarters with encircling colures, though neither of these attains the point of completion. She sets in place the sign-bearing circle: its greater arc extends southward, the lesser toward the starry oxen and their icy wagon. Next is drawn across the sky that path which bears the name "Milky," derived from stars clustered together from all directions.

Solstitiale caput Cancro vicinius exit,
aequidialis item linea Libra fuit.
Anguis, ad Arcturos medius, distinguit utrumque.
Figitur in Borea nautica stella polus,
antipodesque suos nunquam visura. Bootes
descensus supero temptat ab axe breves.
Innixusque genu tractus insistit eosdem
caeli quos Helice, quos Cynosura minor.
Post humeros micat Herculeos Adrianna corona,
praeiacet inventum Mercuriale, Lyra.
Succedit Ledaeus olor; statione propinquum
continuant Cepheus, Cassiopaea locum.
Lacteus Andromaden mediam secat editus auro.
Perseus ignitae Gorgonis ora tenet.
Heniochus quos ipse gerit nascentibus Haedis,
in pluvium multi commaduere dies.
Inde loci micat herbipotens Ophiuchus in astris,
incinctus rigido molle dracone latus.
Clarus et ad vultum spatiosi corporis Anguis
tenditur astrorum splendidiore nota.
Ardet et insigni splendore notabile Telum,
subvolat inferior praepes adunca Iovis.
Iunctior attingit Aquilae confinia Delphin,
stat prope Delphinum Bellerophontis equus.
Vectori, Phrixee, tuo superinsita splendet
quae notat Aegypti deltica forma situm.
Tauri fronte madent Hyades, septemque sorores
cauda: Pleiades Vergiliasque voces.
Morbidat aestatem Procyus qua cardine summo
Signifer erigitur celsior in Geminos.

The point of the solstice emerged close to Cancer, and Libra became the equidial boundary.

Draco, passing between, separates the two Bears. The pole is marked by Boreas, the mariner's star, which may never behold its own antipodes. Bootes attempts brief sorties from the upper region. The Kneeler travels the same regions of the sky as Helice and the lesser Cynosura. Behind his Herculean shoulders gleams the crown of Ariadne, and the Lyre, the discovery of Mercury, lies before. The Ledean Swan is next; Cepheus and Cassiopeia follow in close succession. An effulgence of milk-white gold cuts through the center of Andromeda. Perseus holds up the face of a glowing Gorgon. At the birth of those Kids whom Heniochus carries, many days were filled with rain. In the next position among the stars shines Ophiuchus, master of the powers of herbs, his pliant body girt by an unyielding snake. The brilliant Serpent is stretched forth to display its vast body in a still more splendid pattern of stars. The Weapon, also remarkable for its outstanding splendor, burns brightly; lower down hovers the bird of Jove with curving beak. The Dolphin impinges closely upon the domain of Aquila, and the horse of Bellerophon stands close by the Dolphin. Set above your vessel, o Phrixean, shines that deltaic form which indicates the position of Egypt. The weeping Hyades are set in the forehead of the Bull, and seven sisters form his tail: call them the Pleiades or the Vergiliae. Procyon brings on the blighting heat of summer at that time when the Zodiac attains its highest point in Gemini.

Triste rubet malus egregie notique caloris
Sirius, ad Cancri solstitiale caput.
Aethereum Praesepe suos ostendit Asellos,
sub Cancro positos Herculeaque fera.
Nunc quoque sidereo tractu venatur Orion,
acceleratque vias anticipare Lepus.
Quod primum temptarit aquas famosior Argos
aethereum nullo Tiphyde temptat iter.
Vergit ad austrinum latus inclinatior Ara,
circiter Haemonium semiferumque senem.
Assequiturque locum Pistris Neptunia, qua se
caelesti nodo Piscis uterque ligat.
Influit Eridanus caelum quoque, climate nostro
notus, et ad superos non leve nomen habet.
Cum Corvo loca nota tenet distentior Hydrus,
et Crater, Cancri sub regione situs,
sed Piscis susceptat aquas madidantis Aquarii.
Effulsere suis cetera signa locis.

Phrixeo contra pecori, radiata resultat
exaequans nocti pendula Libra diem.
Oppositum Taurum duris aspectibus urit
Scorpio, natura perditiore gravis.
In Geminos Helenae, lucentia sidera, fratres
tenditur Haemonii nota sagitta senis.
Aestuat ambustus Cancer, contraque madescit
altera solstitii linea, Capra Iovis.
Cretaeo Capra fida Iovi, confulgurat astro
retrogradi Cancri pestiferoque Cani.
Obiacet Herculeo deferventique Leoni
Urceolus pueri continuantis aquas.

Sirius, notorious for heat, burns in baleful brilliance at the point of the Solstice in Cancer. The heavenly Manger reveals its twin Asses, set before Cancer and the Herculean beasts. Now too Orion hunts across the starry regions, and the Hare is quick to anticipate his course. The voyage which the famous Argo first attempted on the deep, it pursues in heaven with no Tiphys at the helm. The Altar, set still lower in the sky, inclines toward the southern region, close by the Haemonian, an old man half a beast. The seaborne Whale occupies the next position, where the two Fish are joined to one another by a celestial bond. Eridanus, famous in our clime, flows also in heaven, and bears a name not without meaning for the gods. The sprawling Hydra, and the Bowl, placed below the seat of Cancer, occupy a common position with the Crow. But the Fish takes in the waters of brimming Aquarius. Other signs shine forth in their several places.

Poised in opposition to the Phrixean Ram, Libra gives forth brilliant beams, setting day and night in equal measure. Scorpio, burdened by his incorrigible nature, rages with fierce glares against his opposite, the Bull. The well-known arrow of the aged Haemonian is drawn against the gleaming stars of the twin brothers of Helen. Cancer rages with scorching heat, and Jove's Goat, at the opposite solstitial boundary, brings drenching rain. The Goat, so devoted to Jove in his Cretan boyhood, shines with the brilliance of the retrograde star of Cancer, and the ravaging Dog. The little Vessel of a boy pouring forth water stands opposed to the rage of the Herculean Lion.

Astraeam, bona fructiferi quae colligit anni,
occiduam surgens Piscis uterque videt.

Sidera, quae praesens sic vel sic nominat aetas,
temporis ex ortu caelicus ignis erant.
Communi ne voce rei generalis oberrret,
quae modo sunt stellis nomina fecit homo.

Sub caelo quo signa meant, septena planetas
sidera devexum currere mandat iter.
Naturam moresque suos praeiudicat illis,
quid mundo moveant singula iure suo.
Luna, quibus vicina meat, terrena marina
legibus exagitat imperiosa suis.
Subsequitur qui lege magis variante viarum
circuit ancipiti limite Solis iter.
Inde loci Venus est, quae seminis et geniturae
vires humecti plena caloris habet.
Sol iubar est medius, quo plenius astra niterent
hinc illinc lucis collaterata deo.
Militat ad Solem Mars iunctior urbibus altis,
saepe super reges prodigiale rubens.
Sexta Iovis bonitas, alio nisi laesa veneno,
format ad eventus hospita signa bonos.
Postremos pigrosque movet diffusius orbes
infecunda suo frigore stella senis.

Opposito spirare sibi de limite certo
mandat ab instabili flamina nata freto.
Obriguit Boreas, maduit Notus; Auster et Eurus,
hic tempestates, ille serena facit.

The two Fish, as they rise, behold the setting of Astraea, who gathers in the wealth of the fruitful year.

The stars, which the present age calls by this name or that, existed from the birth of time as heavenly fire. Lest he should go astray by applying a common name to this class of beings, man created the names that even now denote the stars.

Below the heaven where the signs move, an inclined path determines the courses of the seven planets. Noys preordains their nature and behavior, and what influence each in its own right may exert on the world. The Moon, tyrannical, draws land and sea into conflict by those laws which bring her close to the earth. He who comes next, by a system of widely varying paths, passes back and forth across the route of the Sun. Next in position is Venus, suffused with humid heat, who has charge of the vital powers of sowing and generation. The Sun is the central splendor, that the planets on either hand, sustained by the god of light, may give off a fuller radiance. Mars, following next after the Sun, visits war upon proud cities, and his red glare often works strangely upon kings. Sixth is the goodness of Jove, which, where not tainted by some extraneous evil, creates signs that promise welcome events. Last of all the star of the old man, barren and cold, moves in wide and sluggish circles.

Noys commanded the winds, born of the shifting sea, to blow in opposition to one another from their fixed positions. The north wind is crisp with frost, the south dripping wet, the east wind brings storms, the west fair weather.

Sic ubi sub caelo Tellus stetit, unda refluxit,
et stellata novum reddidit aethra iubar,
cum reptante pecus, cum pisce volatile factum
arripuit proprium dispare sorte locum.
Serpat an incedat, natet an volet, impare fato
vivit, et ad mores non sibi sentit idem.
Nanciscuntur enim fera silvas, bestia campos,
anguis humum, volucris aera, piscis aquas.
Pisce natantur aquae, volucri discurritur aer,
incedunt pecudes, vipera serpit humo.

Ad medium Tellus puncti subsederat instar,
mobilibus stabili sede parata quies.
Scissuris vel tota tribus divisa recedit,
vel sub septeno climate sparsa iacet.
Pars operitur aquis, pars montibus, altera silvis,
cetera sub tractu terra relicta brevi.
Montibus in morem nervorum stringitur orbis.
omnia cum caelo sidera fulcit Atlas.
Partis ad aethereae confinia, clarus Olympus
sub Iove depresso nubila densa videt.
Tractantes humana deos septemque planetas
visere Parnasus temptat utroque iugo.
In cedros Libanus silvescit; libera Sina,
quo sacra sub sacro lex Moysete data est.
Surgit Athos, consurgit Eryx, sic alta Cithaera,
sic Aracyntheus, sic Aganippus apex,
sic Apenninus, sic Herculis Oeta sepulcrum,
sic ardens Liparis, sic Terebinthus olens;

Now when Earth stood firm beneath the heavens, the sea ebbed and flowed, and the starry ether gave off a new radiance, the beast of the field together with the reptile, flying creatures and fish were made, and took over the regions proper to their diverse conditions. Whether it creep or walk, swim or fly, each lives by its own law, and none agree as to their mode of life. For savage creatures are native to the wilderness, other beasts to the field, the serpent to the barren ground, the bird to the air, fish to the waters. The waters are swum by fish, the air is traversed by birds, beasts walk abroad, the viper creeps along the ground.

The Earth had settled at the center of things, a kind of central point; rest from motion was afforded by its stable position. Marked by three great divisions, all the land either withdrew from sight or, in scattered spots, lay open to the seven climates. One part was covered by waters, another by mountains, another by forest; the small expanse of land remaining was left bare.

Earth's orb is bound by mountains as if with sinews. Atlas supports the firmament and all the stars. On the border of the ethereal region renowned Olympus beholds the dense clouds of lowering Jove. Parnassus with its twin peaks seeks to behold the gods disposing the affairs of men and the seven planets. Lebanon bristles with cedars; Sinai, where the blessed Law was given into the charge of blessed Moses, lies open. Athos rises, together with Eryx and lofty Cithaeron, the Aracynthean peak, and the peak of Aganippe; the Apennines too, and Oeta, sepulcher of Hercules; glowing Lipari, hills redolent of terebinth;

Pindus, et in superos suspectius Ossa cacumen,
Othrys, et medici Pelion antra senis.
Caucasus, excubiae vigilantis in astra Promethei;
plectricano Rhodope gratior ora viro.
Vertice Gargano tumet altior Itala tellus,
Trinacris erigitur monte, Pelore, tuo.
In caelum Pholoe gemina cervice minatur,
cognita Centauros ferre biforme genus.
Candent arctoi Riphea cacumina montis
quas illo Boreas parturit axe nives.
Continuat situs ipse suus lateraliter Alpes;
solis ad occiduum devia claustra rigent.

Quod spatii montana tenent deperdit aratrum,
articuloque iacet sub breviore solum.
Cepit enim fruticosa lupos, deserta leones,
arida serpentes, pars nemoralis apros.

Distrahitur genus in species, Naturaque simplex
unaque non uno particulata modo.
Ossibus extruitur elephas, dorsoque camelus
surgit, et in bubalo cornua frontis honor.
Ad cursum cervus succingitur; erigit altis
poplitibus dammas tibia longa pedum.
Substitit in pectus leo fortior, ursus in ungues,
tigris atrox morsu, dente timendus aper.
Velleribus mollescit ovis; capraeque maritus
et capra vestitur asperiore toga.
Cor fervens erexit equum, deiecit asellum
segnities; animos praegravat auris onus.
Rugiit ad praedam pardusque lupusque sititor
sanguinis; ille nemus, hic iuga montis amans.

Pindus, and Ossa, a peak menacing to the gods; Othrys, and Pelion, retreat of the ancient healer; the Caucasus, watch-tower of stargazing Prometheus; Rhodope, a clime favored by him who sang to the lyre. The Italian land swells higher with the peak of Gargano, and Sicily is exalted by your peak, O Peloris. Pholoe, known for bearing the biform race of Centaurs, threatens heaven with her double peak. Snows which Boreas brings to birth in that clime whiten the peaks of the northward-lying Rhipean mountains. Their very situation links the Alps together on every side; and toward the setting sun lonely passes lie frozen.

The terrain that mountains occupy never knows the plow, and the small areas of open ground lie idle. For the thickets harbor wolves, the deserts lions, the dry wastes serpents, and the woodland boars.

Genus is separated into species, and Nature, simple and one herself, is particularized in diverse ways. The elephant is fortified with tusks, the camel's back rises high, and horns grace the forehead of the buffalo. The stag is equipped for flight, and long slender legs with knees drawn high lift the doe. The bold lion relies on his stout heart, the bear on his claws, the tiger breeds terror by his fangs, the fearsome boar by his tusks. The sheep is soft with fleece; the she-goat and her spouse are clad in a coarser robe. An ardent spirit emboldens the horse, but sluggishness burdens the donkey; the weight of his ears lies heavy on his spirit. The panther and the bloodthirsty wolf roar for prey; the one loves the forest,

Grandior in tauro virtus, sed parvula vulpes
plenius angusta sub brevitate sapit.
Nascuntur servire boves, animalque timoris
crescit in auriculas, res fugitiva, lepus.
Ad montes onager fugiens emancipat usum
officiumque negat corporis ipse sui.
Morato canis ingenio vel amicior usu
pertulit humanas extimuisse minas.
Prodit, ut ignoti faciat miracula visus,
lynx, liquidi fontem luminis intus habens.
Prodit et in risus hominum deformis imago
simia, naturae degenerantis homo.
Prodit item castor, proprio de corpore velox
reddere, quas sequitur hostis avarus, opes.
Cisimus obrepsit, et vestitura potentes
martix, et spolio non leviore bever,
Carior et redolens, et bursae praedo sabellus,
guttura complectens deliciosa ducum.
Per gremium telluris aquae diffunditur humor,
qui vada, qui fluvios, stagna lacusque facit.
Influit Euphrates terras, ubi magna virago
in Babylone sua coctile duxit opus.
Telluris loca Tigris obit, qua sorbuit aurum
Crassus, et in Crasso cognita Roma fuit.
Nutrices fert Nilus aquas ubi, Magne, probasti
quam male sub puero principe tuta fides.
Abana dissiluit, expectavitque Damascus
surgeret, ut riguis culta foveret aquis.
Parvaque sed felix Siloe visura prophetam,
immo reformantem saecula nostra Deum,

the other the mountain ridge. Though the bull's power is greater, the little vixen has more intelligence within her spare frame. Oxen are born to slavery, and that creature of fear, that fugitive thing, the hare, waxes great in ears. The wild ass, fleeing to the mountains, claims for himself the use of his body, and refuses to offer it up. The dog, devoted through native understanding or by habit, submits to living in fear of human threats. The lynx comes forth to create miracles which none may behold, for he possesses within himself a fountain of liquid light. The ape comes forth to receive men's laughter, a deformed image, a man of degenerate nature. The beaver comes forth, prompt to give up from his own body those treasures which a greedy enemy pursues. The squirrel creeps forward, and the marten, destined to clothe the great, and the beaver, with a pelt no less rich. Costlier still is that ill-smelling plunderer of purses, the sable, wrapping himself about the pleasure-glutted throats of princes.

Throughout the womb of earth water is diffused, creating streams and rivers, marshes and lakes. The Euphrates flows through those lands where the great virago raised an edifice of clay in her Babylonian capitol. The Tigris passes through the region of the earth where Crassus drank down gold, and Rome was recognized in his example. The Nile bears nourishing waters where you, great Pompey, confirmed how unsafe is loyalty when the prince is a boy. Abana rushes forth, and Damascus waits for it to rise and nourish its plantations with irrigating waters. Shiloah, small but blessed, will behold a prophet, nay, God himself, renewing

Iordanisque sacer, sumptoque futurus honore
  nobilis, auctoris tinguere membra sui.
Ambitur Simoente suo Segeia tellus,
  felix, si melius sciret amare Paris.
Alpheos amnes Arethusaque flumina vidit
  Trinacris, in dominos excrucianda malos.
Romanas habiturus opes, et culmina rerum,
  distulit obliquas ad mare Tibris aquas.
In Ligurum campos cecidit Padus, impulit undas,
  et tulit ad Venetos imperiosus iter.
Influxit Rhodanus, ubi nobile vidit Agauno
  certamen turbae martyris ante mori.
Fluxit et Eridanus quae sub Phaethontide flamma
  unica communi restitit unda malo.
Secana prosiliit, ubi grandia nomina regum—
  Pippinos, Karolos—bellica terra tulit.
Emicuit Ligeris, ubi Martinopolis inter
  sidereos fluvios pictaque rura sedet.

Texuntur musco fontes, et caespite ripae.
  vestitur tellus gramine, fronde nemus.
Fronduit in plano platanus, convallibus alnus,
  rupe rigens buxus, litore lenta salix,
monte cupressus olens, sacra vitis colle supino,
  inque laborata Palladis arbor humo.
Populus albescens, lotus cognatior undis,
  et viburna magis vimine lenta suo;
in nodos et lata rigens venabula cornus,
  in validos arcus flexile robur, acer;
mobilibus tremulus et acutis frondibus ilex,
  et mala Cecropias perdere taxus apes;

our world. Jordan, sacred as well, will be ennobled by the honor of bathing the limbs of its creator. Simois winds through the land of Troy, a happy land, had Paris loved more wisely. Sicily, fated to suffer under cruel tyrants, beholds the river Alpheus, and the stream of Arethusa. Tiber, destined to possess the wealth and worldly eminence of Rome, bears its waters slanting toward the sea. The Po descends to the Ligurian plain, drives its waters along, and makes its way majestically toward the Venetians. The Rhone flows where Agaune saw her band of martyrs fight nobly to be the first to die. Eridanus flows forth, the one stream which withstood the general disaster of Phaethon's flames. The Seine wells forth where a warlike land has borne great dynasties of rulers—the Pippins, the Charleses. The Loire shimmers where the city of St. Martin lies between starry waters and brightly tinted fields.

Springs are wreathed with moss and riverbanks with turf. The field is clad with grasses, the grove with leaves. The plane tree flourishes on level ground, the alder in valleys, the sturdy box tree on rocky cliffs, the supple willow on the shore, the scented cypress on the mountain, the sacred vine on the hillside, the tree of Pallas in hard-worked soil. There is the silvered poplar; the lotos, lover of the stream; the wayfaring tree, more supple, with its shoots; the cornel, gnarled and bristling with long spears; the maple, hard and flexible, suited for strong bows; the holm oak, quivering with sharp and trembling leaves; the yew, fell destroyer of the Cecropian bees;

quercus alumna, gigas abies, pygmaea mirica.
Dumus, et armato corpore spina nocens,
ruscus inhorrescens, et eisdem rhamnus in armis,
non nisi callosas extimuere manus.
Fagus amans hederas, et coniuga vitibus ulmus,
quaeque parum cinus matre recedet humo;
concava sambucus, frangique levis sycomorus,
quique novae frondis gaudet honore frutex.

Alcinoi modo sponte nemus, modo stirpe renascens,
et modo fortuito semine, poma tulit.
Arrisit pater Autumnus, potuitque novellus
fructus in arboribus complacuisse suis:
nux vestita togis, contractaque carica rugis,
fructus Adae ficus, mensa secunda pirus;
cognita vis sorbae ventrem retinere fluentem.
Coctana pallescunt, punica mala rubent.
Castana dura togis, velataque pessica lana,
et quae perdurant cerea pruna brevi;
aesculus alta solo, caelo directa cacumen
pinus, et exiguae Phyllidis esca nuces;
cedrus poma ferens triplici sensata sapore,
iuniperus tereti semine paene piper;
festino quae flore solet prodire sub auras,
gessit amagdaleas ardua virga nuces;
grata suae Veneri mirtus, sacra laurea Phoebo,
et quaecumque notam nominis arbor habet.

Inter felices silvas generosior arbor
balsamus ignotas protulit orbe comas.
Myrrhaque, de cuius lacrimis in corpora functa,
ne resoluta fluant, altera vita redit.

the nurturing oak; the giant pine; the pigmy tamarisk. The bramble, and the menacing hawthorn with its well-armed body, the bristling butcher's broom, and the buckthorn, similarly armed, fear nothing but the calloused hand. The beech, lover of ivy; the elm, bride of the vine; the wild briar, which scarcely separates itself from mother earth; the arching elder; the mulberry, easily broken; every kind of tree rejoices in the splendor of new foliage.

The grove of Alcinous, arising sometimes spontaneously, sometimes by the renewal of a parent stock, sometimes by a random seeding, brought forth its fruits. Father Autumn smiled and in his orchards the fruit, though young, attained a pleasing ripeness: the walnut, clad in its jacket, the Carian fig, creased with wrinkles, the fig that was Adam's food, the pear, a common dessert, the sorb apple, known to have power to curb the flow of the bowels. The quince is pale colored, the pomegranate red. There is the hard-shelled chestnut; the downy-coated peach; the waxen sheen of the plum, which endures but a short time; the lofty winter oak, bowing to the earth; the pine, thrusting its top toward heaven; nuts that are the food of scrimping Phyllis; the cedar, bearing fruits endowed with a threefold essence; the juniper, with polished berries of an almost peppery tang; the almond, which is wont to issue forth in an early flowering, and whose topmost branches bear its nuts; the myrtle, dear to Venus, the laurel, sacred to Phoebus, and every tree that enjoys the distinction of a name.

Amid the flourishing forest the balsam, a noble tree, produces foliage unregarded by the world. The myrrh tree, too, by whose weeping over deceased bodies, lest they disintegrate and flow away, a second life is imparted.

Thurea stirps consurgit olens, quae munera Christo
Persis adorator primitiata tulit.
Cinnamus exoritur, quae suaviter exteriore
cortice, sed melius interiore sapit.
Utilis et medicos aloe specialis ad usus
defluit a ligno, succida gutta, suo;
sic liquor Heliadum, sic cedria, sic quoque gummi
quod trasmittit Arabs, quod terebinthus habet.
Cetera solemnes adeo facientia gustus
ad rapidos soles Indica gignit humus.

At potius iacet Aurorae vicinus et Euro
Telluris gremio floridiore locus,
cui Sol dulcis adhuc primo blanditur in ortu,
cum primaeva nihil flamma nocere potest.
Illic temperies, illic clementia caeli
floribus et vario germine praegnat humum.
Nutrit odora, parit species, pretiosa locorum,
mundi delicias angulus unus habet.
Surgit ea gingiber humo, surgitque galanga
longior, et socia baccare dulce thymum;
perpetui quem floris honos commendat acanthus,
grataque conficiens unguina nardus olet.
Pallescitque crocus ad purpureos hyacinthos;
ad casiae thalamos certat odore macis.
Inter felices silvas sinuosus oberrat
inflexo totiens tramite rivus aquae;
arboribusque strepens et conflictata lapillis
labitur in pronum murmure lympha fugax.
Hos, reor, incoluit riguos pictosque recessus
hospes—sed brevior hospite—primus Homo.

The sweet-scented frankincense tree rises up, which the Persian worshipper brought as a first offering to Christ. The cinnamon appears, sweet flavored in its outer bark, but sweeter within. The lign-aloe, specially useful in the practice of medicine, exudes drops of juice from its bark; so too the tears of the Heliades, so cedar resin, and so the gum that Arabia sends, which the terebinth harbors. Beneath the blazing sun the soil of India generates other essences, which lend relish to high feasts.

But still nearer to the dawn and the abode of Eurus, in the flowering bosom of Earth there lies a region upon which the Sun, still mild at its first rising, shines lovingly, for its fire is in its first age, and has no power to harm. There a temperate climate and benign heaven impregnate the soil with flowers and various fruits. This one little retreat nurtures the scents, bears the species, contains the riches and delights of the regions of the world. In this soil ginger grows, and the taller galingale, sweet thyme, with its companion hazelwort; acanthus, graced with the token of a perpetual blossom, and spikenard, redolent of the pleasing ointment which it bears. The crocus pales beside the purple hyacinth, and the scent of mace competes with beds of cassia.

Amid the flourishing wood strays a winding stream, continually shifting its course; rippling over the roots of trees and agitated by pebbles, the swift water is borne murmuring along. In this well watered and richly colored retreat, I believe, the first Man dwelt as a guest—but too brief a time for a guest.

Hoc studio curante nemus Natura creavit;
surgit fortuitis cetera silva locis.
Nascitur Aonium nemus oblectare poetas.
Ad Paridis raptus Ida datura rates.
Frondet Aricinae, fontanis marcida guttis,
frondet et herbosis silva Lycaea iugis.
Grandiloquis habitanda sophis, habitanda Platoni
frondet Academici gratia multa loci.
Signiferi convexa novem liquere sorores,
Pierii nemoris tantus abundat honor.
Inter odoratas Gryneo vertice lauros
vatibus et vatum gratior umbra deo.
Robora verticibus caelo certantia gignit
India; fertque suum Celtica terra nemus,
Silaque, piniferum quae tollit ad astra cacumen,
prospectans gemini candida vela maris.
Briscelim sinus Armoricus, Turonia Vastem,
Ardaniam silvam Gallicus orbis habet.

Dividit in species tunicata legumina tellus:
in cicer Italicum, Pictoniasque fabas,
et caecas lentes, et pisa moventia ventrem,
nigrantes vicias phaseolasque leves.
Macra siligo riget, frumentaque plena tumescunt;
surgit avena levis, ordea parva sedent.

Cum sensim reptantis aquae persensit odorem,
Explicuit varias quas habet hortus opes.
Pectoris herba, cavas rupes insedit ysopus;
plana soporatum terra papaver habet.
Purgatura caput tenet arva sinapis, et altos
obsedit muros frigida barba Iovis.

Nature created this grove with affectionate care; elsewhere the wilderness sprang up at random. The Aonian grove is born to be the delight of poets. Ida will provide ships' timber for the theft of Paris. The glade of Aricia, enervated by the mere trickle of its fountains, and the Lycean grove on its grassy ridge put forth leaves. The great beauty of the grove of the Academy, destined to be home to high-sounding philosophers and Plato himself, comes into bloom. The Nine Sisters have abandoned the vault of the firmament, so great is the renown of the Pierian grove. The shade of scented laurels about the Grynean temple is cherished by poets, and by the god of poets. India produces trees which assail heaven with their tops; the Celtic lands, too, have their groves, and Sila, who raises her pine-covered summit to the stars, looking out upon the gleaming sails of twin seas. Brittany has Broceliande, Touraine her Gâtine, and Gaul has the forest of Ardennes.

Earth divides the jacketed vegetables into species: Italian chickpea and beans of Poiteau; eyeless lentils, and peas which activate the belly; dark vetch and light kidney bean. Sparse winter wheat grows hard, and ripe grain swells; the slender oat grows tall, barley remains short.

As it slowly feels the scent of seeping water, the garden spreads forth the wealth it possesses. Hyssop, an herb for the lungs, dwells in the hollows of rocks; open ground bears the drowsy poppy. Mustard, with power to clear the head, takes over the fields, and chill houseleek besieges lofty walls.

Narcissos fontana tenent, saepesque ligustra;
   horti forma rosae, lilia vallis honor.
Et cum scariola surgit lactuca sopora,
   portulaca iacens, intiba fixa solo,
caepa repleta notis, Liguris sapor allia dirus,
   quodque relativo caespite gaudet olus;
latius aspirans mentaster, discolor iris,
   cumque dialtea supplice, malva levis;
plena voluptatis eruca, libens satirea,
   satyricon revocans ad iuvenile senes,
quaeque die clauso sibi clauditur, et reserato
   se reserat, Solem sponsa secuta suum.
Purgatura quibus aegrotat femina causas,
   pullulat in glaucas artemisia comas.
In festis epulis emendatura sapores,
   salvia de calamis prodit odora suis,
quam medicinalem tulit ad pulmenta culinae
   prodigus et longe deliciosus homo.
Prodit feniculus tenui crinita capillo,
   confusos oculos extenebrare potens;
quando retardantes cum pellibus exuit annos,
   in marathro serpens lumina functa novat.
Substitit origanum, serpillum serpere coepit,
   contra vipereum gramina nota genus.
Maxima nervorum calaminthis conciliatrix,
   cum per membra furit articulare malum.
Res rata pulegium contra suspecta veneni
   pocula, cerfolium non secus herba valens.
Vulgago, terrae fumus, jocunda buglossa
   surgit, ut expurgent menstrua, splen, cerebrum.

Fountains possess the narcissus, hedges the bindweed; the fair form of the rose adorns the garden, lilies grace the vale. Sleep-inducing lettuce rises, together with prickly lettuce; low-lying purslane, and endive, set firmly in the ground; the onion, filled with wind; garlic, a harsh taste for the Ligurians, and cabbage, which rejoices in a bed of turf; mint, diffusing its scent far and wide; the streaked iris; the supple mallow, with the suppliant marshmallow; lustful rocket and willing savory; the orchid , recalling old men to youthful ways; and she who is closed upon herself at close of day and reappears at the day's reappearance, responding to the Sun like a bride. Mugwort, empowered to purge the causes of women's sicknesses, burgeons into bright foliage. Sage, which improves the flavor of festive meals, gives off its odor from its stalks; medicinal though it is, prodigal man, far gone in luxury, makes it a dressing for his meat. Fennel appears, decked with delicate foliage, and empowered to dispel the shade from clouded eyes; when the snake casts off his burdensome years together with his skin, it is with fennel that he restores his exhausted vision. Marjoram takes root, and wild thyme begins twining, an herb well known as an antidote against the serpent race. Calamint is the best pacifier for aching muscles when rheumatism rages through the limbs. Pennyroyal is a proven measure when there is suspicion of a poisoned draft, and chervil is a no less efficacious herb. Wild nard, fumitory, and merry bugloss arise, to purge the effects of menstruation, spleen, and brain fever.

Thymbra iuvans renes, et quae perfectius ipsum
altera plantago lanceolata facit.
Ruta Mithridati, brassisque probata Catoni,
Herculeis apium grata corona comis;
tussibus elna valens, faciens urtica podagrae,
insomni cerebro grata camilla quies;
dictannus defixa trahens, panaceaque crudis
cognita vulneribus ferre salutis opem;
quodque calens rivis genialibus obstat anethum
et patulum contra semina claudit iter;
quaeque malos chymos sudore absinthia tollunt;
et violae, contra caumata consilium.
Tithymalus septena gravem quae mollitat alvum
nascitur: ecce tibi proelia, venter, habes!
Lacteris egreditur, stomacho factura tumultum,
et tempestates purga datura suas.
Socraticae cum iusquiamo crevere cicutae,
cognatusque neci surculus hellebori.
Gramina mandragoras, nostros imitantia vultus
partu terra novo prodigiosa tulit.

Diversumque tulit variumque natatile Proteus,
obtinuit regnum squamea turba suum:
Armorici balaena sinus, delphinus aduncus,
qui mage suspecto tempore ludit aquis;
suspectus murena cibus, suspectior ipsa
congrus, et causas febris echinus habens;
morius insipidus, et amico dorea gustu,
piscis item succo nobiliore lupus;
ostrea, sive genus quibus ampla palatia conchae,
quae nova sunt quotiens luna novavit iter;

Summer savory, good for the kidneys, and the lesser plantain, with its little pointed leaves, which performs the same function even better; rue, commended by Mithridates, and wild cabbage, the choice of Cato; parsley, a crown fit for the locks of Hercules; elecampane, effective against coughs; nettle, a cure for gout; chamomile, pleasant rest for the sleepless brain; dittany, to draw out embedded objects; panacea, known to bring the gift of healing to open wounds; anise hot to the taste, which congests the genital ducts and closes the open canal to the flow of semen; wormwood, which purges evil fluids from the stomach through perspiration; and violets, a prescription against the heat. Tithymal, which sooths a troubled stomach, is born in seven forms; behold, O belly, the fights in store for you! Wild cucumber appears, to create disruption in the stomach and spurge, to produce its stormy effects. Socrates's hemlock springs up, together with henbane, and hellebore, a plant intimate with death. In a new fit of productivity the earth brings forth mandragora, prodigious plant, to imitate our human countenance.

Proteus bears the various kinds of swimming life, and the scaly host lays claim to its dominion: the whale, who frequents the coast of Brittany; the dolphin, with curved snout, who is more playful in the waves at moments of impending danger; the lamprey, a suspect food, the conger eel, still more suspect, and the sea urchin, harboring the causes of fever; the tasteless cod; the pleasant-tasting dory, and the sea pike, likewise a fish of finer flavor; oysters, and the conch tribe, possessed of spacious palaces which are made anew as often as the moon renews her journey;

Lethaeus piscis qui, cuius harundine pendet,
 oblitum reddit immemoremque sui;
in venerem prurire senes vis improba stincus
 quique sepulta diu surgere membra facit.
Sirenes, portenta maris, vel denique multa
 id genus aequoreos incoluere sinus.

Multa peregrinis excursibus hospita turba
 descendit fluvios regnaque dulcis aquae.
Concordes commune natant fluvialibus undis
 aequorei fetus indigenaeque loci:
sturgio quadratus, mulus teres, hispida perca,
 gardo brevis, longus barbalus, ampla plais;
turcra rubens, salmo sapidus, praepinguis alosa,
 lucius exactor praepositusque gravis.

Has aluit species substantia mollis aquarum;
 aethereo plures tacta calore tulit.
Tractibus aeriis insultavere volucres,
 sed neque cognatas pars bona liquit aquas:
lunares veniente mari quae praevolat aestus
 et refugum sequitur alba moota fretum;
hirsutus buter, et cruribus ardea longis,
 pisce satur mergus, et male fortis anas;
et solus qui sentit olor discrimine quanto
 vivitur, et spreto funere cantor obit.
Plurima pars caelo sustollitur: unica phoenix,
 quae de se potuit se reparare sibi;
rex avium, cui praeda puer qui Bacchica miscet
 munera, per noctem munus et ipse Iovi;
nisus et accipiter, quorum praedaria vita;

that Lethean fish who visits oblivion and self-forgetfulness on anyone to whose line he attaches himself; the stickleback, whose wicked power makes old men itch with lust, and causes members long dormant to rise again. The Sirens, prodigies of the deep, or at any rate many creatures of that order, dwell in hidden recesses of the sea.

Great throngs of fish, journeying abroad, move as guests through the rivers and the realms of fresh water. In the river waters ocean-born fish and those native to this region swim peacefully together: the angular sturgeon, round mullet, spiny perch; the short roach, long barbel, broad plaice; the rosy trout, tasty salmon, shad, surpassingly plump; the pike, cruel tyrant and taskmaster.

The fluid substance of water supports these kinds of life; that element touched by ethereal warmth bears still more. In the expanses of the air the winged creatures dance about, but a good number never abandon familiar waters: the white gull, which flies before the lunar surge of the incoming sea, and follows the waters as they withdraw again; the densely feathered bittern and the long-legged heron; the diver, glutted with fish, and the duck, foolishly bold; the swan, who alone senses the terms on which its life is lived, and goes out singing in defiance of death.

The greater number are borne upward toward the heavens: the singular phoenix, which has the power to renew itself by its own means; the king of birds, whose prey was the boy who prepares the gifts of Bacchus, borne through the night, himself a gift, to Jove; the sea—eagle and the hawk, whose way of life is predatory,

In reliquum volucrum degere vulgus habent.
Quaeque figuratos apices describit eundo,
cum de Strimoniis grus peregrinat aquis;
Naturae ludentis opus, Iunonius ales,
albaque nec lateris parca columba sui;
deque suis Philomena malis quae vere querelam
integrat, et pectus sanguine tincta soror;
gallus uterque, domi privatior et peregrinus,
Medeae patria Phaside nomen habens;
fidus amans turtur, et decurtata coturnix,
et turdus sapiens conciliansque cibus;
cuique foret didicisse minus, plus vivere perdix,
et quae laeta novum laudat alauda diem;
ambiguus passer, visuraque saecula cornix,
picaque quam dubiam pingit uterque color;
degeneres tam vultur edax quam milvus in armis;
struthio deserti cultor amansque loci;
in teneros praedulce canens acalanthis amores,
garrulus et nostro psittacus ore loquens;
quique novae sobolis viridi sub fronde relictos
non meminit nidos Delphica corvus avis;
litoris alcyone, nemoris custodia picus,
quique lacus patulos anser amare solet;
et bubo, solis quem caecat amabile lumen,
et strix, in lacrimas exequiale canens.
Has ubi per formas species pennata recessit,
distarunt volucres, corpore, mente, loco.

for they subsist upon the host of lesser birds. The crane, who describes in flight the shapes of written letters, whenever he ventures forth from Strymonian waters; Juno's bird, a sport of Nature; the white dove, unsparing of her body; Philomena, who renews each spring her lament for her wrongs, and her sister, whose breast is stained with blood; the two cocks, that confined at home and that roaming one which takes his name from Phasis, the land of Medea; the turtle dove, faithful lover; the bobtailed quail; the thrush, a tasty and agreeable food; The partridge—would that he had studied less and lived longer!—and the lark, who joyfully hails the new day; the sparrow, hopping here and there; the crow, who will behold ages to come; and the magpie, whose twofold coloring gives her an uncertain appearance; the greedy vulture and the quarrelsome kite, degenerates both; the ostrich, denizen and lover of the desert; the finch, singing sweetly of tender love; the chatty parrot, who speaks with our voice; the raven, Delphic bird, who does not recall nests of new offspring abandoned among the leafy branches; the kingfisher and the woodpecker, guardians of shore and forest; the goose, who loves the open waters of the lake; the owl, whom the sun's kindly light makes blind, and the screech owl, chanting doleful tidings in funereal tones. When the feathered race had separated into these several forms, the birds differed greatly in bodily shape, inclination, and habitat.

Megacosmus 4

Iam igitur generatorum subolem multiformem cum ignita caeli substantia, levitate qua trahitur, circuiret in gyrum, secutum est ut elementa, partes Mundi primarias partesque partium, porrectiore contineret cingulo circumferentia firmamenti. Quicquid enim ad essentiam sui generis promotione succedit ex caelo, tanquam ex deo vitae, subsistentiae suae causas suscipit et naturam. Unde enim stellae irrequieto circumferuntur excursu, nisi quia aethereum fomitem imbiberunt? Unde terrestre, unde aequoreum, unde aerivagum genus se suis vestigiis emoverent, si non de caelo motus vivificos insumpsissent?

2. Ignis namque aethereus, sociabilis et maritus gremio telluris coniugis affusus, generationem rerum publicam, quam de calore suo producit ad vitam, eam inferioribus elementis commodat nutriendam. Spiritu animantium de convexis caelestibus evocato, terra corporibus praebet operam nutriendis, et a nutricationis officio non desistit adusque naturalibus satisfecerit incrementis.

3. Sic igitur Providentia de generibus ad species, de speciebus ad individua, de individuis ad sua rursus principia, repetitis anfractibus rerum originem retorquebat. Ex eo incipientis vitae primordio, cum volvente caelo de motu quoque

Megacosmus 4

Now since the fiery substance of the celestial sphere, drawn by virtue of its lightness, was moving in a circular course around the manifold progeny of created life, it followed that the circumference of the firmament embraced within its vast compass the elements, the primary parts of the Universe, and the parts of these parts. For anything which is brought forth to assume the essential character of its kind receives the causes and nature of its substantial existence from the heavens, as though from a life-giving god. For how are the stars borne about in their ceaseless journey, if not because they have imbibed ethereal tinder? How would the creatures of the land, the waters, the air, move along their paths if they had not received life-giving impulses from the firmament?

2. For ethereal fire, intimate partner and husband diffused into the womb of earth, his bride, entrusts all the generation of creatures which he has brought to life by his heat to the nurture of the baser elements. Once the spirit of animate life has been summoned from the vault of heaven, earth applies herself to the nurturing of bodies, and does not cease from the task of nourishment until she has ensured their natural development.

3. Thus Providence brought the course of created life full circle, from genus to species, from species to individual, from individual out again to first principles, in continual revolution. When from the first motion of incipient life, the revolving of the firmament and the movement of the stars,

siderum substantia temporis nasceretur, quae successerunt saecula, simplici aeternitatis initiata principio, cum sua numerus varietate suscipit.

4. Rerum porro universitas, Mundus, nec invalida senectute decrepitus, nec supremo est obitu dissolvendus, cum de opifice causaque operis utrisque sempiternis, de materia formaque materiae utrisque perpetuis ratio cesserit permanendi. Usia namque Primaeva, aeviterna perseveratio, fecunda pluralitatis simplicitas, una est: sola ex se vel in se tota natura Dei, cuius quicquid loci est, nec essentiae nec maiestatis infinibile circumscribit. Huiusmodi si virtutem, si salutem, si vitam diffiniendo dixeris, non errabis.

5. Ex ea igitur luce inaccessibili splendor radiatus emicuit—imago nescio dicam an vultus, patris imagine consignatus. Hic est Dei sapientia, vivis aeternitatis fomitibus vel nutrita vel genita. De sapientia consilium, voluntas consilio nascitur, de divina Mundi molitio voluntate.

6. Porro Dei voluntas omnis bona est. Dei ergo vel voluntas vel bonitas summi Patris est eiusque Mentis in eadem operatione consensus. Quisnam ergo Mundo et aeternitati eius audeat derogare, ad cuius continentiam causas aeternas videat convenisse? Dei quidem de voluntate consensum, de sapientia consilium, de omnipotentia causas pariter et effectum. De stabilitate, de aeternitate sibi Mundus conscire praesumit, quod gradatim, firmeque dispositis causarum sibi succedentium ordinibus, mundus sensibilis integrascit.

the substance of time was born, number with its variations assumed control of the succession of the ages, which had had their beginning in the primal simplicity of eternity.

4. The totality of creatures, the Universe, is never wasted away by the infirmity of old age, nor will it be abolished by ultimate destruction, for the basis of its permanence is due to a maker and an operative cause, both of them eternal, and a material substance and form, both existing in perpetuity. For the Primal Being, eternal permanence, simplicity fecund of plurality, is one: the unique nature of God, complete in and of itself, whose infinitude of being and majesty no amount of space can circumscribe. If in defining such a being you should call it "virtue" or "health" or "life," you will not be wrong.

5. From this inaccessible light a radiant splendor shone forth—I know not whether to call it an "image" or a "face," inscribed with the image of the Father. This is the wisdom of God, conceived or nourished by the living fire of eternity. From this wisdom arises the deliberation, from deliberation the will, and from the divine will the shaping of the Universe.

6. Moreover the will of God is wholly good. The divine will or goodness of the supreme Father, then, is the harmonious expression of his Mind in a single action. Who then would dare to disparage the Universe and its eternity, when he may behold eternal causes working together for its maintenance? From the will of God issues harmonious volition, from his wisdom deliberation, from his omnipotence both cause and effect. Through its stability and eternity the Universe possesses a prior knowledge of what the sensible world gradually brings to full realization through the fixed ordering of a series of secondary causes.

7. Praecedit Hyle, Natura subsequitur elementans; elementanti Naturae elementa, elementis elementata conveniunt. Sic principia principiis, sed a principe principio, cohaeserunt. Nisi caelum, nisi motus sidereus illis quas importat varietatibus afficiat elementa, pigra iaceant, iaceant otiosa. Luminaria, Sol et Luna et qui dicuntur erratici, quorum conversio non quiescit, elementa quae subiaceant non perferunt non moveri. Est igitur elementans Natura caelum stellaeque Signifero pervagantes, quod elementa conveniant ad ingenitas actiones. Sua igitur in Mundo non fatiscunt ligamina, nec solvuntur, quod universa a cardine nexu sibi continuo deducuntur.

8. Rerum incolumitas vitaque Mundi causis quidem principalibus et antiquis—spiritu, sensu, agitatione, ordinatione—consistit. Vivit Noys, vivunt exemplaria: sine vita non viveret rerum species aeviterna. Praeiacebat Hyle: praeiacebat in materia, praeiacebat in spiritu vivacitatis aeternae. Neque enim credibile est sapientem opificem insensatae materiae nec viventis originis fundamina praelocasse. Mundus quidem est animal; verum sine anima substantiam non invenias animalis. De terra porro pleraque consurgunt, sed sine vegetatione non stirpea, non plantaria, non cetera compubescunt.

7. First there is Hyle; then Nature bringing to life the elemental qualities; the elements appear in response to this elementing Nature, and elemented substances take their rise from the elements. Thus the principles of existence came to cohere among themselves, but depend on one sovereign principle. For if the firmament and the movement of the stars did not infuse the elements with that capacity for change which they transmit, these would remain sluggish and inactive. But the great lights, the Sun and Moon and those which are called the wandering spheres, whose circling never ceases, do not suffer the elements of the underlying world to remain unmoved. This elementing Nature, then, is the firmament, and those planets which traverse the circle of the Zodiac, for these adapt the elements to their natural activity. Thus these universal bonds do not weaken and are not undone, for all creation, indivisibly interrelated, is derived from one cardinal principle.

8. The soundness and vitality of the Universe depend on sovereign and ancient causes—spirit, sentience, a source of movement, a source of order. Noys and the exemplars are living beings; without their life the visible creation would not live everlastingly. Hyle was in existence before it, preexistent in matter, preexistent in the spirit of an eternal vitality. For it is not to be believed that the wise creator of insensate matter did not first establish for it a living source. The universe is an animal, and one may not detect the substance of animal life apart from soul. Moreover, many things spring from the earth, but without the stimulus of a principle of growth neither tree nor shoot nor anything else will thrive.

9. Ex Mentis igitur vita, Silvae spiritu, Anima Mundi, mundalium vegetatione, rerum aeternitas coalescit. In Deo, in Noy scientia est; in caelo ratio, in sideribus intellectus. In magno vero animali cognitio viget, viget et sensus, causarum praecedentium fomitibus enutritus. Ex Mente enim caelum, de caelo sidera, de sideribus Mundus, unde viveret, unde discerneret, linea continuationis excepit. Mundus enim quiddam continuum, et in ea catena nihil dissipabile vel abruptum. Unde illum rotunditas, forma perfectior, circumscribit. Si se igitur influentis Silvae plerumque necessitas vel turbidius vel inpensius importabit, qui multiplex inest Mundo vel sensus vel spiritus malitiam non patitur ultra lineas excursare.

10. Quicquid extenditur spatiis, vel annosum vel saeculare vel perpetuum vel aeternum. Annosum senio, saeculare dissolvitur aevitate. Aeterno perpetuum durabilitate concertat, sed quia quandoque coeperit, ad supremam aeternitatis eminentiam non aspirat. Mundus igitur quaedam annosa, quaedam saeculari, quaedam agitatione perpetua vel continuat vel evolvit. Aequaeva namque generatione Mundus et tempus quibus innascuntur principiis, eorum imagines propinquas et simillimas aemulantur. Ex mundo intelligibili Mundus sensibilis perfectus natus est ex perfecto. Plenus

9. Thus from the life of the divine Mind, from the spirit of Silva, from the World Soul, from the growth principle of created life, the eternity of things has its growth. Knowledge reposes in God, in Noys; a rational plan exists in the firmament and intelligence in the stars. In this great animal understanding thrives, and sentience, too, thrives, drawing nourishment from its antecedent principles. The firmament receives from the divine Mind, the stars from the firmament and the Universe from the stars, by a chain of continuity, the capacity for life and understanding. For the Universe is a continuum, a chain in which nothing is out of order or broken off. Thus roundness, the perfect form, determines its shape. And so, although the inevitable flux of Silva often occurs in a confused or excessive way, that complex faculty or spirit which is present in the Universe does not permit the hostile force to overflow its bounds.

10. Whatever has spatial extension is annual, or temporal, or perpetual, or eternal. The annual is dissolved by old age, the temporal by the end of time itself. The perpetual vies with the eternal in endurance, but because at some time it had a beginning it does not attain the surpassing excellence of eternity. The Universe sustains or prolongs the lives of its creatures, some by an annual, some by a temporal, some by a perpetual motion. For the Universe and time, owing to the principles from which they are sprung by a simultaneous act of creation, conform to closely related and very similar models. From the intelligible universe the sensible Universe was born, perfect from perfect. The generative

erat igitur qui genuit, plenumque constituit plenitudo. Sicut enim integrascit ex integro, pulchrescit ex pulchro, sic exemplari suo aeternatur aeterno.

11. Ab aeternitate tempus initians, in aeternitatis resolvitur gremium, longiore circulo fatigatum. De unitate ad numerum, de stabilitate digreditur ad momentum. Momenta temporis: praesentis instantia, excursus praeteriti, expectatio futuri. Has itaque vias itu semper redituque continuat. Cumque easdem totiens et totiens itineribus aeternitatis evolverit, ab illis nitens et promovens nec digreditur nec recedit. Quod ubi finiunt inde tempora renascuntur, relinquitur ad ambiguum quaenam praecessio in tempore, ut non eadem et consecutio videatur.

12. Ea ipsa in se revertendi necessitate, et tempus in aeternitate consistere, et aeternitas in tempore visa est conmoveri. Suum temporis est quod movetur, aeternitatis est ex qua nasci, in quam et resolvi habet, quia in inmensum porrigitur. Si fieri possit ne decidat in numeros, ne defluat in momentum, idem tempus est quod aeternum. Solis successionum nominibus variatur, quod ab aevo nec continuatione nec essentia separatur.

source exists in fullness, and this fullness ensured the fullness of its creation. For just as the sensible Universe participates in the flawlessness of its flawless model, and waxes beautiful by its beauty, so by its eternal exemplar it is made to endure eternally.

11. Setting out from eternity, time returns again into the bosom of eternity, wearied by its long journey. From oneness it issues into number, from the unmoving into movement. The instant present, the flowing away of the past, the anticipation of what is to come: these are the stages of time. It moves along these paths in perpetual departure and return. And though it will have traveled these same roads over and over again in the course of eternity, still striving and forging ahead, it neither strays from them nor turns back. And because its journeys are renewed from the point at which they end, it remains uncertain in what way preceding time might not be considered the same as what follows.

12. By virtue of this very necessity of returning upon itself, it may be seen both that time stands fast in eternity, and that eternity is moved in time. It is the property of time to be in motion, and that of eternity, from which time is born, and into which it must be released, that its extent is immeasurable. Were it possible for time not to divide into quantity or issue into movement, then time would be identical with the eternal. Only by the names of its progressions is it distinguished, for it differs neither in its extent nor in its essential nature from the everlasting.

13. Aeternitas igitur, sed et aeternitatis imago tempus, in moderando Mundo curam et operam partiuntur. Ignes sidereos aeternitas naturaeque aethera purioris utraque vegetanda suscepit. Depressas et ab aere subtus declinatas materias, vel continuat vel evolvit agitatio temporalis. Mundus igitur tempore, sed tempus ordine dispensatur. Sicut enim divinae voluntatis semper est praegnans, sic exemplis aeternarum quas gestat imaginum Noys Endelichiam, Endelichia Naturam, Natura Imarmenen quid Mundo debeat informavit. Substantiam animis Endelichia subministrat; habitaculum animae, corpus artifex Natura de initiorum materiis et qualitate conponit; Imarmene, quae continuatio temporis est, et ad ordinem constituta, disponit, texit, et retexit quae complectitur universa.

FINIT *MEGACOSMUS*

13. Eternity, then, but also time, the image of eternity, share the responsibility and labor of governing the Universe. Eternity undertakes to impart life to the fiery bodies of the stars, as well as the purer substance of the ether. The activity of time sustains or prolongs those heavier material existences borne downward by the lower atmosphere. Thus the universe is governed by time, but time itself is governed by order. For as Noys is forever pregnant of the divine will, she in turn informs Endelechia with the exemplars she conceives of the eternal forms, Endelechia impresses them upon Nature, and Nature imparts to Imarmene what the well-being of the Universe demands. Endelechia supplies the substance of souls, and Nature the artisan compounds the soul's dwelling, the body, out of the qualities and materials of the elements; Imarmene, who is temporal continuity in its aspect as a principle of order, disposes, weaves together, and unravels the Universe she encompasses.

HERE ENDS *MEGACOSMUS*

INCIPIT *MICROCOSMUS:*
LIBER SECUNDUS, DE
HOMINIS PLASMATIONE

Microcosmus 1

In praedecoro longeque artifici Mundi sensilis apparatu cum iam Providentiae conplaceret, Naturam evocat, ut pariter commiretur et gaudeat, ad quorum exornationem totis desideriis anhelarat. "Ecce," inquit, "Mundus, O Natura, quem de antiquo seminario, quem de tumultu veteri, quem de massa confusionis excepi. Ecce Mundus, operis mei excogitata subtilitas, gloriosa constructio, rerum specimen praedecorum, quem creavi, quem formavi sedula, quem ad aeternam ideam ingeniosa circumtuli, mentem meam propiore vestigio subsecuta. Ecce Mundus cui Noys vita, cui ideae forma, cui materies elementa. Ecce, de opere meo num ad animum tuum officiosa perveni? Num quod Mundus iam nascitur votis felicibus amplexaris?

2. "Missum facio quantam turbam Silvae asperitas fecerit attrectanti, quid diligentiae contulerim adversus intemperiem reluctantis, adusque manus artifices insuevit. Missum facio quanam cote de antiquis rubiginem elementis effricui, et recoctas essentias splendore quo decuit innovavi.

HERE BEGINS *MICROCOSMUS:*
THE SECOND BOOK, ON THE
CREATION OF MAN

Microcosmus 1

When at last Providence was content with the eminently beautiful and surpassingly skillful preparation of the sensible Universe, she summoned Nature, that she too might marvel and rejoice at that embellishment which she had so desired. "Behold, O Nature," she said, "the Universe which I have brought forth from the ancient seedbed, from the turbulence of old, from the chaotic mass. Behold the Universe, the subtle inventiveness of my work, the splendid construction, the surpassingly beautiful display of created life, which I have created, carefully shaped, ingeniously conformed to its eternal idea, following as closely as possible the path of my own thought. Behold the Universe, whose life is Noys, whose form is ideal, whose substance is that of the elements. Behold: Have I not been attentive to your wishes in my labor? Do you not greet with joyful prayers the Universe now born?

2. "I say nothing of the great tumult with which the fierceness of Silva resisted my touch, and what diligence I brought to bear upon her unruly reluctance, until she grew tame under my shaping hand. I say nothing of how with flint I chipped away the rust from the ancient elements, and endowed their reforged essences with the splendor that befits

Missum facio unde sacer controversantia sibi genera foederavit amplexus, unde nata medietas disparatas potentias exaequavit. Missum facio unde formae substantiis obvenerunt, unde terris, unde aequoribus, unde aere, unde vivitur in convexis.

3. "Caelum velim videas multiformi imaginum varietate descriptum, quod quasi librum, porrectis in planum paginis, eruditioribus oculis explicui, secretis futura litteris continentem. Zonas velim videas, quemadmodum intra polos certis legibus exporrectae, terras sibi subpositas afficiunt qualitate. Coluros velim videas, quemadmodum quadrifida lineatione caelum ambire conveniunt, sed continuationem quam coeperant non obsolvunt. Signiferum velim videas, quem ratio secretior obliquavit: rerum enim incolumitati provisum est, quae perpetuo non duraret, si directo semper limite Solem Signifer excandentem terrae per medium reportaret. Galaxem velim videas, frigoribus hyperboreis temperantem; quia locis longe sepositis Solis calefactio remedium non ferebat. Lineam velim videas utrisque solstitiis respondentem, itemque illam quae diurni nocturnique temporis excrescentias ad momentum parilitatis affigit.

4. "Ignita, clara, teretique forma solare corpus composui; cui planetarii orbes concinerent ad medium collocato. Luna,

them. I say nothing of how a sacred embrace united conflicting elements, and how a newborn mean rendered equal forces formerly imbalanced. I say nothing of how forms encountered substances, how it is that there is life on earth, in the sea, the air, the arching firmament.

3. "I would have you survey the firmament, inscribed with its manifold array of symbols, which I have set forth for learned eyes like a book with its pages spread open, containing things to come in secret characters. I would have you regard the zones, and how, extending by fixed laws between the poles, they determine the climates of the underlying terrain. I would have you note the colures, and how in their fourfold delineation they join to encircle the heavens, but never finish the extended journey which they had begun. I would have you consider the Zodiac, which a hidden plan has set atilt: hereby provision is made for the safety of the natural world, which would not endure perpetually if the Zodiac always conducted the blazing Sun in an unvarying course across the center of the earth. I would have you gaze on the Galaxy, moderating the cold of the northern regions; for to regions lying so distant, the heat of the Sun does not bring its relief. And I would have you notice the line which corresponds to the two solstices, and likewise that which marks the prolongations of day and night to the time at which they are equal.

4. "I have fashioned the body of the Sun with a fiery, brilliant and rounded form; for him, set at the center of things, the planetary spheres join in harmonious chorus. The Moon,

aeris aetherisque intervia, qualitates mutat et facies, Solem aliter et aliter de latere circumspectans. Venerem Solis assistricem Mercuriumque conserui, currus luciferos vicinius obeuntem. Exporrecto Iovem circulo, Martem aspicis castiore, hunc rutilare sanguineum, illum amici fulgore sideris eblandiri. Saturnum superextuli hactenus efficacem, ut cuius elementi signa possiderit, ad eam naturam anni contorqueat qualitatem.

5. "Sed quid ergo positiones sidereas caelique leges enumerem, cum ad oculos pateant universa? Terra vides quomodo, ex elementorum fecunditate concepta, nunc fluviis, nunc graminibus, nunc silvis comantibus hilarescit. Amphitrite, limitibus circumplexa, victum animantibus de medio subministrat: pars frugibus, pars virescit arboribus, pars odoramentis aspirat, pars gemmis, pars metallorum generibus est fecunda. In lubrico pisces elemento, itemque facies beluinae regna lucentia pervagantur. Neve rerum tranquillitas violentis passionibus temptaretur, contra fontem caloris, Solem, quem linea medialis exportat, fontem humoris, mediterraneum mare, medio telluris infudi. Quodque illud et oceanum in plurimas distraxerim sectiones, regionibus provisum est, ut ad eas navali evectione necessaria commearent.

6. "Pennati generis turba multicolor liquidum transnat aera, patentis itineris libertate. Pluviarum vehiculo ventos

placed at the boundary between ether and atmosphere, changes in influence and appearance, and beholds the Sun now from this side, now from that. I have set Venus in attendance on the Sun, and assigned Mercury to travel close beside his light-bringing chariot. You observe that Jupiter moves in an extended circle, Mars in a more contained one, that the latter glows bloodred, and that the former has the mild gleam of a friendly star. Saturn I have elevated to such power that whatever be the elemental nature whose sign he occupies, to its influence he subjects the climate of the year.

5. "But why should I catalog the positions of the heavenly bodies and the laws of heaven when all lies open to view? You see how the earth, by a fertility derived from the elements, rejoices now in streams, now in meadows, now in dense forests. Amphitrite, surrounded by bordering land, brings forth from within herself sustenance for living things: one region flourishes with fruits, another with trees, another with herbs and spices. One region teems with gems, another with different kinds of metal. In the fluid element fish move about, even as the shapes of great beasts roam through the realms of day. And lest the harmony of earthly life be assailed by violent passions, to counter the Sun's fountain of heat, which the meridian bears along, I have poured out at the center of earth a fountain of water, a mediterranean sea. And because I have drawn out this sea and the great ocean into many sectors, provision has been made for isolated regions, that the necessities of life may reach them by ocean voyages.

6. "The many-colored host of the feathered race swim along the flowing air, with the freedom of the open road. I

in aere discursare praecepi, ut quibusdam in locis solutae terrae pulveres infecundos pluvialis humiditas alligaret. Vastitatem aeris zonarum inpressione distinxi, ut earum qualitatibus tellus inferior consentiret."

Microcosmus 2

Iam sectum per membra chaos, iam Silva, decorem
  nacta suum, vero nomine Mundus erat.
Siquid adhuc ruris vetus inportabat origo,
  expulit, artifices usque secuta manus;
et, nihil obtrectans operi rerumque figuris,
  continuam sese morigeramque dedit.
"In laudem titulosque meos, Natura, repono
  tam bene materias excoluisse rudes.
Induxi rebus formas, elementa ligavi,
  concordem numero conciliante fidem.
Ascripsi legem stellis, iussique planetas
  indeclinatum currere semper iter.
Substrinxi mare limitibus; ne terra labaret,
  in medio sedit pondere fixa suo.
Mandavi, calor aethereus produceret herbas,
  quas calor aethereus parturit, humor alat;
corpora cuncta creet tellus, resolutaque rursus
  excipiat placido mater amica sinu;

have taught the winds to roam abroad through the air bearing rain, that in regions of crumbling soil showers of moisture may reagglomerate the sterile dust. I have sectioned off the vast ether by the imposition of the zones, that the underlying earth may conform to their conditions."

Microcosmus 2

Now chaos had been divided into parts; now, since Silva had attained her proper beauty, there existed a Universe worthy of the name. If her ancient origin intruded any trace of rusticity, she banished it, ever submissive to the shaping hand; offering no resistance, she presented herself, coherent and obedient, to the work of Noys and the formation of creatures.

"I count it to my praise and glory, O Nature, that I have so well cultivated my coarse materials. I have brought form to creatures and yoked the elements by a proportion which has elicited peace and trust. I have given a law to the stars, and ordered the planets always to pursue an undeviating course. I have curbed the sea with boundaries, and lest the earth should totter, it rests, fixed by its own weight, at the center of things. I have decreed that ethereal warmth should bring forth vegetation, and that moisture should sustain what this ethereal warmth has produced; that the earth, loving mother, should give birth to all things, and at their dissolution receive them back again into her tranquil bosom;

ex Endelichia Mundi res quaeque creata
sementem vitae principiumque trahat."

Microcosmus 3

"Ad contemplanda igitur quae fecerim si diligens speculatrix intendis, ea sunt omnia quorum figuram, speciem, firmitatem, ordinationem debeas admirari. Sed quoniam par est diligentem opificem claudentes partes operis digna consummatione finire, visum est mihi in Homine fortunam honoremque operis terminare. Impensioribus eum beneficiis, impensioribus eum impleam incrementis, ut universis a me factis animalibus quodam quasi dignitatis privilegio et singularitate concertet.

2. "Verumtamen in iugandis principiis, in rigentis Silvae partibus excolendis, adversusque omnes importunitatesque manum ego meam potenter apposui, quia rerum necessitas expetebat. Ventum est ad Hominem, in cuius compositione bonum est, mihi nec displicet, si sodalis societas operam quoque suae sedulitatis adjungat.

3. "Humanae quidem sementem animae, et in anima iubar vivacitatis eternae vel facere vel fundare, utrumque subtilitati meae singulare perspicio, quia id operis et tuam, Natura, prudentiam et cuius velis numinis facultatem sicut aestimatione ponderis, sic auctoritate maiestatis excedit. Velle meum est, Uraniam, Physim, utramque sciam, utramque

that every creature should derive the seed and principle of its vitality from Endelechia, soul of the Universe."

Microcosmus 3

"Thus if you apply yourself as a careful observer to contemplating what I have done, all these are things whose form, beauty, stability, and ordering you must admire. But since it befits the careful craftsman to make the final portions of his work a worthy consummation, I have decided to complete the success and dignity of my creation with Man. I will bestow upon him abundant favor and abundant resources, that he may excel all my creatures by a certain privilege, as it were, a distinctive attribute of dignity.

2. "Now in harnessing the principles of things and refining the components of resistant Silva, I have applied my own strong hand against all unruliness, since the necessity inherent in created things demanded it. But we have come to Man, and for his composition it is good and not displeasing to me if a group of companions should also contribute their zealous efforts.

3. "Yet I recognize that the sowing of the human soul, and the creating or instilling in this soul of the radiance of eternal vitality, are both tasks for my subtle power alone, for this work exceeds both your understanding, Nature, and the capacity of any power you might muster, either to gauge its difficulty or to realize its solemn significance. My wish is that Urania and Physis, both of whom are knowing and

providam, utramque ad id de quo agitur ingeniis expeditam, ubi locorum fuerint, tuo, Natura, studio, tuo labore perquiri. Uraniam mearum sedium assistricem, Physim in inferioribus reperies conversantem."

4. Ad hoc Natura, gratulantis vultu pariter et volentis, amicis Providentiae iussionibus officiosa concurrit. Quid enim gratius accepisset quam creationem, quam Hominis plasmaturam, quas vocatis artificibus iri perspicit properatum? Uraniam igitur, quod personatu dignior, quod mansione propior videretur, in primis investigare disponit. Caelo licet mansitare non dubitet, errorem tamen potuit ambagesque itineri locus diffusior importare. Omni lato latior est circumferentia firmamenti. Cum toti caelo debeat, cunctis debeat Urania sideribus interesse, unde sciri potuit quas ex partibus partes excoleret potiores?

5. Anastros in caelo regio est, ad unius modum qualitatis affixa, indefecto lumine, serenitate perpetua; aethereae puritati conterminans et affinis, invenitur etiam qualitate conformis. Ea igitur sicut aerem altitudine supergressa, sic aeris passionibus libera; non densatur pluviis, non procellis incutitur, nec nubilo turbidatur. Eo Uraniam Natura prosequitur, si vel eam loci proximitas vel species invitasset otiosis discursibus evagatam. Sed reginam sideream locus alius detinebat. Cassa voto, cassa proposito non est morae questa

competent, both endowed with the intelligence to perform the task in question, be sought by your own zeal and effort, Nature, wherever they reside. You will find Urania seated close by my abode, and Physis sojourning among the lower creatures."

4. At these words, Nature, her countenance equally expressive of gratitude and eagerness, readily concurred with the agreeable commands of Providence. For what gift could she have received more pleasing than the creation, the formation of Man, which she saw would be hastened to fulfillment by the summoning of these artisans? Accordingly she decided to seek out Urania first, since she seemed the more distinguished, and her abode seemed nearer. But though Nature had no doubt that she dwelt in the heavens, so vast a region was likely to produce a wandering and uncertain journey. For the circumference of the firmament is broader than any breadth. And since Urania must be concerned with the whole of heaven and all the stars, how could Nature know which regions she might frequent in preference to others?

5. Anastros is a region of the heaven held to the norm of a uniform quality, its light unwavering, its calm perpetual; bordering upon the ethereal realm and partaking of its purity, it is similar also in quality. Therefore, just as it is set above the air in altitude, so it is free from the passions of the air; it does not grow heavy with rain, is not attacked by storms or disturbed by clouds. Here Nature sought Urania, if by chance the accessibility or the beauty of the place had attracted her when wandering at her leisure. But the queen of the stars was engaged in another region. Denied what she sought to accomplish, Nature did not complain of the loss

dispendium, quia gratiosi splendore luminis suum saltem pavisset aspectum.

6. Itineris ergo promotione longissimi, extremos inter vertices quinque caeli ligamina, parallelos scrutabunda conscendit. Sed diversa quidem intemperie fervoribus unus, sed medius, frigiditate duo, sed extremi, impatientem habitationis duritiem praeferebant. Diversis qualitatibus temperamentum contraxerat ille vel ille qui fuerat parallelus extremorum mediique lateribus circumclusus. Per eorum diffusas sed distinctas latitudines sollicito et disquisito intuitu pervagatur. Colurum it reditque alterutrum, commissuras ad ultimas per concurrentiam linearum. In coluris, in parallelis, in utrisque disquiritur, in neutrisque reperitur.

7. Splendorem quem de pluralitate confecerat globus siderum circumfusus quasi semitam prosecuta, Galaxiam incidit, qua duobus tropicis Signiferum ambiendo contingit. Itaque Cancri circa confinium turbas innumeras, vulgus aspicit animarum, quae quidem omnes vultibus quibus itur ad exequias et quibusdam quasi lacrimis exturbatae. Quippe de splendore ad tenebras, de caelo Ditis ad imperium, de aeternitate ad corpora per Cancri domicilium quae fuerant descensurae, sicut purae, sicut simplices, obtusum caecumque corporis quod apparari prospiciunt habitaculum exhorrebant. Ad huius rei spectaculum mora consumpta est aliquanta, et quae quaeritur non inventa.

8. Ergo per solstitialem lineam viam flectit ad circulum planetarum hospitiis et potentiis deputatum, cuius partes

of time, for she had at least nourished her vision with the splendor of this benevolent light.

6. Setting out again on her long journey, she ascended to search the five parallels, the bonds of the firmament, set between the polar extremities. But in their contrasting inclemency, the central zone with its heat and the two outermost with their icy cold, as habitations they promised unremitting hardship. Each of the two zones enclosed on either side by the borders of the middle zone and the two extremes had established a temperate balance between divergent climatic conditions. Through their spreading but distinct latitudes Nature traveled, searching with anxious care. She went back and forth along each of the two colures, to the concurrence of their arcs at the final meeting point. Among the colures, among the zones, though sought in both, Urania was to be found in neither.

7. Following like a highway that radiance which a crowded mass of stars produces through its numbers, she enters the Galaxy at the point in its course where it meets the Zodiac at the two tropics. Here she saw a numberless throng, a mob of souls clustered about the boundary of Cancer; the faces of all were such as one sees at a funeral, and they were shaken by a kind of sobbing. And certainly they who were about to descend, pure and simple as they were, from splendor into shadow, from heaven to the kingdom of Pluto, from eternal life to that of the body, grew terrified at the clumsy and blind fleshly habitation which they saw prepared for them. Some little time was spent pondering this spectacle, and she who was sought was not found.

8. Then she made her way along the line of the solstice, to that circle assigned to the houses and powers of the

duodecim laborosior visa est peragrare, obliquitate circuli retardante. Reliquorum siderum itineribus destitutis, viam Solis ingreditur, quia, minus inflexionis habens, medio dirigitur libramento. Ex eo quidem elevatiore Signiferi dorso despiciens, et suspiciens universa, nec visu, nec vestigiis, nec quaestionibus invenit requisitam. Supremo igitur consilio Aplanon destinat veniendum, superiores et extimi finales terminos firmamenti.

9. Aether omnisque compago siderea non elementale est conpositum, sed ab elementis numero quintum, ordine primum, genere divinum, natura invariabile. Si enim ex elementis, natura quorum convertibilis, caelum stellaeque caeligenae substantiam contraxissent, certum nihil, nihil veridicum nuntiarent. Circulus igitur, et ambitor et extimus, nec quidem ignis est nec ignitus. Unus eisdemque semper ad punctum reditionibus circumferens planetarum globos, et corpora violenta secum rapacitate convertit.

10. Hoc igitur in loco Pantomorpho, persona deus venerabili, et decrepitae sub imagine senectutis, occurrit. Illic Oyarses idem erat, et Genius in artem et officium pictoris et figurantis addictus. In subteriacente enim mundo, rerum facies universa caelum sequitur, sumptisque de caelo proprietatibus, ad imaginem quam conversio contulit figuratur. Namque impossibile est formam unamquamque alteri simillimam nasci horarum et climatum distantibus punctis.

planets. She seemed to traverse the twelve sections of this circle with more difficulty, as its slanted position was a hindrance. Leaving behind the orbits of the other planets, she entered the path of the Sun, for, since this is less curving, it is determined by a leveling mean. Looking down from this, the lofty arc of the Zodiac, and surveying the universe, she gained no sight or sign, nor any information about her whom she sought. As a last resort she decided to visit the Aplanes, highest terminal boundary of the outermost firmament.

9. The ether and all the starry assemblage are composed, not of the material elements, but of a fifth element, the highest in order, divine in kind, and of an unvarying nature. For if the firmament and the stars it bears derived their substance from the material elements, whose nature is changeable, they would reveal nothing certain, express no truth. This circle, then, outermost and all encompassing, is neither fire nor derived from fire. Alone encompassing the spheres of the planets with its continuous and identical circlings, it causes these bodies to orbit by its own forceful rapacity.

10. In this, the region of Pantomorphos, a god of venerable aspect, and with the signs of the ravages of old age upon him, confronted her. For he himself was Usiarch here, and also the Genius devoted to the art and office of delineating and shaping. For the aspect of all things in the subordinate world conforms to the heavens, whence it assumes its properties, and it is shaped to whatever likeness the motion of the heavens imparts. For it is impossible that one form should be born identical with another at points separate in time and region. And so the Usiarch of that sphere which is

Oyarses igitur circuli quem Pantomorphon Graecia, Latinitas nominat Omniformem, formas rebus omnes omnibus et associat et ascribit.

11. "Heus," inquit, "O Natura, et ad axes astriferos devenisti? Digna quidem tu caelo recipi, cuius qualitatibus et cuius essentiis indefessae studio sedulitatis inservis. Assistricem indigetemque caeli Uraniam, quam quaeritas, eam aspice te propter assistere, sideribus inhiantem, reditusque stellarum et anfractus temporarios sub numerum et ad certas observationis regulas colligentem."

12. Ad consessum sidereum, et contra iubar aetheris inaccessum, retusos et conniventes oculos Natura qua poterat intendebat. Urania venientem et quid veniat primis aspectibus recognovit. Intercepto salutantis officio, parantem dicere ingenio diviniore praevenit.

Microcosmus 4

"Supremi decreta Dei, Natura, reportas,
quidve recens fieri sacra Mens velit.
Velle Dei, formetur Homo, cui corpus ab imis,
a superis animus super influat.
Quadret opus, faciatque suum junctura decorem,
velle Dei, desit solido nihil.
Velle Dei, mixtura modum, modulatio nexum,
nexus amicitiam pariat sacer,

called in Greek Pantomorphos, and in Latin Omniformis, composes and assigns all forms of creatures.

11. "Hail, O Nature," said he, "have you come even to the star-bearing heights? Indeed you are worthy to be received in heaven, since you care for heavenly properties and essences with the zeal of unflagging devotion. And that native ministress of the heavens whom you seek, Urania: behold her standing before you, gazing attentively at the heavens, calculating the stars' recurrent motions and the periods of their orbits, by exact measure and sure standards of observation."

12. Nature turned her dazzled and blinking eyes as best she could toward the assembled stars, and full into the impenetrable brilliance of the ether. Urania knew at first sight who had come and why she had come. Cutting short the business of greeting by her more divine insight, she forestalled Nature's attempt to speak.

Microcosmus 4

"You bring, O Nature, the decrees of the most high God, what the divine Mind has willed even now to come to pass. It is God's will that Man be formed; his body will be made of lowly matter, his spirit will issue from the powers above. That the work may be perfect, and the joining of its parts produce beauty, it is God's will that nothing be lacking in his composition. It is God's will that the mixture be balanced, that balance effect a bond, that this divine bond give rise

ne pigeat mentem caecas habitare tenebras
 hospitiumque pati grave corporis;
ne propria de carne queat fecisse querelam
 spiritus imperiis subiectior.
Ut concors sibi disparitas coniuret amice,
 huius ad artis opus comes evocor.
Non aliena subis nostros, Natura, penates,
 me tibi germanam Noys edidit.
Nempe tuum genus unde meum; te publicus orbis,
 unus me recipit locus aetheris.
Cum superis delector ego, delector in astris,
 officiisque meis gravis abstrahor;
in terris Homo terrenus fabricabitur hospes,
 et descensus eo mihi non levis.
Umida colluvies, humili contermina terrae,
 laeserit e facili nostrum iubar.
Sed quod ab archetypis ea res decorata figuris,
 excusare viam minus expedit.
Iuxta divinae summaeque sacraria Mentis
 exsequar iniuncti rem muneris.
Principis exempli formam modumque secuta,
 inducam temere vacuum nihil.
Mens humana mihi tractus ducenda per omnes
 aethereos ut sit prudentior:
Parcarum leges et ineluctabile Fatum
 Fortunaeque vices variabilis;
quae sit in arbitrio res libera, quidve necesse,
 quid cadat ambiguis sub casibus.
More recordantis quam multa reducet eorum
 quae cernet, penitus non immemor.

to harmonious relation, lest it disgust the mind to dwell in shadowy blindness and suffer the burdensome hospitality of the body, lest the spirit have cause to complain that it is too much subject to the dictates of its own flesh. That this concord of unlike powers may come about peaceably, I am summoned to assist in this skillful work.

"You come to my home no stranger, O Nature, for Noys gave birth to me, your sister. Your origin is assuredly one with mine; but the universe at large is your domain, mine this single portion of the ether. My delight is in the heavens, in the stars, and I am drawn away from my post reluctantly; Man, of earthly nature, is to be made a sojourner on earth, and the descent thither is not easy for me. The dank impurity that surrounds the base earth will quickly mar my brilliance. But since this creature owes his form to archetypal patterns, it is useless to plead the journey as an excuse. In accordance with the sacred purpose of the divine and most high Mind I will execute the work of the office assigned me. In following the form and manner of this noble model I shall produce nothing random or worthless.

"The human soul must be guided by me through all the regions of heaven, that she may learn wisdom: the laws of the Fates and inexorable Destiny, and the shiftings of unstable Fortune; what matters are open to our judgment, what is determined by necessity, and what is subject to uncertain accident. By the practice of reflection she will recall as much as she can of that which she discerns, being not wholly without memory.

Ingeniis animoque deos caelumque sequetur,
ut regina suum vas incolet.
Quae virtus stellis, et quanta potentia caelo
et quis sidereis vigor axibus,
quid valeant radiis duo lumina, quinque planetae,
sentiet ingrediens vas corporis.
De caelo speciem vultus, animique tenorem
et morum causas sibi contrahet.
Legibus astrorum vivendi tempora nactus
extremique viam discriminis,
corpore iam posito cognata redibit ad astra,
additus in numero superum deus.
Sic erit, adde fidem; mea vox plenissima veri:
sidera mentiri nec enim licet.
I, Natura, sequar; nec enim vagus incidet error,
si directa tuis via ductibus."

Microcosmus 5

Divinam igitur interpretem Natura constupuit, quam et opus et causas operis modumque executionis intelligit exponentem. Captatis itaque non interfata colloquiis, ad concurrentes voluntatis suae sententias gestu quodam, ut assolet, et nutibus aplaudebat. Ad tam sanctum igitur et religiosum opus itinere destinato, ut concessam apud superos licentiam et auspicium insumerent recedendi, locis longe

"In mind and spirit she will emulate the gods and the heavens, that she may dwell as a queen within her earthly vessel. As she enters the vessel of the body she will have experienced what influence the stars, what power the firmament possesses, what vital force is in the starry vault, what force the two luminaries exert by their rays, and the five planets. From the heavens she will derive a comely aspect, stability of mind, and principles of conduct.

"Having received through the law of the stars her term of life, and the path to the final separation, her body cast off at last, she will come again to her native stars, one more divinity in the host of celestial powers. So shall it be, be assured; my voice is charged with truth: for it is not permitted to the stars to lie.

"Go forth, Nature, I will follow; for no stray wandering can befall us if the path is determined by your guidance."

Microcosmus 5

Nature was astounded by the divine interpretress, as she understood her exposition of their task and its principles and means of execution. And after receiving the whole speech without interrupting she expressed her approval of these declarations which so concurred with her own wishes by the customary gesture and by nodding. That they might gain the express consent and favor of the heavenly powers for their departure, now that the course of their solemn and sacred task had been determined, they entered the realm of

corpulentis sepositam et abstractam purgati defaecatique luminis introeunt mansionem. Ibi summi et superessentialis Dei sacrarium est, si theologis fidem praebeas argumentis.

2. Dextra laevaque caelum aethereis divinisque potestatibus habitatum; quorum quidem ordinibus per ordinem collocatis, unusquisque de superis, de medioximis, de infimis ascripti legem muneris pensumque sui operis recognoscit. Contingentes invicem mansiones, et linea continuationis annexas, uniformis pervadit spiritus, qui vires sufficit universis. Verumtamen non uniformiter a spiritu suscipiunt uniformi: qui enim propiores ad consessum deitatis assistunt, nudatisque ostensisque interdum consiliis internam adusque mentem propius deducuntur. Ceteri, pro qualitate distantiae, decisum nec adeo integrum retinent contemplatum, gustantque parcius deitatis notitiam, scientiam futurorum.

3. E sedibus quidem quas Tugaton suprema divinitas habitatrix insistit, splendor emicat radiatus, non utique perfunctorius, sed infinibilis et aeternus. Ea igitur lux inaccessibilis intendentis reverberat oculos, aciem praeconfundit, ut, quia lumen se defendit a lumine, splendorem ex se videas caliginem peperisse. Ex splendore igitur vel infinibili vel aeterno alter se radius exerebat, ut ex primo secundoque suboriretur et tertius. Qui quidem radii, uniformes et claritatis parilitate consimiles, cum omnia collustrassent, se rursus sui fontis liquoribus admiscebant.

pure and uncontaminated light, far removed and wholly distinct from the physical world. Here, if you give credence to theological arguments, is the secret abode of supreme and superessential God.

2. The heavens on either hand are inhibited by ethereal and divine powers; their ordered ranks being themselves arranged in order, each and every power of the highest rank, the intermediate, or lowest, understands the rule of his assigned function, the amount of his work. For a single spirit pervades their neighboring stations, conjoined with one another and arranged in unbroken succession, and imparts sufficient power to them all. However they do not receive a uniform power from this uniform spirit: those who stand closer to the seat of the deity are drawn, at times, when his decisions are openly and directly revealed, even closer to his inner mind. The others, by virtue of being more distant, retain only a reduced and incomplete vision, and enjoy the experience of the deity and knowledge of the future in a more limited way.

3. From that seat where Tugaton, the supreme divinity, has his dwelling, a radiant splendor shines forth, nowhere partial, but infinite and eternal. This inaccessible light strikes the eyes of the beholder and confounds his vision, so that since one light shields itself from another, you may perceive the splendor producing of itself a darkness. From this infinite and eternal splendor a second radiance extended forth, in such a way that from the first and the second there proceeded a third. These radiances, uniform and identical in brilliance, when they had together made all things bright, reabsorbed themselves again into the well of light which was their source.

4. Istic Urania pariter et Natura, cuidam trinae maiestati, plurima precum devotione, auspicium propositumque itineris conmendarunt. Exinde promoventes, exporrectam aetheris diffusamque planitiem comitato vestigio metiuntur. Neque in eundo Natura sufficeret, nisi solitam ingenitamque celeritatem Urania moderatius inhiberet. Spatiis igitur deductioribus evolutis, eas caeli partes iam linea vicinante contigerant, ubi aether, itemque obtusior nec adeo subtilis planetarum regio, participatis sibi qualitatibus immiscentur. Primo regionis ingressu de puro ad obtusum, de temperato ad frigidum, utramque contrarietatis incurrentiam facili Natura cognitione praesensit.

5. Eo ex loco, multa tamen depressione inferius, Oyarses erat Saturnus, accusatissimus veteranus, crudelioris quidem et detestandae malitiae, dirisque ac cruentis actibus efferatus. Quotquot illi filios uxor fecundissima peperisset, interceptis vitae primordiis recens editos devorabat. Parturienti sedulus excubator non torpuit consideratione, non relanguit misericordia, ut quandoque parceret vel sexui vel decori. Natura senis crudelitatem exhorruit, et, ne sanctos oculos foedo violaret obtuitu, faciem suam virginea pavitatione devertit.

6. Fuit seni unum malum: unde saevitiam exerceret, si quando defuit quem voraret? Crudus adhuc, nec citra vires emeritus, insumpto falcis acumine, quicquid pulchrum, quicquid florigerum demetebat. Rosas et lilia et cetera

4. To this threefold majesty, with an offering of many prayers, Urania and Nature together entrusted the purpose and success of their journey. Then setting forth, they traveled side by side across the wide and extensive surface of the ether. Nor indeed could Nature keep pace, did not Urania carefully curb her native and customary speed. When these more withdrawn regions had been left behind, they entered the region of heaven where, along a neighboring border, the ether and the denser, less refined planetary heaven commingle, imparting their properties to one another. At their first passage into this region, from pure to dense, from temperate to cold, Nature easily divined and understood the force of the opposition between the two.

5. Further on, but placed at a far lower level was the Usiarch Saturn, an ancient to be most strongly condemned, cruel and detestable in his wickedness, savagely inclined to harsh and bloody acts. As many sons as his most fertile wife had borne him he had devoured newly born, cutting short the beginning of life. Ceaselessly on guard when she was giving birth, he neither paused for deliberation nor succumbed to pity, whereby he might sometimes have been sparing because of the sex or comeliness of the child. Nature was horrified by the old man's cruelty, and lest she should profane her divine gaze with the foul sight, turned away her face in virginal alarm.

6. One thing troubled the old man: how could he practice his savagery if ever there were lacking someone whom he might devour? Still vigorous, his strength still unimpaired, he mowed down with a blow of his sickle whatever was beautiful, whatever was flourishing. Just as he would not accept childbirth, so he forbade roses, lilies, and the other

olerum genera, sicut nasci non sustinet, non sustinet et florere. Huius spectaculi praefigurabat imagine, quam pestilens, quam contrarius immineret humanae soboli mox futurae, veneno sui sideris et pernecabili qualitate. Ex contemplatu operum, durum licet adiudicet et impositum, ex eo tamen Natura senem credidit venerandum, quod aeternitatis filius Chronos paterque temporis diceretur.

7. Licet igitur quietem pausamque via productior postularet, non fuit tamen consilium illic hospitium collocare, ubi gelidis et pruinosis rigoribus demutata caeli tranquillitas inhorrescit. Praesumpto igitur animi robore, infecunda Saturni frigora transcurrentes, qua mulcebris et salutaris est Iupiter restiterunt. Huius regionis Oyarses adeo praesens, adeo benevolus, ut eum Latinitas Iovem nominet, a iuvando. Fidesque est quam certissima, per omnia Mundi membra indulgentiarum Iovis beneficia permeare. Amoenitatem circuli blandientis ingressae, laevorsum primo Iovis in limine duo dolia conspicantur, quorum alterum tristis absinthii, mellis alterum dulcorati. Circumstabant et animae alterutrum vicissim poculum, si quando prodirent in corpora, gustaturae. Ea enim conditione sub Iove vivendum universis, ut si quando de temporalibus causae delectionis obveniant, obveniant et doloris.

8. In consistorio suo Iupiter regia praenitebat maiestate: manum quidem sceptratus dexteram, de sinistra suspenderat momentanam, ad cuius aequilibritatem nunc hominum nunc res superum pensitaret. Quicquid igitur statera fidelior iustis ponderibus aequasset, imperiosi vultus femina,

kinds of sweet-scented flowers to flourish. By the spectacle he presented he prefigured how plaguing, how destructive a threat he would pose to the future race of men by the poisonous and deadly property of his planet. While Nature, after observing his labors, judged him harsh and treacherous, yet she believed the old man must be respected, inasmuch as it was said that Chronos was the son of eternity and the father of time.

7. Nevertheless, though their extended journey demanded an interval of rest, it was agreed not to make this their resting place, where the peace of the firmament had been broken, and shivered with chill and icy harshness. Accordingly they mustered their courage, and crossing the barren and frozen wastes of Saturn, paused at the seat of mild and beneficent Jupiter. The Usiarch of this region is so propitious and well-disposed that he is called in Latin "Jove," from "lending aid." And one may believe with absolute certainty that the beneficial effects of Jove's favor permeate every part of the Universe. Entering the pleasant atmosphere of this delightful sphere, they beheld two vessels, placed to the left at Jove's very threshold, one of bitter wormwood, the other of sweet honey. Souls stood about each vessel in turn, and would taste of them, if ever they were to enter bodily life. All life in the Universe is subject to this condition imposed by Jove, that if ever reasons for joy occur in temporal life, reasons for sorrow will occur as well.

8. Seated in his council chamber, Jupiter shone in regal majesty: wielding in his right hand a scepter, he held suspended from his left a scale, in the balance of which he weighed the affairs, now of men, now of the higher powers. Whatever his most trustworthy balance had weighed with

Clotho, per ordinem successionibus temporum explicabat. Ea igitur, quod exaequatam refixamque rerum seriem et distribuat et evolvat, tam plenissime sibi nomen maiestatis insumpsit, ut quicquid spatii Lunam interiacet et Saturnum regnum Clothos appelletur.

9. Loco igitur evidentiore conpositas Uraniam magnifice, sed et Naturam magnificentius, rerum novus et infrequens delectavit aspectus. Verumtamen, ne novitatibus intuendis morosius indulgerent, rursus accinguntur itineri, et laborem iam initum continuatione qua coeperant prosequuntur.

10. Martis igitur ad subteriacentem circulum, anfractuosis quidem sed non adeo distortis lineis, propinquantes, murmur aquae velut in abrupta vallium praecipitantis accipiunt. Cumque de proximo fideles oculos infixissent, Natura Pyriphlegethontem, qui Martio demanaret e circulo, de rivis liventibus et sulphureis recognovit. Sed et Pyrois, sidus Martium, cum forte de Scorpione, suo loco consentaneo, et nativis erectus potentiis, in quartum signumque septimum minaces radios intorquebat, opportunitatemque quaerebat ex circulo ut, cometa factus sanguineus, crinito sidere terribilis appareret. Suspectam intemperie mansionem dirisque vaporibus aestuantem citatis accelerant excursionibus transvolare, et ad Solis vivifici tabernacula deferuntur.

such measure, Clotho, a woman of commanding aspect, unfolded in sequence through the order of time. Inasmuch as she measures out and sets in motion the precisely determined sequence of events, she claims for herself a title of such majesty that all the area lying between the Moon and Saturn is called the realm of Clotho.

9. Reposing at this fine vantage point, Urania was entertained splendidly, and Nature still more splendidly, by this new and unfamiliar view of creation. However, lest they allow too long a delay for contemplating these novelties, they girded themselves once again for travel and resumed their initial laborious journey along the path they had been following.

10. As they approached the sphere of Mars, lying just below, by winding but not wholly distorted tracks, they heard a roar like that of water cascading down a steep slope. When, drawing closer they had concentrated their clear gaze, Nature recognized by its seething and sulfurous waters the river Pyriphlegethon, which issues from the sphere of Mars. But Pyrois, the Martial planet, emboldened by the favoring position of Scorpio and aroused by his own native propensities, shot out menacing beams into the fourth and seventh signs, and sought an opportunity of leaving his orbit, so that, transformed to a comet, he might appear, bloodred and terrifying, with a starry mane. Traveling quickly, the goddesses hastened to pass by this realm, suspect in its uncontrolled behavior and seething with hostile vapors, and proceeded to the dwelling place of the life-giving Sun.

11. Profecto limes Heliacus, per quem annuo Sol circumfertur excursu, non uniformis erat, sed quaternis varietatibus discolorus. Quarta prior e circulo, more viridantis Aegypti, in diversa florum germina novamentis vernalibus herbidabat. Secunda, contra veris teneritudinem ignitis vaporibus adaestuans et abiecta, ariditate sitiebat aestiva. Porro tertia, ex croceo viridique confectam, autumnali maturitate coloris speciem praeferebat. Extrema et ipsa signorum trium spatiis exporrecta; specie tenus fluctuabat instar aquae quam in concretam glaciem rigor solidasset hibernus. Utque maioris esset spectaculi una unius excursio totiens alterata, per mutatum quater circulum mutatis quater vultibus ferebatur. De puero conpubescens in iuvenem, de iuvene virum, de viro senem induerat, canis intermiscentibus albicantem. Eas igitur varietatis species alternabat, per inflexum obliquumque Signiferum, altis pressis et mediis Sol itineribus circumvectus.

12. Inter Oyarsas Geniosque caelestes quos aeterna sapientia mundano vel decori vel regimini deputavit, Sol, illustrior lumine, praesentior viribus, augustior maiestate; mens Mundi, rerum fomes sensificus, virtus siderum, mundanusque oculus. Tam splendoris quam caloris inmensitate perfuderat universa. Instrumenta deo familiaria, arcus et cithara,

11. Now the "Helian highway" by which the sun is borne on his annual journey was not everywhere the same, but was divided into four diversely colored segments. The first quarter of the circle, like verdant Egypt, waxed green and produced an array of flowers under the renewing influence of spring. The second suffered thirst, raging against spring's tenderness with fiery vapors, and enervated by the aridity of summer. The third presented an appearance compounded of the saffron and green of autumnal ripeness. The last, too, extended through three signs of the Zodiac; as far as one could see it shimmered like water that the chill of winter had hardened into solid ice. That the single journey of this single power, so often changing, might present a more imposing spectacle, as he was borne through the fourfold change of his orbit he underwent a fourfold change of countenance. Passing from boyhood through pubescence into youth, from youth to manhood, from manhood he put on hoary age with its intermingling of white hair. The sun assumed these various appearances in turn as it was borne through the upper, lower, and intermediary stages of its journey around the slanting circle of the Zodiac.

12. Among the celestial Usiarchs and Genii whom eternal wisdom has appointed either to adorn or to govern the Universe, the Sun is the most brilliant in its light, preeminent in power, venerable in majesty; it is the mind of the Universe, the spark of perception in creatures, source of the power of the stars and eye of the Universe. It bathed all creation with an immensity of both radiance and warmth. The instruments proper to the sun god, his bow and lyre, hung

de loco sibi proximo dependebant, ut siquando iracundus armaretur in pharetra, tranquillus et placidus fidibus insonaret.

13. Veris Fructus, persona deus venerabili, Phaethonque innoxius, uterque Solis filius; Psyche, Celeritas, ambae proles Apollinea. De dextra iuvenes; de sinistra virgines, currus luciferos ambiebant. Psyche de paterna lampade quos in caelum terramque diffunderet igniculos insumebat. Celeritas, Solis iter perpetuo prosecuta, ita motus temporum hactenus ordinavit, ut diei substantiam unius efficeret semel facta conversio firmamenti; mensurna spatia lustris lunaribus conplerentur; ex numero mensium, orbes annorum; ex annorum multitudine texeretur series saeculorum.

14. Hic igitur Urania, proprii speciem recognoscens officii, nisi proposito moras innecteret, cum cognatis virginibus voluntaria resideret. Verumtamen, quia circa Solis admirationem spectaculo steterat longiore, amoenus Lucifer communisque Cyllenius sine morae dispendio Natura suggerit excurrantur.

15. Intrant igitur, neque enim fas erat divertere, Mercurii Venerisque circulos, ad se invicem et ad Solem perplexius intricatos. Et nisi conmissuras nodosque intersectionum Urania intentior deprehendisset, viarum ambagibus ad Solem, unde venerant, ferebantur.

close at hand, so that if wrathful he might arm himself with his quiver, if calm and at peace he might play upon the lyre strings.

13. Fruit of the Spring, a god of venerable aspect, and harmless Phaethon are both sons of the sun god; Psyche and Swiftness are both Apollo's daughters. On the right hand the youths, on the left the maidens stood about the light-bearing chariot. Psyche was gathering from her father's burning lamp those fiery beams that she would spread through the heavens and the earth. Swiftness, following always in the path of the Sun, governed the movement of time in such a way that a complete revolution of the firmament simultaneously determined the extent of a single day; the spans of the months were resolved by the phases of the moon, and the years' cycles by the number of the months; and by the accumulation of years the sequence of the ages was composed.

14. Urania, recognizing here an office like her own, would willingly remain with these kindred maidens, were it not that this would impose delay on their undertaking. However, as they had spent so long in admiring contemplation of the Sun, Nature suggested that charming Lucifer and promiscuous Cyllenius should be visited without loss of time.

15. Accordingly they entered, for it would have been wrong to pass them by, the circles of Mercury and Venus, intricately connected with one another and with the Sun. And had not Urania noted carefully the junctures and points of intersection, they would have been carried by a roundabout path back to the Sun whence they had come.

16. De contiguo proximoque Mercurius, solaris orbitae circumcursor, ab eadem quam praevenit praevenitur, et pro lege circuli reportantis, nunc supra Solem promovet, nunc inferior delitescit. Communis ambiguusque, Cyllenius in rebus quas siderea qualitate convertit venientem de moribus malitiam non ostendit, sed sodalis eum societas vel iustificat vel corrumpit. Fervori Martio vel Iovis indulgentiae copulatus, de proprietate participis suam constituit actionem. Epicoenum, sexus promiscui in communi, signoque bicorpore hermaphraditos facere consuevit. Huic igitur deo virga levis in manibus, pes alatus, expeditus accinctus, quippe qui deorum interpretis legatique muneribus fungebatur.

17. Porro Venus et ipsa, Mercurii Solisque lineam certis in partibus attingendo, utriusque circuitus amplitudine circumcludit. Mediam inter humectum calidumque temperiem consecuta, naturae suae beneficio germinantium fetus provehit, et publica rerum semina genialibus adiuvat incrementis. Benivolarum quoque stellarum superadiuta testimoniis, nativitates quas aspicit indulgentiore felicitate componit. Ex Venereo sidere, credit astrologus, proveniat incitatum quicquid humanis desideriis obrepserit voluptatum. Vultus quidem Veneris perlucidus ad gratiam inspectoris. Gestamen eius facula, nunc subfumigans, nunc accensa. Sinistro super ab ubere Cupido parvulus dependebat.

16. Mercury, next and nearest, circling around the solar orbit, is preceded by the very planet he precedes; and because of the law of the orbit which bears him, he rises at times above the Sun, and sometimes lurks beneath him. Promiscuous and ambiguous, Cyllenius does not himself reveal the misfortune that results from his behavior in the affairs which he governs by his planetary quality; instead his alliance with companions shows him just or perverse. Joined with the madness of Mars or the liberality of Jove, he determines his own activity by the character of his partner. It is his practice to create epicene and sexually indeterminate beings, and hermaphrodites of bicorporeal shape. This god held a slender wand in his hand, and his feet were winged, lightly shod and bound, as befitted one who performed the office of interpreter and messenger of the gods.

17. Venus, while she touches the orbits of Mercury and the Sun at certain points, encompasses both with the fullness of her own. Attaining a median climate between the extremes of heat and moisture, she draws forth by the benevolence of her nature the fruits of budding plants, and inspires the renewal of all creatures by her generative impulses. Further, aided by the evidence of favorable stars she ensures for those births over which she presides a more bountiful happiness. Astrologers believe that a stealthy arousal of the human longing for pleasure becomes vehement through the influence of Venus's star. The radiant countenance of Venus gives delight to the beholder. Her distinguishing ornament is a torch, now smoldering, now bursting into flame. Infant Cupid clung to her left breast.

18. Inter circulos igitur nunc dividuos nunc altrinsecus limitantes, Urania, Natura, circumspectis itineribus ad vacuum evolutae, de conplexu quem viderant colloquuntur. Quia igitur in depressum citimumque Lunae circulum via declivior et pronior deferebat, longa licet non sentitur excursio; iter promovent nescientes; deveniunt quo intenderant citius expectato. Erat limes aeris aetherisque intervius, qui Lunae mediantis obiectu naturam regionum disparabat alterutram. Supra, quies intermina, serenum perpetuum, tranquillitas aetheris inconcussa. Unde superna, quia non ad aliud et aliud momento mutationis emigrant, eo ab incolumitate et decore proprio nullatenus alterantur. Ea quidem in parte caeli, quia natura est invariabili mulcebris et quieta, sollers Graecia Campos consentit Elysios, et felices animas alma sacrata et numquam desitura lucis amoenitate vestiri.

19. Infra, aeris qualitas turbidior infunditur, cuius mutabilis convertitur species, quotiens expositas passionibus materias contrarietas accidentium interpellat. Unde homines, quia locum incolunt inquietum, tumultus instar veteris, motus permutationum necesse est experiri. Quippe quae de caelo sideribusque decesserat potentius expurgata, in inferioribus remansit ad plurimum, Silvae necessitas influentis.

20. Luna igitur, divisorem et mediastinum limitem intercurrens, feculentae quidem et reliquorum comparatione

18. Amid those spheres which are far apart at one moment and border closely upon one another the next, Urania and Nature, turning to look back along their route as far as the ultimate void, discussed the complex order they had seen. Since an easy and sloping path led downward to the neighboring circle of the Moon, the journey, though long, did not seem so; they made haste unawares, and arrived at their goal more swiftly than they had expected. Here a boundary was interposed between the ether and the atmosphere, which separated the natures of the two regions by the interposition of the Moon as mediator. Above was endless quiet, perpetual calm, the unshaken peace of the ether. Hence the higher powers, as they do not pass into one state and another by the process of change, undergo no alteration of their inviolability and intrinsic dignity. In this region of the heavens, since it is mild and quiet because of its unvarying nature, sagacious Greece agrees to place the Elysian Fields, and blessed souls are clad in the loveliness of a light sustaining, sacred, and everlasting.

19. Below is spread abroad the more turbid quality of the atmosphere, whose changeable appearance is altered whenever some conflict between accidental movements disrupts substances exposed to its passions. So mankind, because it inhabits this unquiet region, the very image of ancient chaos, must necessarily experience the force of its upheavals. For the necessity which arises from the fluctuating state of Silva, and which had ceased when rigorously purged from the heavens and the stars, remained fully active in the lower regions.

20. Thus the Moon, traveling along her divisory and lowly path, is crude and heavy of body by comparison with the

siderum corpulentiae grossioris; divinas et inmortales vivacitates ignium pascens, ethin etiam quae crescendi natura est inferioribus subministrat. Cuius corpus lucidum, et solaris cui resplendet luminis redditivum, ordinatis semper et eisdem invectionibus et solvitur et reparatur. Unde, quia ex alieno lumine lumen nascitur, planetam Solis Ptolemaeus eam Memphiticus appellavit. Ad haec, sicut maris excrescentias et sollicitat et exponit, sic terrenis substantiis quanto vicinior tanto potentior invenitur. Itum reditumque, per eadem signa, assidua et infatigabili velocitate convertens, in res et fata hominum vim praesentissimam vendicavit. Unum idemque numen, pro diversitate potentiae et officii, nunc Lucinam in lampade, nunc Venatricem in pharetra, nunc Reginam Tartaream sertato capite praeferebat.

Microcosmus 6

Exhaustus pro parte labor, superata viarum
ardua tam poterant exhilarasse deas.
In sphaeris titulata suis septena planetum
corpora transierant sidereasque domos.
Sermo viae: falx curva senis, galeata cruenti
militis effigies, inter utrumque Iovis;

other spheres; feeding upon the divine and immortal vitality of the heavenly fires, she also transmits that property which ensures natural bodily growth to the lower world. Her gleaming body, reflecting back to its source the solar light with which it glows, is consumed and restored by regular and unvarying transferals. Because her radiance is produced by the radiance of another, Ptolemy of Memphis named her the planet of the Sun. Moreover, just as she both arouses and allays the swellings of the ocean, so she is known to influence earthly existence more powerfully when she is closer to the earth. Passing through the same constellations in her withdrawal and return with ceaseless and unwearying speed, she has claimed the most immediate power over the affairs and destiny of humankind. Her divinity, one and the same, presents itself according to her various powers and duties, now as Lucina in her radiance, now as the Huntress with her quiver, and now as the Queen of Tartarus with garlanded head.

Microcosmus 6

The part of their task now accomplished and the hardships overcome on their journey gave the goddesses cause to rejoice. They had traversed the seven planetary bodies, reigning in their spheres, and the realm of the stars. Their talk as they went was of the old man's curved scythe, the helmeted form of the bloodthirsty warrior, and Jove between the two;

Mundanum Sol, Luna, iubar; sub utroque ligati
  Mercurius Veneri, Mercurioque Venus.
Mirari libet in caelo stabilita profundae
  Mentis, et argutum Primipotentis opus:
quo iaceant tractu caeli, cinctura, coluri,
  vincla paralleli, robur uterque polus;
Signifer obtortus, neque caelo recta Galaxe,
  qualiter inflexi dispositique loco;
quod tropicis contenta suis via Solis, et ultra
  legitimos fines exspatiata nihil;
quod neque perlustret aequali lumine terras,
  quas super obtorto limite ducit iter;
et quod Phrixeus Aries nocturna diurnis
  tempora iustificat, aequidiemque facit;
quod tenebras abolere die rebusque colorem
  et caelo speciem reddere Solis opus;
quod consectatrix Solisque pedissequa Luna
  sic terrena movet corpora, sicut aquas.
Artificem testata suum, pulcherrima rerum
  machina de forma materiaque placet;
quod, meliore polo melius morata, relinquunt
  sidera, paulatim degenerante loco.
Defectus fluxusque sui ratione timendum,
  quicquid sub caelo turbidiore iacet.
Hac igitur regione poli Natura resistens,
  fixit ad aspectus lumina certa novos.

the Sun and Moon, illuminating the Universe, and the two who are bound to one another, Mercury to Venus, Venus to Mercury.

It was pleasant in heaven to marvel at the steadfast creation of the unfathomable Mind, the intricate work of the Almighty: where the colures lie like a girdle across the plane of the sky; the binding zones; the two steadfast poles; how the slanted Zodiac and the Galaxy, not squarely aligned, are unalterably set in place; that the path of the Sun is contained by its tropics, and never strays beyond these established limits; that it does not shine with equal radiance on all the lands over which it is borne along its slanting path; that the Phrixean Ram balances the periods of night and day, and determines the equinox; that it is the Sun's task to banish the shades with daylight, to restore color to the world, and beauty to the sky; that the Moon, eager follower and handmaid of the Sun, has power over earthly life, as over the tides.

Bearing witness to its maker, the supremely beautiful frame of creation gives pleasure by its form and substance; preserving this finer quality in the higher heavens, life descends from the stars, each stage a little more subject to decay. For whatever lies beneath our turbid sky is to be regarded with mistrust because of its imperfect and fluctuating condition.

Pausing in this region of the heavens, Nature directed her clear gaze upon new sights.

Microcosmus 7

In lunari enim limite, ubi aureae Homeri quasi medietas est catenae, superioris inferique Mundi videlicet umbilicus, spirituum numerus ad milia circumfusus populosae more civitatis laetabundus occurrit. Ad quorum multitudinem formasque dissimiles cum defixis Natura irrevocatisque luminibus inhaereret: "Nosce," inquid Urania, "neque enim conveniens Natura dubitet, rerum prudentior indagatrix; nosce, inquam, O Natura, qui spiritus, et quae eorum differentia, quantisque locorum distinctionibus supremae serviunt potestati.

2. "Caelum, aether, aer, tellus, quaterna quidem regio, universam Mundi continentiam circumcludunt. Caelum simplex est, una eademque quantitate continuum, nec qualitatibus disparatum. Binam aetheris, binam item aeris, trinam telluris partitionem cognoveris. Suum numen, suos habent angelos, et principaliter singuli et subdivisio singulorum.

3. "Caelum ipsum Deo plenum est; neque enim credibile deiectioribus elementis, terrae sordidae, aeri turbulento, sancta et incommutabilis divinitas suarum affixerit sedium mansionem. Posteriora et minora se omnia de loco celsitudinis Deus dispositor intuetur. Divinae licet maiestate caliginis abscondatur incognitus, de suorum vestigiis operum perspicuis innotescit. Eius opera Angeli, quos hactenus ordinavit ut, iuxta rationem continui competentis, copularet

Microcosmus 7

Now along this lunar boundary, as if at the midpoint of Homer's golden chain, the node uniting the higher with the lower Universe, a crowd of thousands of spirits thronged joyously around them, like citizens of a populous city. As Nature stared at this multitude of diverse figures, unable to withdraw her gaze, Urania spoke: "Learn, for it is not fitting that Nature, so diligent in investigating created life, should be in doubt; learn, I say, O Nature, what spirits these are, what their differences, and in what diverse stations they serve the almighty.

2. "The heavens, the ether, the atmosphere, the earth: this fourfold realm encompasses the whole content of the Universe. The heavens are uniform, of one and the same density throughout, unchanging in quality. Know that the ether has two parts, the atmosphere has two parts, and the earth has three. Each of these realms, first of all, and each of their subdivisions has its divine power, each has its angels.

3. "Heaven only is filled with God; for it is unthinkable that the sacred and unchanging godhead should have established the site of its dwelling place among the lowly elements, the impure earth and the turbulent atmosphere. From his lofty position God the disposer views all things as lower and lesser than himself. Though he remains unknown, concealed in the majesty of divine darkness, yet he is manifest in the clear traces of his handiwork. The Angels are his creation, whom he has so ordered that by a system of unbroken continuity he may link the highest with the

ad invicem primos cum mediis, medioximos cum extremis. Sua caelo animalia, ignes siderei: huius generis animal, rationale quidem, nec morte dissolvitur nec afficitur passione.

4. "Extimum telluris globum sapiens genus Homo, quem pergimus fabricatum, digno possederit incolatu. Porro sedem Mundi mediam genus insistit tertium, de extremorum proprietate vel participatione confectum. Participat enim angelicae creationis numerus cum siderum divinitate quod non moritur; participabit cum homine quod passionum affectibus incitatur.

5. "In sublimiori igitur fastigio, siquid caelo sublimius, tabernaculum Tugaton, suprema divinitas, collocavit. Quem circumsistunt obeuntque vicinius agmina ignitae flammantisque naturae perlucida, ex pyr spiritus et creata pariter et vocata. Ea, propter infatigabilem et perpetuam ad Deum conversionem, vel membra vel divinitatis partes specie similitudinis aestimantur; non enim verum est quippiam in divinitate dividuum. Illi ergo, ex proximitate, Deo convertuntur plurimo, et de mente eius excipiunt futurorum arcana quae in Fatum Mundi publicum, per inferiores spiritus, ineffugibili necessitate constituunt proventura. Quia aeternae visione beatitudinis perfruuntur, ab omni distrahentis curae sollicitudine feriati, in pace Dei, quae omnem sensum superat, conquiescunt. Ab ortosphaera igitur firmamenti princi-

middle orders, and the intermediate with the lowest. The firmament, too, has its animate beings, the starry fires: an animal of this kind, certainly rational, is neither destroyed by death nor moved by passion.

4. "The intelligent race of Man, whom we are preparing to fashion, will claim as a worthy habitation earth, the lowest sphere. Moreover a third race occupies the middle realm of the Universe, combining the attributes and participating in the condition of the extremes. For the multitude of angelic beings share the divinity of the stars in that they do not die; they will share the condition of man in that they are impelled by the effects of passion.

5. "On a still loftier height, if there be any place higher than the heavens, Tugaton, the supreme divinity, has established his tabernacle. Those gleaming hosts whose nature is blazing fire, who are both created and named from spiritual fire, stand about him and approach him closely. Because of their unwearied and unceasing inclination toward God, beings of this order are deemed limbs or parts of the divine by a form of similitude; for in truth there is no division whatsoever in the godhead. Owing to their proximity, these beings are drawn most strongly to God, and from his mind they learn the hidden determinations of future events that establish what will come to pass as the revealed Fate of the Universe, by inescapable necessity, through the agency of inferior spirits. Because they enjoy the vision of eternal blessedness, being free from all vexations and distracting concerns, they repose in the peace of God which is beyond understanding. Such a company, pure, wise, and attendant

piisque aetheris purioris usque ad Solem, huiusmodi pura, prudens, et ministra Deo legio continetur.

6. "Abhinc linea continuationis ad Lunam qui interiacent alii, minoratione quadam et luminis et numinis, tantum a superiorum maiestate degenerant, quantum et localiter infimantur. Verumtamen huius ordinis species, intelligentia, memoria, utraque felici, oculorum intuitu adeo subtili, adeo penetrabili, ut, animae pervadens latebras, concepta pectoris deprehendat arcani. Quorum ita benevola, ita communis est servitus, ut hominis indigentias ad Deum, indulgentiarum Dei beneficia ad hominem reportantes, et obsequium caelo et terrenis diligentiam studeant impertiri. Unde Angelus officii nomen est, non naturae.

7. "Cum igitur Homo, condictante quidem Providentia, novum figmentum, nova fuerit creatura, de clementissimo et secundario spirituum ordine deligendus est Genius, in eius custodiam deputatus, cuius tam ingenita, tam refixa est benignitas, ut, ex odio malitiae displicentis, pollute fugiat conversantem. Et cum quid virtutis agendum insumitur, sacris per inspirationem mentibus assolet interesse.

8. "In sublunari aere pars superior, pars inferior: potius qualitatibus quam spatiis localibus disparatur. Cuius primae partes tenuiores, et aliquatenus vaporatae, quia ignitis continuisque aetheris affinitatibus attingantur, quantum parva magnis, quantum possibile rapidis pigriora contingi.

on God, is located from the celestial sphere of the firmament and the brink of the purer ether down to the sphere of the Sun.

6. "Other spirits, who are interspersed along the line of descent from this point to the Moon, are inferior in majesty to the powers above, through a certain diminution of brilliance and power, insofar as their place is lower. Nevertheless a spirit of this rank has an aptness of both understanding and memory, and powers of vision so subtle and penetrating that by probing the inner depths of the spirit, it perceives thoughts hidden in the breast. So benevolent is their service, so devoted to the common good, that in reporting the needs of mankind to God, and returning the gifts of God's kindness to man, they eagerly demonstrate at once their obedience to heaven and their attentiveness to earthly beings. Hence the name Angel denotes their office, not their nature.

7. "Thus when Man, a new form, a new creation, has come to be by the determination of Providence, a Genius responsible for his safekeeping must be selected from this most kindly and serviceable order of spirits, whose benevolence is so ingrained and unalterable that they shun, from a hatred of offensive evil, whoever traffics with impurity. And when some virtuous act is undertaken, they are ever wont to assist the devoted mind with their inspiration.

8. "In the sublunar atmosphere there is a higher part and a lower: they differ more in their qualities than their spatial location. The highest levels are more refined, and to some extent vaporized, since they are affected through affinity by the contiguous fires of the ether, insofar as small things can share the condition of great, or the sluggish that of the swift.

Ea igitur spirituum distinctio quae in aere mansitat, sed sereno, tranquillas mentes contrahunt, quia cohabitant in tranquillo. Ex istorum quoque numero secundus est Genius qui, de nascendi principiis Homini copulatus, vitanda illi discrimina vel mentis praesagio, vel soporis imagine, vel prodigioso rerum spectaculo configurat.

9. "Horum quidem non adeo sincera, non usquequaque simplex est divinitas, verum corpore, sed aethereo, circumplexa. Ex aetheris namque serenitate et liquore aeris defaecatam opifex puritatem excepit, unde divinas extrinsecus animas materiis, ut ita dixerim, simplicibus alligavit. Cum corpore igitur velut incorporeos, subtiliores inferis, sed superis grossiores, imbecilla non sufficit humanitas intueri.

10. "Ex medio porro aeris inferius turbulenti, spiritales nequitiae circumcursant, imperiique satellites durioris. Quippe terrena non affici non possunt illuvie, qui vicinos terrae limites intercurrunt. Summa Dei diligentia, minus defectiusque purgati ab antiqua Silvae malitia, angustissima brevique linea recesserunt. Quia igitur in malignitate et nocendi studio perseverant, divino plerumque iudicio potestatem accipiunt, ut tormentis afficiant sceleribus inquinatos. Plerumque ex arbitrio ultroneas inferunt laesiones. Saepe per suggestionem tacitis cogitationibus invisibiles illabuntur; assumpto saepe corpore formas umbraticas induuntur.

The class of spirits who dwell in the atmosphere, but in its serene portion, maintain calm of mind, as they live in calm. Second in rank to these is the Genius joined to Man from the first moment of his birth, who represents to him, by forebodings of mind, by visions in sleep, or by portentous displays of external things, dangers to be avoided.

9. "The divinity of these beings is not wholly simple or pure, for it is enclosed in a body, albeit an ethereal one. For the creator extracted the distilled purity of ethereal calm and aerial fluidity, and then adapted divine souls from above to a material which was, so to speak, simple. Since their bodies are virtually incorporeal, subtler than those of lower creatures, though coarser than those of higher powers, feeble humanity is unable to apprehend them.

10. "Below the midpoint of the teeming air wander evil spirits, and servants of a cruel power. They cannot avoid the taint of earthly foulness, indeed, for they hover close to the surface of earth. These beings, having been only slightly and imperfectly cleansed of the ancient evil of matter, have withdrawn within extremely narrow bounds through the great assiduity of God. And since they persist in wickedness and the desire to do harm, they are often empowered by divine decree to inflict torment on those stained with crime. Frequently, too, judging for themselves, they inflict injury of their own accord. Often they insinuate themselves invisibly into our secret deliberations through the power of suggestion; often, assuming bodily existence, they put on phantasmic forms.

11. "Primos igitur spirituum Praesules, medioximos Interpretes, extremos Angelos dixerim desertores. Telluros, qui terram incolunt, sic habeto. Ubi terra delectabilior, nunc herboso cacumine, tergoque montium picturato, nunc fluviis hilarescit, nunc silvarum viriditate vestitur, illic Silvani, Panes et Nerei innocua conversatione aetatis evolvunt tempora longioris. Elementali quadam puritate compositi, sero tamen obeunt in tempore dissolvendi.

12. "A principiis igitur aeris adusque terrae superficiem contingentis, praecipuus est Oyarses Plutonius, dixerim vel Summanus, quia, summum manium, a lunari iam circulo, imperii regnique sui latitudines ordiatur. Porro numen cuius potestas in aere, maiestatis auctoritate apud conscientiam tuam nolo sordeat aut vilescat. Aer namque spirandi est organum, et sine aeris beneficio rerum incolumitas non subsistit.

13. "Haec est ergo turba, circumfusam quam aspicis, quae super subterque Lunam stationem suam non deserit, et deputati propositum operis non abrumpit."

Microcosmus 8

"Perspice, mente sagax, quae Mundi forma, quibusque
internixa sibi sint elementa modis;
quo studio Noys alma rudem digessit acervum

11. "The first rank of spirits I call the Guardians, those intermediary the Interpreters, and the lowest the renegade Angels. Consider now the Telluri, spirits who dwell on earth. Wherever earth is most delightful, rejoicing now in green hill and flowery mountainside, now in rivers, now clothed in woodland greenery, there Silvans, Pans, and Nerei draw out the term of their long life in innocent communion. They are composed of a kind of elemental purity: yet they too die at last in the season of their dissolution.

12. "From the limits of the atmosphere down to the surface of earth which borders it, the preeminent power is the Plutonian Usiarch, whom I might call Summanus, because, as lord of the shades, the empire over which he rules begins at the circle of the Moon. But I would not have a power whose potency is limited to the air appear to your judgment as mean or base in the scope of his royal power. For the air is the instrument of breathing, and without the gift of the air the health of created life cannot endure.

13. "Such, then, is the multitude whom you behold spread about; who never abandon their positions, above or below the sphere of the Moon, nor cease to perform the duties of their assigned function."

Microcosmus 8

"Observe, O keen-minded one, how the Universe is formed, and in what manner the elements are interwoven; with what care fostering Noys distributed the rude heap, that

ut stabilem teneant contiguamque fidem;
quid mediis extrema liget, quid foedera ungat,
quid caelum moveat, quidve moretur humum;
astrorum motus et quae sit cuique potestas,
ortus, occasus, puncta, gradus, numeri;
cur Aplanen contra septenos impetus orbes
volvat, et anfractus per sua signa vagos;
cur Veneris sint blanditiae, cur proelia Martis,
frigora Saturni, temperiesque Jovis;
quae Solis, quae Mercurii Lunaeque potestas,
et qua discurrant signa gradusque mora;
quod, si praetemptes numeros, si consulis artem,
quid fati series detve negetve probas.
Cur constringat hiems, ver laxet, torreat aestas,
Autumnique metant tempora, mente vides;
cur gelidus Boreas, mollisque Favonius; alter
floribus expoliet, vestiat alter humum;
coniugis in gremium Jove descendente novetur
mundus, et in partu turgeat omnis humus;
inveniatque Ceres quaesitam cum face prolem,
ut proserpendo proferat illa caput;
in silvis volucres, pisces generentur in undis,
floreat omnis ager, frondeat omne nemus.
Quae membris animam numeri proportio iungat,
ut res dissimiles uniat unus amor;
cum terrena caro, cum sit mens ignea, cumque
haec gravis, illa movens, haec hebes, illa sagax;
simplicitas animae sic transit in alteritatem
divisumque genus dividit illud idem.

they might attain a stable and unbroken harmony; what binds extremes to medians, what establishes their bonds, what moves the heavens, and what stays the earth; the motions of the stars, what power belongs to each, their rising and setting, position, motion, and laws; why the rotation of the Aplanes runs counter to the seven planets, and their wandering course through their signs; why pleasure belongs to Venus, wars to Mars, cold weather to Saturn, fair weather to Jove; what are the powers of the Sun, Mercury, the Moon, at what interval they run their course through the signs: for if you investigate their proportions, and have recourse to art, you will discover what the scheme of fate will grant or deny.

"You understand why winter fetters the earth, and spring sets it free, why the summer burns, why autumn is the season of harvest; why Boreas is chill and Favonius mild; why the one lays waste the flowers, while the other adorns the earth; how the world is renewed when Jove descends into the lap of his spouse, and all the earth swells in pregnancy; how Ceres finds the child she had sought, torch in hand, that the maiden, creeping slowly upward, may show forth her head; how birds are engendered in the forest, fish in the seas, how the fields come to flower, and all the groves put forth new leaves.

"You understand what harmonious proportion unites souls to bodily members, so that a single bond of love unites unlike things; though the flesh be earthly and the mind fiery spirit, though one is heavy and inert, the other in motion, one dull, the other keen; thus the simplicity of the soul enters the condition of otherness, and a divided mode of being divides what is one and the same.

Sed quae compedibus, quae carcere clausa tenetur,
en quasi corporea mole sepulta iacet,
ad natale jubar, ad regna paterna redibit,
si sapiat; si non, coniuga carnis eat.
Quid morti licitum, quid mortis causa, quis auctor,
altius evolvens, philosophando vide,
quo trahit imperio sorbetque voragine quicquid
aura levat, tellus sustinet, aequor alit.
Si tamen inspirat verum mens conscia veri,
rem privat forma, non rapit esse rei;
res eadem subjecta manet, sed forma vagatur
atque rei nomen dat nova forma novum;
forma fluit, manet esse rei; mortisque potestas
nil perimit, sed res dissociat socias.

Quid placeat per se, quae sint aliunde petenda,
quid deceat, quid non, philosophando vide.
Iniustum iusto, falso discernere verum
sedula pervideas, et ratione probes."

Microcosmus 9

Ventum erat inter colloquendum ubi aer inferior, Aeoliis fratribus regio decertata, nunc rigescens nunc adaestuans, verberata saepe grandinibus collisis, saepe nubibus intonatur.

But what is thus held by fetters, shut up in prison, yea lies all but buried beneath its bodily burden, will return to the glory of its birth, the kingdom of the father, if it is wise; if not, let it remain wedded to the flesh.

"Reading more deeply and philosophically, behold what is permitted to death, what is death's cause and what its agent, by what tyranny it drags down, in what maelstrom it engulfs everything that air, earth, or water sustains. And yet, if a mind that consorts with truth may inspire true understanding, death deprives a thing of its form, but does not steal the essence of that thing; for the subject matter remains the same, though its form pass away, and a new form only gives this matter a new name; form flows away, the essence of the thing remains; the power of death destroys nothing, but only disunites united parts.

"Learn through philosophy what is pleasing in itself, what must be pursued for another purpose, what is fitting, and what is not. Be zealous to distinguish justice from injustice, truth from falsehood, and to test your observation by reason."

Microcosmus 9

During this conversation they had come to that region of the lower atmosphere disputed by the Aeolian brothers, freezing at one moment and burning the next, often assailed by showers of hail, often resounding with thunderclouds.

De cuius inaequalitate Urania constipuit, quae nihil insueverat in diversa traducibile vel discrepans a tranquillo. Videt lubricam elementi substantiam ad omnes contrarietatis incurrentias convertibili qualitate mutari: nunc offendi pluviis ex oceano comparatis, nunc densari nebulis quas terra parturit crassiores. Quae quidem omnia quantum obvia consuetudini, tantum aegra animo, tantum contraria visioni. Illis innatam regionibus inconstantiam abhorrentes, elementorum excursis interstitiis, iam florentis terrae gremio consistere contendebant.

2. Gramision locus est Eoum ad cardinem secretior in reducto. Is quidem, de recentis puerique Solis teneritudine feliciorem aeris temperiem consecutus, et virescit ad gratiam et germinat ad fecunditatem. Nomen loco Gramision, quia graminum diversitatibus perpetuo compubescit.

3. Quicquid occurrit morbis, quicquid conciliat sanitatem, quicquid deliciosos voluptate sensus irritat, plantas, herbas, odoramenta, species, in diversa mortalium commoda sinus abditus subministrat. Haec in mundo sola est, ut opinor, excepta particula, quae, de elementorum intensione nihil in se suscipiens, plenam consummatamque temperiem adaptata est confiteri. Haec ver habet perpetuum, brumas, aestates, inaequales autumnos, clementiori caelo supposita, sed, quod verius est, munere divinitatis, ignorat. Eo, ergo, quia eisdem in locis Physim reperiendam existimat, Natura suggerit divertendum.

Urania was amazed at this variability, having never encountered a thing capable of being transformed into something different, or anything divergent from calm. She saw that the fluid substances of the elements, by their property of changeability, were altered by every incursion of contrariety: now assailed by rains drawn up from the sea, now burdened with clouds of a denser kind that the earth produced. Insofar as all these were at odds with her customary life, they were oppressive to her spirit, and painful to behold. Recoiling in horror from the inconstancy intrinsic to this region, and having traversed the interstices of the elemental structure, they hastened onward and came to rest in the lap of the flourishing earth.

2. Gramision is a secluded and remote spot near the eastern horizon. Having received, through the tenderness of the Sun in its fresh youth, a most happy evenness of climate, this place flourishes with pleasant greenery and burgeons with rich growth. The name of the place is Gramision because it is perpetually bringing plants of all sorts to maturity.

3. This hidden valley presents to the various uses of mankind whatever allays disease, whatever is conducive to health, whatever provokes the delights of sensual pleasure, be it plant, grass, scent, or spice. This is the one privileged spot in all the world, I think, which, undergoing none of the effects of elemental strife, is capable of claiming a full and perfect evenness of climate. The place maintains perpetual springtime, for it knows nothing of the variations of winter, summer, and autumn, placed as it is under a kinder sky, but more truly due to divine munificence. Since she thought that Physis might be found in this very place, Nature suggested that they turn aside here.

4. Locus utique, suapte perspicuus, speciem pulchritudinis amplioris adiecit; quippe matrem generationis Naturam praesenserat adventare. De Naturae igitur Genio fecunditate concepta, derepente tellus intumuit, et comfortatis caespitibus vis occulta subrepsit. Heliadum silva uberiora sudavit unguenta, Sabaea virgula suam certavit distillare pinguedinem. Amomum, cinnamomum vicinos tractus, hoc lenius, illud diffusius, odoravit. Quicquid ergo deliciosus oriens parturit et educit, ad adventum Naturae vultu quodam festivitatis occurrit.

5. Erat rivus, oriundis ex alto cursibus in plana praecipitans, non ut tumultus violentos incuteret, verum auribus amico murmure blandiretur. Blandus auditu, blandior fuerat visione: aethereae liquidum puritatis excedens, tanquam corporalitate deposita, ad purum fere transierat elementum. Is quidem gyris, anfractibus suos hactenus differebat effectus, ut humoris materiam, graminibus sufficeret universis. Totam loci continentiam utrobique silva lateraliter circumplectens, geminato commodo et temperabat solibus et communes arcebat ingressus. Claudentes intra terminos agebat calor aethereus in humecto, ut ibi flores varii, ibi odoramenta, ibi seges aromatum cresceret vel invisa.

6. Eo igitur in loco Physim residere super aspiciunt, Theoricae et Practicae individuo filiarum consortio cohaerentem. Studiosa rerum, in seposito et tranquillo ubi nihil

4. Wholly splendid in itself, the place assumed an even more beautiful aspect; for it had had a premonition that Nature, mother of generation, was at hand. The earth, its fecundity conceived through the Genius of Nature, suddenly swelled with life, and its hidden powers crept forth in sturdy greenery. The grove of the Heliades emitted a more abundant resin; Sabaean boughs vied in exuding their richness. Balsam and cinnamon scented the air nearby, one lightly, the other more amply. Thus everything to which the delightful east gives birth and nurture rose up at Nature's arrival with a certain festive air.

5. There was a stream, flowing swiftly in its descending course from the height to the floor of the glade, not striking the ear with a tumultuous roar, but rather soothing with its gentle murmur. Charming to hear, it was more charming to behold: its water was of a more than ethereal purity, as if it had cast off its bodily state and been nearly transformed to the pure element. By way of bends and windings it distributed its benefits to provide a sufficiency of moisture for the entire plantation. A wood, which surrounded the place and all it contained on every side, served the twofold purpose of tempering the sun's heat and preventing ready access. Within this confining boundary an ethereal heat was at work in the moist soil, so that in one place an array of flowers, in another herbs, at still another spices sprang up even unbidden.

6. From above, they saw that Physis was seated in this place, closely attended by Theory and Practice, her daughters and inseparable companions. She was occupied with the study of created life, in this place, calm and sequestered, where nothing would disturb her. She had taken as the

offenderet, mansitabat. Naturarum omnium origines, proprietates, potentias, effectus, postremo universam omnemque Aristotelis categoriam, materiam cogitationis effecerat. Sumptis a suprema divinitate principiis, per genera, per species, per individua, naturam, et quicquid eo nomine continetur, indeflexo vestigio sequebatur. Siquando caelo vel sideribus inferius excogitavit, de complexione mores animalium studuit iudicare: pavitationem leporis ex frigido, leonis audaciam ex ignito, in vulpe versutiam, tarditatem in asino, alterum phlegmatis, alterum melancholiae qualitatibus importari.

7. Animati conditionem corporis per inconstantiam mutabilitatis videbat effluere; inde subortas morborum molestias animam primo lacessere, domum eius labefactare corpoream, evictam denique sedibus exturbare. Ea contra inveniendis invigilabat remediis, ad quorum temperamentum inaequalitas frenaretur, cum se dirigeret ad nocendum. Verum id disquisitiori pertractabat ingenio, ut elementa, partes mundi primariae partesque partium, in hiis, ex hiis, et per haec quae generant, causis physicalibus deservirent. Non herbis, non plantis, non contenta graminibus, de lapidibus, de metallis remediales etiam extorqueret effectus. Id suae visum est superaddendum scientiae, ut per mixturam calidam venenis etiam mortiferis ad curam medicam salubriter uteretur.

8. Plasmaturam quoque Hominis, de naturae possibilitate coniciens, quadam velut sub imagine somniabat, cum venientis Uraniae radius praecucurrit, et de fontis contigui

subject of her thought the origins of all natural things, their properties, powers, and functions, and, in sum, the whole range of the Aristotelian categories. Drawing her first principles from the supreme divinity, she pursued nature, and whatever is included under that name, by an undeviating path through genera, species, and individuals. Whenever her thoughts descended from the heavens and the stars, she sought to explain by their composition the behavior of animate creatures: the timidity of the hare was due to coldness, the boldness of the lion to fire; cunning in the fox and sloth in the donkey are caused by the property of phlegm in the one and of melancholy in the other.

7. She observed that the state of an animate body fluctuated under the shifting influence of mutability; thence arise the afflictions of disease, first troubling the spirit, causing its bodily dwelling to totter, and finally casting it out, dispossessed of its home. She took pains to seek out remedies against this, by whose tempering influence imbalance might be restrained when it sought to do harm. Indeed she accomplished this with such penetrating insight that the very elements, primary components of the world, and the components of these components, in and of themselves and by virtue of what they produce, lent themselves to medical causes. Not content with herbs, plants, and grasses, she wrung curative effects even from stones and metals. It must seemingly be added to the sum of her wisdom that by artful mixing she could use even deadly poisons effectively in the work of healing.

8. Physis was dreaming, constructing an imaginary version of the creation of Man from the potentiality of Nature, when a ray of light gave notice of the approach of Urania,

repercussione faciem demonstravit absentis. Prior igitur Theorica, divas hospites recognoscens, matrem sublevat, sororem excitat ad surgendum. Concurritur ad osculum et suis sese nominibus consalutant. Collata est quae debetur hospitibus reverentia susceptando. Ire sessum commonitae, succincte quid veniant prosequuntur, nulla in medium mora. Et ecce Noys praesentiam intulit, et monstrato silentio, sic incepit.

Microcosmus 10

"Pignora cara, deae, quas ante creata creavi
  saecula: de partu glorior ipsa meo.
Summa voluntatis haec est: venistis ad istas
  consilii partes propositique mei.
In rebus formisque suis si defuit orbi,
  suppleat id nostro numine vestra manus.
Plena minus, perfecta minus, minus esse decora
  quae feci totiens, est mihi turpe 'minus'!
Sensilis hic Mundus, mundi melioris imago,
  ut plenus plenis partibus esse queat,
effigies cognata deis et sancta meorum
  et felix operum clausula fiet Homo,
qualis ab aeterno sub mundo principe vivit,
  digna nec inferior mentis idea meae.
Mentem de caelo, corpus trahet ex elementis,
  ut terras habitet corpore, mente polum.

and by reflection in the nearby spring revealed the countenance of the still absent goddess. Theory, the first to recognize the divine guests, awoke her mother and bade her sister rise. Kisses are quickly given and they greet one another by name. That reverence was observed which the entertainment of guests demands. Once invited to seat themselves, the goddesses explained briefly why they had come with no interruption. And behold, Noys appeared before them, and, having appealed for silence, began to speak.

Microcosmus 10

"Goddesses, beloved children, whom I created before the creation of time: I myself take pride in my progeny. This is the completion of my wish: you have come to the final stage of my plan and enterprise. If there is anything lacking among the creatures and forms of the universe, your hands, through my inspiration, must make it good. That so often what I have wrought is less than complete, less than perfect, less than beautiful: this 'less' is a disgrace to me! That this sensible Universe, the image of an ideal universe, may be completed through the completion of its parts, Man will be made, his form closely akin to the divine, a blessed and happy conclusion of my work, such as he has lived from eternity, a subject of the primary universe, a worthy and in no way inferior idea in my mind. He will derive his mind from heaven, his body from the elements, so that he may dwell bodily on earth, mentally in heaven.

Mens, corpus, diversa licet, iungentur ad unum,
ut sacra conplacitum nexio reddat opus.
Divus erit, terrenus erit, curabit utrumque,
consiliis mundum, religione deos.
Naturis poterit sic respondere duabus,
et sic principiis congruus esse suis.
Ut divina colat, pariter terrena capessat,
et geminae curam sedulitatis agat,
cum superis commune bonum rationis habebit:
distrahet a superis linea parva Hominem.
Bruta patenter habent tardos animalia sensus:
cernua deiectis vultibus ora ferunt.
Sed, maiestatem mentis testante figura,
tollet Homo sanctum solus ad astra caput,
ut caeli leges indeflexosque meatus
exemplar vitae possit habere suae.
Dii superi stellaeque sibi caelumque loquetur,
consilium Lachesi notificante suum.
Viderit in lucem mersas caligine causas,
ut Natura nihil occuluisse queat—
aerios tractus, tenebrosa silentia Ditis,
alta poli, terrae lata, profunda maris.
Viderit unde vices rerum, cur aestuat aestas,
siccitat autumnus, ver tepet, alget hiems.
Viderit unde suum Phoebo iubar, unde sorori,
unde tremit tellus, unde marina tument,
cur longis aestiva dies extenditur horis,
parvaque contrahitur nox breviore mora.
Ut sua sint elementa volo: sibi ferveat ignis,
Sol niteat, tellus germinet, unda fluat;

His mind and body, though diverse, will be joined into one, such that a sacred union may render the work agreeable to both. He shall be both divine and earthly, and will devote himself to both spheres, dealing wisely with the world, reverently with the gods. Thus can he conform to his dual nature and remain in harmony with his two defining principles. That he may both worship things divine and fully embrace earthly life, and meet the demands of this double commitment, he will possess the gift of reason in common with higher powers; only a thin line will separate Man from the gods.

"Brute beasts make plain the dullness of their faculties: their heads are bent forward, their faces downcast. But Man alone, his form bearing witness to the majesty of his mind, will raise his blessed head toward the stars, that he may claim the laws of the heavens and their unalterable courses as a model for his own life. The gods above, the stars, the firmament will speak to him, and Lachesis reveal to him her deliberations. He shall behold clearly principles shrouded in darkness, so that Nature may keep nothing hidden—the aerial realms, the shadowy stillness of Dis, the vault of heaven, the breadth of the earth, the depths of the sea. He will perceive how change occurs: why the summer swelters, autumn parches the land, spring is balmy, winter cold. He will see whence comes the radiance of Phoebus, and that of his sister, why the earth trembles and the ocean swells, why the summer day draws out its long hours, and night is reduced to a brief interval.

"It is my will that the elements be his: that fire burn for him, the Sun shine, the earth be fruitful, the sea ebb and

Terra sibi fruges, pisces sibi nutriat unda,
  et sibi mons pecudes et sibi silva feras;
omnia subiciat, terras regat, imperet orbi.
  Primatem rebus pontificemque dedi.
Sed cum nutarit, numeris in fine solutis,
  machina corporeae collabefacta domus,
aethera scandet Homo, iam non incognitus hospes
  praeveniens stellae signa locumque suae."

Microcosmus II

"Trina igitur tribus superincumbit opera, cuique sua: compositio animae, ex Endelichia et virtutum aedificatione; corporis, ex materiae praeparatione; utrumque corporis et animae formativa concretio, de caelestis ordinis aemulatione. Prior igitur ad Uraniam, secunda ad Physim, tertia ad te, O Natura, dinoscitur pertinere.

2. "Verumtamen indultum vobis plurimum; vestro plurimum detractum est operi vel labori. In vestra manu est sumere, cum velitis, humanae sementem animae, ex Endelichia iam creata; corpus, ex elementis massa confusionis exceptis. In quorum creatione vel expolitione quid studii, quid diligentiae, quid putatis sedulitatis impendi? Grave quidem et subtile et difficillimis implicitum rationibus quod iniungo.

flow; that Earth bear its fruits for him, the sea its fish, the mountains their flocks, the wilderness its beasts for him, that he subordinate all to himself, rule on earth and govern the universe. I have established him as ruler and high priest of creation.

"But when the tottering structure of his bodily dwelling falls, its binding harmony dissolved, man will ascend the heavens, no longer an unacknowledged guest, passing beyond the place of his star among the constellations."

Microcosmus II

"A threefold task is imposed on you three, with a portion for each: the composition of a soul from Endelechia and the edifying power of the virtues; the composition of a body from the matter prepared; and the formative uniting of the two, soul and body, through emulation of the order of the heavens. The first task plainly belongs to Urania, the second to Physis, the third, O Nature, to you.

2. "However you have been shown much consideration; your task and labor have been much reduced. It remains for you, when you see fit, to undertake the sowing of a human soul from the already created Endelechia, and a body out of those elements extracted from the mass of chaos. Do you realize what zeal, what perseverance, what effort is to be devoted to the creation and refinement of these things? It is, indeed, a weighty and intricate task that I impose, involving most difficult analysis.

3. "Verumtamen si, prae rerum multitudine, auctoritate, et pondere, vestra , ut solet, memoria vacillabit in aliquo, ad monimenta quae dedero fuerit recurrendum: Providentiae Speculum Uraniae, Tabulam Fati Naturae, et tibi, Physi, Librum Recordationis exhibeo. Trina haec est, ut verum fatear, consiliorum dei notitia, veritas, et purgatissima certitudo."

4. Erat igitur Speculum Providentiae, cuius magna admodum circumferentia, intermina latitudo, extersa superficies, prospicuus introspectus, ut quas olim contineret imagines non rubigo deterreret, non deleret antiquitas, non turbaret incursus. Vivebant ideae, vivebant exemplaria, rerum species, nullo nata tempore, nulloque in tempore desitura. Speculum igitur Providentiae Mens aeterna, in qua sensus ille profundissimus, in qua rerum genitor, extortorque omnium, intellectus.

5. Erat in exemplaribus invenire simulacrum cuiusvelis generis, quale, quantum, quando et quomodo proventurum. Illic Silva, prioris adhuc nubiculo vetustatis obducta; exinde sub aedificatore Deo vultus novicios induebat; illic elementorum amicitia, mediator et complectibilis, ex se, in se concidens, et mutuus internexus; illic orbiculata caelique volubilis magnitudo. Illic fomes ille vivificus Endelichia, molem illam intrinsecus atque extrinsecus circumplexa. Illic ignes siderei, illic proprietate parili ministra mundo lumina, Sol vitalis et generans, Luna coadiuvans incrementis.

3. "Nevertheless, if in the face of the many details, the heavy responsibility of the task, your memories, as is likely, should falter at any point, recourse may be sought to records which I shall provide: to Urania I present the Mirror of Providence, to Nature the Table of Destiny, and to you, Physis, the Book of Memory. This threefold gift embodies, to speak truly, insight into the deliberations of God, true knowledge, and the clearest kind of certitude."

4. The Mirror of Providence was of vast circumference, its breadth was boundless, its surface was polished, and one could see deep within that whatever images it had ever received no rust might eat away, nor age make faint, nor intrusion disrupt. There lived ideas and exemplars, the images of things, not born in time and destined not to pass away in time. This Mirror of Providence is the eternal Mind, in which resides that most profound understanding, that intellect which is the creator and remover of all things.

5. Among the exemplars might be discovered the model of anything whatsoever, its quality and quantity, and when and how it would come to exist. Here was Silva, still covered by the darkness of her ancient condition; now through God's craft she assumed new shapes; here the agreement of the elements, mediating and embracing, dividing them and bringing them together, and their mutual bonding; here the rounded and revolving vastness of the heavens. Here was the vital fire, Endelechia, embracing the whole, within and without. Here were the starry fires, here those orbs who minister to the world in complementary ways, the vivifying and generative Sun, and the Moon, lending assistance to

Illic planetae, illic signa, planetarum hospitiis et potentiis deputata. Illic pedestrium, natatilium, pennatorum genera, sicut suas conplectitur species familiaritas elementi. Ea igitur formarum diversitas Uraniam plurimo labore distraxit, longasque in curas ante dissecuit, quam imaginariam Hominis imaginem certis indiciis inveniret.

6. Erat quoque et Tabula Fati, magnae quidem continentiae, sed finitae. Non lubrici, non luminosi corporis, sed de ligni materia grossiore. Illic, eodem prope modum genere quo et in speculo, rerum facies omnium lineata coloribus apparebat. Ea Speculi Tabulaeque differentia, quod in Speculo speculatur status naturarum caelestium indeflexus, in Tabula quidem quam maxime temporales qui permutantur eventus.

7. Unde Atropos, Clotho, Lachesis, iurata Providentiae Fatoque germanitas, similem, sed dissimili loco, mundanae administrationis diligentiam curamque sunt sortitae. Ortosphaeram firmamenti Atropos, planetarum erraticam Clotho, Lachesis terrena disposuit.

8. Non igitur aliud Fati Tabula quam eorum quae geruntur series, decretis fatalibus circumscripta. In ea divinorum quidem operum vestigia, sed summatim, naturalia et quae temporis sunt porrectiore spatio tenebantur. Illic causae unde antiquissimus tumultus in Silva, miraculumque opificis quod in tanto rerum divortio pax inventa. Illic unde species, unde formae substantiis obveniunt, et quae quatinus miro

births. Here were the planets, here the constellations delegated to be the houses of the planets and transmit their influence. Here were the races of land-going, swimming, and feathered creatures, as the friendly quality of their element embraced their species. This array of different forms presented Urania with a hard and perplexing task, and she wearied herself in long and anxious seeking before she discovered by clear indications the still imaginary image of Man.

6. The Table of Destiny, too, was of vast extent, but finite. Its surface, neither smooth nor luminous, was the coarser material of wood. Here, in much the same manner as in the Mirror, appeared the shapes of all creatures, tinted with their colors. There was this difference between Mirror and Table: in the Mirror was reflected the unvarying state of heavenly natures, while in the Table were seen most of all events in time that were subject to change.

7. Hence Atropos, Clotho, and Lachesis, a sisterhood pledged to Providence and Fate, were assigned to keep a common careful watch, though in separate realms, over the direction of the universe. Atropos governed the sphere of the firmament, Clotho the planets' wandering, Lachesis the affairs of earth.

8. Thus the Table of Destiny is nothing else but the sequence of those things which come to pass as determined by the decrees of Fate. Here too there were traces of the divine handiwork, but they were slight. The works of Nature and whatever exists during the extended course of time were contained here. Here were the causes of the ancient tumult in Silva, and the miracle of the creator whereby peace was contrived amid so vast a disunity. Here was shown how species and form come together with substance, and how, in a

quodam modo idearum impressione signantur. Illic unde caelo sit spiritus et virtus defluens in terrena, stellarum motus efficax quid importat; illic unde rebus occiduis rediviva substantia, unde factum Mundo seminarium quo repullulet et resurgat. Illic omne animal, omnis species, omnisque natura. Fatalem igitur mater generationis Tabulam cum fidelius inspexisset, quae tantas inter species latitabat humanitas vix reperta.

9. Primum igitur Hominem, quem pagina designabat ab occipitis regione, longa longis historiis fatorum series sequebatur. In ea namque Fortuna calcata plebis humilitas, in ea regum venerabilis celsitudo. In ea vel paupertas miserias vel redundantia fecerat voluptates. Sortis plerique mediae ab alterutro temperabant. In ea vel sudatum militiae vel litteris vigilatum, ceteraque operum functione vita fataliter actitata. Saecularis illa continentia, purioribus ex auro initiata principiis, paulatim degenerante materia, in ferrum visa est terminare.

10. Erat quoque Liber Recordationis, non communibus litteris, verum charactere notisque conscriptus, brevis ad sententiam et pagina pauciore contentus. In ea quidem brevitate res Providentiae Fatique congestae subnotari poterant, poterant subintelligi, non poterant provideri. Liber enim Recordationis non aliud quam qui de rebus se ingerit et compellat memoriam intellectus, ratione saepe veridica, sed probabili saepius coniectura.

certain marvelous manner, they are distinguished by the impress of divine ideas. Here were shown the spirit and power flowing down from the firmament into earthly life, and what the influential motions of the stars portend; how the substance of dead creatures is restored to life, and how a seed plot is established for the Universe where it may sprout forth and grow afresh. Here were every animal, every species and every nature. And thus, when the mother of generation had studied carefully the Table of Destiny, humankind, lurking among so many species, could barely be discovered.

9. A long chain of fate and much history stemmed from the first Man, whom the page distinguished by the position of his head. For here were the lowly peasantry trampled underfoot by Fortune, and the venerable loftiness of kings. Here either poverty bred misery, or abundance afforded pleasure. Most preserved the balance of a middle course between the two extremes. Here a life was assigned by Fate to the sweaty work of soldiery, or the vigils of study, or employed in work of some other kind. The succession of the ages, introduced by the pure primal state of gold, could be seen degenerating little by little, to end in an age of iron.

10. There was also the Book of Memory, written not in ordinary letters, but rather in signs and symbols, its contents brief and contained in a mere page. In this brief compass the combined workings of Providence and Fate could be observed, and partially understood, but they could not be foreseen. For the Book of Memory is nothing else but the intellect that studies the world, and commits to memory knowledge based often upon accurate reasoning, but more often upon probable conjecture.

11. Illic eadem, sed non eodem iudicio, naturarum omnium quae praecesserant argumenta. Verumtamen eorum quae visuntur corporea consummatior inibi et multo plenior disciplina. Illic quattuor mundani corporis materiae, ad aeternam sententiam de nativo litigio revocatae. Suberat ratio unde amor, unde parta sodalitas, ut componentia compositum membra corpus efficerent, et divisa se traderet pluralitas unitati. Illic aquaei pennatique generis cognata germanitas, divisiva per species, qualitatibus differens et figuris. Suberat ratio unde squamas, unde plumas alterutris Natura comparet tegumentum, unde avibus lingua dulcissona, pisces perpetuo conticescunt. Illic pedestrium alia domesticae mansuetudinis, alia moribus ad malitiam efferatis. Suberat ratio cur leonibus et apris excandentior iracundia, cur in cervo vel lepore relanguit vis ignita. Illic de herbarum potentiis familiarior contemplatus. Suberat ratio unde illa seminibus, sucis altera, haec efficacior in radice. Illic quicquid vel ingressus ad substantiam generatio provehit, vel egressus a substantia destruit corruptela. In tanta igitur naturarum multitudine, labore Physis plurimo speciem deprehendit humanum, sublustrem, tenuem, et paginae terminantis extremum.

11. Here appeared, though not with the same certainty, the accounts of created natures that had been shown before. Here, however, much fuller and more careful information was given regarding those creatures that are beheld in bodily form. Here the four components of the world's body were shown, summoned from their natural litigiousness to accept eternal determination. Next was shown the plan whereby love and compatibility were imparted, so that component parts might compose a compound body, and sundered plurality give itself over to unity. There was shown the close kinship between the watery and feathered races, though distributed into species distinct in property and shape. Next appeared the plan whereby Nature provides scales as a covering for one creature, feathers for another, whereby birds possess a language of sweet song, while fish remain perpetually silent. Here appeared the various four-footed creatures of a domestic gentleness, and others naturally driven to cruelty. The plan appeared whereby blazing anger is a property of lions and boars, while in the deer and the hare the fiery power grows weak. Here were attentive observations concerning the powers of herbs. The plan was shown whereby the potency of one is in the seed, another's in the sap, that of a third in the root. Here was everything that generation brings forth to enter substantial existence, and corruption destroys at its departure from substantial existence. Amid so great a host of natures Physis discovered only by great effort the human image, dim and faint, at the very end of the final page.

Microcosmus 12

Quicquid in exemplis rerum distinxerat ordo
corripuere deae.
Se prius accingens operi, Natura sorores
participesque vocat.
Exprομptas Urania manus traducit ad artem
ingeniumque movet.
Sed Physis, nil questa palam, taciturna moleste
murmura mentis habet.
Ingeniis aptaret opus, sed pondere visa est
succubuisse minor.
"Brutorum factura levis, minimumque decoris
et nihil artis habens.
Alter mundus, Homo, sensus curaeque prioris
et melioris eget.
Vera Dei facies Homo, fomes sumptus ab astris,
mentis et artis opus."
Usias, elementa, rudes diffindit, ad omnem
commoderanda modum;
in quibus et maculas et inextricabile Silvae
cernit inesse malum.
Territat artificem veteri collisa tumultu
turbida materies:
ignis in humorem compugnat et humor in ignem,
convariantque vices.
Limitibus quicumque suis intensior exit,
hunc revocare, labor.
Naturae mala corporeae partesque fluentes
extimuisse potest,

Microcosmus 12

The goddesses took in all that had received ordered expression in these exemplars of things. Nature, the first to gird herself for work, summoned her sisters and fellow laborers. Urania brought ready hands and an active mind to her work. But Physis, outwardly uncomplaining, was hard put to contain the silent murmuring in her mind. She would plan the work according to her ability, but she felt herself inadequate, overcome by the weight of the undertaking. "The fashioning of brute beasts is easy," she thought, "demanding little grace and no art. But Man, the second universe, requires understanding and care of a nobler and abler kind. For Man is God's true likeness, a spark drawn from the stars, a work of intellect and art."

Physis divides the coarse substance of the elements, which must be adapted to every form; she sees inhering in them the stains and the inextricable evil of Silva. The violent and teeming state of matter in its primordial confusion terrifies the artisan: fire wars against moisture, and moisture against fire, and they adopt one another's roles. It is her task to recall to order whatever has transgressed its bounds through too much force. She may well fear that when she makes an attempt on the evil in bodily nature and its

ne, cum temptarit, neget inconstantia formam
    ludificetque manum.
Corrixansque globus numeris ut forte ligetur;
    haec quoque pugna gravis.
Tota per esse suum, perfectaque viribus, orbis
    semina continuit;
sed neque sic mortalis Homo, sed longius impar
    aedificandus erat.
Aevi Mundus opus, Homo temporis; alter in illo,
    spiritus alter in hoc.
Non consentirent mortalis vincula formae
    ut diuturna forent.
Hic opus ingeniis et acuti pectoris igne
    doctificaque manu,
ut, quia contextu non durat ab exteriore,
    duret ab intus Homo.
Materias, operum fundamina prima suorum,
    compositumque hominem
astra videt caelumque sequi, lunaeque potentis
    conditione trahi.
Sunt mala quae soleant etiam cum corpore nasci,
    Physis et illa timet.
Haerentem rubuere duae partesque laboris;
    has Urania subit:
expugnare malum Silvae, fluidamque tenere
    limite materiam.
Humanumque genus, quamvis mortale trahatur
    conditione sua,
tale reformandum, quod demigrare supernos
    possit adusque deos,

teeming components, their instability will reject form and mock her effort. Perhaps the tumultuous mass may be subjected to proportion; but this too will be a grim struggle.

The universe, complete and perfect in its powers, contained seminal forces throughout its being; but mortal Man is not so made, and must be constructed very differently. For the Universe is a work of perpetuity, Man of time; there is one spirit in the Universe, another in Man. The bonds of the human form would not agree to be long lasting. Here intelligence was needed, the fire of a keen mind, and a well-schooled hand, so that Man, who might not survive through connection with the external world, might survive through a power within himself.

She sees that the materials, the primary foundations of her task, and the man composed of them will follow the stars and the heavens, and be affected by the state of the powerful moon. Moreover certain evils are wont to be born together with the body, and Physis fears them. Two parts of the task make her blush in confusion, and Urania undertook these: to overcome the evil taint of Silva, and to contain fluid matter within a boundary.

The human race, although, being mortal, it is constrained by its condition, must yet be so reformed that it may rise to dwell among the heavenly powers, subject to its laws what-

et dare sub leges quicquid torquente rotatu
stellifer axis agit,
cognatas sordes innataque crimina certis
extenuare modis.
Physis in ora redit, frontemque reducit, et ecce:
tutior intrat opus.

Microcosmus 13

Erant igitur duo rerum principia: unitas et diversum. Diversum longe retro antiquissimum. Unitas non inceperat: simplex, intacta, solitaria, ex se in se permanens, infinibilis et aeterna. Unitas Deus, diversum non aliud quam Hyle, eaque indigens forma. Primiparens igitur deitas diversitatem excoluit, limitavit interminam, figuravit informem, explicuit obvolutam, Hylem ad elementa, elementa ad usias, usias ad qualitates, qualitates et usias ad materiam circumscribens. Ea ergo materia, ex ingenito Silvae vitiosa contagio, ex elementorum conversionibus transformabilis, ex usiis substantialibus facta est corpulenta.

2. Corpulentam vero essentiarum quattuor continentiam, prima molitionis suae fundamina, cervices nervosque operis Physis argumentosa subiecit. In supremis operum magisteriis, divinae tantum sapientiae lineas prosecuta, deplanatum iterque liberum decucurrit. Opificis Dei diligentia,

ever the star-bearing sphere impels by the force of its circling, and in these decisive ways redeem the taint of its earthly beginnings and its innate evil. Physis recovers herself, knits her brow, and begins her work with more assurance.

Microcosmus 13

Now there were two principles of created life, unity and diversity. Diversity was by far the oldest of things. Unity, simple, inviolate, solitary, abiding unchanged in itself and through itself, infinite, and eternal, had no beginning. Unity is God, and diversity nothing else but Hyle, and that which lacks form. The deity, primal parent, refined diversity, limited the boundlessness, gave shape to the formless, separated what was intermingled, dividing Hyle into elements, defining those elements by essences, essences by qualities, and containing essence and quality in substance. Thus substance, though tainted by the innate contagion of Silva, was rendered capable of transformation through the conversion of the elements, and assumed a bodily state through these substantial essences.

2. Full of purpose, Physis established the bodily coherence of these four essences as the primary foundation of her creation, the spine and sinews of her work. In the ultimate plan of her work, adhering strictly to the pattern of the divine wisdom, she traveled a smooth and open path.

quae praecesserat, Silvam edocuerat iam se submittere, iam parere. Promiscuam revocarat ex turbido, tumultuantem a litigio. Splendore vestierat impolitam. Conditiones partium, in plerisque contrarias, fundatis ad pacem legibus foederibusque connexuerat inconvulsis. Ne quid vagis liceret erroribus, distinctas singulis praefinierat mansiones. In his utique nihil aut exiguum est quod obiaceat attrectanti.

3. Suberat tamen importuna, tacita, surrepensque Silvae necessitas influentis. Ad id malignans intendebat illuvies, ut divini splendorem operis vel inficeret vel damnaret. Contra Physis invigilat, ut vel evertat huiusmodi, si possibile est, vel saltem deliniat imposturam. Ad haec cum subiceret materiam operi destinato, defluens quidem eliquavit in digitos et a specie quam intenderat artifex lubricavit. Obviam propositis inconstantiam Physis exhorruit, effrenemque licentiam exsecravit. Curat, agit et promovet quantum Natura patitur, lubricantem detineat, coerceat effluentem.

4. Praeterea non elementa, sed elementorum reliquias aedificationi suae traditas recognoscit, quas utique de mundana concretione extremas et superstites invenisset. Non igitur esse in opifice, vel perito, de minus integris corporibus vel opus facere vel absolvere consummatum. Ad tantas tamque importunas difficultates ingenium Physis circumducit argutum. Sed, omissis quam pluribus, ad materiam

The diligence of God the creator had gone before, and taught Silva already to submit, already obey. It had recalled the unruly from turmoil, the quarrelsome from strife. It had adorned the unrefined with splendor. It had joined factions whose conditions were incompatible in many ways, establishing laws and unbreakable bonds to ensure peace. Lest any room be afforded to random error, it had established separate dwellings for the individual elements. There was nothing anywhere among them, however small, that might oppose itself to her control.

3. Nonetheless the necessity of unstable Silva was lurking close at hand, silent and dangerous. And a malignant foulness sought to injure or destroy the splendor of the divine handiwork. Physis kept watch, that she might avert, if possible, or at least contain such treachery. Moreover, when she was shaping the material for her destined task, it flowed away, slipping through her fingers and sliding out of the shape the artisan had sought to fashion. Physis was appalled at the instability which hindered her project, and cursed this unbridled lawlessness. She took pains and labored mightily to check its fluctuation and contain its flowing away as far as Nature would admit.

4. Besides, she realized that not the elements themselves but the remains of the elements had been given her to build with, scraps and leavings from the forming of the Universe which she had found here and there. Thus it was beyond even a skilled craftsman to perform this task or bring it to completion with imperfect materials. Physis applied her keen understanding to these stubborn difficulties. But as so much was lacking she decided to reexamine the material

quae susternitur operi visa est recursare. In ea solas elementorum contemplatur imagines, non veritatem de integro substantiae purioris: siquidem non elementa quae perficiunt, sed elementorum usias faeculentas, a simplicibus et reliquias grossiores.

5. Igneum, terreum, sic cetera sensu grossiore contingens, plenas et integras, ubi plena et integra sunt, eorum potentias arbitratur. De materiali quod ad oculos praeiacet fundamento, humidi, sicci, ferventis et frigidi qualitates eliciens, aut explicuit singulas, aut sociatas permiscuit, magnum quidem quod fuerat consilium disponentis.

6. Explicuit singulas, quae simplices fuerant, ex substantiali videlicet et nativo. Permiscuit sociatas, ut compositae fierent ex adiuncto. Igni, aquae, huic calido, huic frigidae, si siccum, humidum alterutris socialiter adiungitur, quaedam de cohaerentia et vicinitate germanitas invenitur. Aeri, terrae, huic humido, huic siccae, si calidum, frigidum alterutris socialiter adiungitur, societas huiusmodi permixtio nominatur. Eam ergo qualitatum mixturam impensiori Physis prosequitur diligentia; praesentis res erat illa negotii, nec videlicet otiosa.

7. In humani corporis anatomia, quaedam de simplicibus, quaedam de compositis membra meminit reformanda. Sic igitur de contiguo et proximo cum se sibi traderent elementa, cohaerentia quae in animali complexio dicitur est inventa. Complexiones igitur elementarias humanae sic

which was the foundation of her work. In this she beheld only images of the elements, and not their true nature in the integrity of its purer substance: not those elements which achieve perfection, but the dregs of the essences of the elements, gross remnants of their original simplicity.

5. Forming a rough sensory impression of the fiery, earthy, and other bodies, she concluded that their powers were full and entire insofar as they themselves were full and entire. Drawing forth the qualities of moist, dry, warm, and cold from the material substrate which presented itself to her scrutiny, she either separated them individually or blended together those closely related, for such had been the great design of the all-disposing one.

6. She separated those properties which were substantially and in their natures simple. She mingled those closely related that they might become compound substances through this joining. Of fire and water, one is hot, the other cold; if dryness or moisture is joined by association to one or the other, a certain kinship is revealed by their cohesion and closeness. Of air and earth, one is moist, the other dry; if heat or cold is joined by association to one or the other, such a relationship is called a mixture. Thus Physis worked with extreme care at this mixing of qualities; for it pertained to the task at hand, and was clearly no idle matter.

7. She recalled that in the human anatomy certain parts were to be formed from simple, others from compound materials. And when the elements, through contiguity and proximity, adapted themselves to one another, that coherence appeared which in an animal is called complexion. Physis applied these elementary complexions to the construction of Man in such a way that what arose from them would

applicat aedificationi ut, quibus innascuntur principiis, eorum origines consequantur. Melancholia, phlegma, alterum terreni ponderis, alterum inventum est aquaticae levitatis. Ignita fervet cholera; sanguis, aerius, commitescit.

8. Ceterum non ea quae in Homine et in ceteris animantibus Naturae diligentia reperitur. Intemperans enim humorum cohaerentia brutorum complexionem saepius assolet depravare. Asinus hebes est ex phlegmate, leo iracundus ex cholera; canis aerio totus inficitur odoratu. Sola et singularis, hominum conditio de humorum conplexu facta est in qualitatibus et quantitatibus temperato. Compacta est humanitas quantum curari potuit, vel indigentia vel redundantia multo parcius felicitatem operis attemptante. Futurum enim intelligentiae et rationis habitaculum non oportuit inaequalitatem aut turbatricem consilii diffidentiam pateretur.

9. Collibratis igitur humoribus et eorum potentiis exaequatis, cum usiae substantiam qualitates confecissent, secuta est partium quae corpus efficit plenitudo. Cumque formam exposceret consummata soliditas ad perfectum, totam concretionis materiam per ternas primum partitiones oculis fidelibus commetitur. Eas rudi primum inpressione in liniamenta distrahit, subinde in eam quae membrorum est speciem configurat. Primam caput, secundam pectus, tertiam renes de proprietate quam viderat appellavit. Has utique corporis partes de multis singulas, de communibus exceptavit angustas: cerebrum, cor, epar, trina vitae fundamina suscepturas.

conform to the principles from which it arose. Melancholy and phlegm are the result, in the one case, of earthly gravity, in the other, of the lightness of water. Choler is kindled by fire, the sanguine is airy and mild.

8. Moreover, that carefulness on the part of Nature which is seen in Man is not also found in other animals. For an imbalanced mixture of humors is often apt to distort the complexion of brute beasts. The donkey is made sluggish by phlegm, the lion wrathful by choler; the dog is wholly imbued with his airy sense of smell. The human condition, unique and remarkable, is the product of a complexion of humors in which quality and quantity are balanced. Human nature has been wrought with all possible care, so that insufficiency and excess have very little effect on the healthy state of the work. For it was not right that the future abode of intellect and reason suffer imbalance or disordering uncertainty in its deliberations.

9. When the humors had been set in balance and their powers balanced, when their qualities had combined to produce the essential substance, that fullness of parts ensued which constitutes the body. And since this achieved solidity demanded form for its perfection, Physis, observing closely, first divided all the combined material into three portions. These she first gave the rough outline of lineaments, next shaped them into the form of each member. The first she called the head, the second the breast, and the third the loins, according to the properties she observed in them. These three in particular of the body's many parts, these narrow chambers out of the whole structure she selected to receive the brain, the heart, and the liver, the three foundations of its life.

10. In minori mundo, Homine, Physis intelligit non errandum, si maioris Mundi similitudinem sibi sumpserit in exemplum. In illo subtili mundani corporis apparatu, fastigio caelum supereminet altiore. Aer, terra, terra de infimo, aer de medio, circumsistunt. De caelo deitas imperat et disponit. Exsequuntur iussionem quae in aere vel in aethere mansitant potestates. Terrena quae subteriacent gubernantur. Non secus et in homine cautum est, imperaret anima in capite, exsequeretur vigor eius constitutus in pectore, regerentur partes infimae pube tenus et infra collocatae.

11. Physis igitur, sollers ut erat artifex, cerebrum animae, cor vitae, epar appetentiae futurum destinat fundamentum. Unde et divinis hospitibus divinum satagit habitaculum praeparare. Loco namque principe, de firmamenti sphaeraeque superioris exemplo, caput aedificat in rotundo. Caput tanquam arcem, tanquam totius corporis Capitolium, tollit et erigit in excelso. Regionem capitis eam condecuit superattolleret, ubi sincerae rationis divinitas habitaret. Optimam corporis et deputatam intelligentiae portionem ab esculentis membrisque grossioribus longissime relegavit, ne ab ea quae cibo alimentisque nascitur sensus illuvie tardarentur.

12. Secretis itaque rationibus, mollem cerebri liquidamque quam crearat essentiam tegumentum intra testeum occuluit, ne ei facile noceretur. Molle et delicatum ad

10. Physis understood that she would not go astray in creating the lesser universe, Man, if she took as her example the pattern of the greater Universe. In the intricate structure of the world's body, the firmament holds the highest place, the summit. Air and earth position themselves, earth at the lowest point, air in the middle region. From heaven the deity rules and disposes. The powers who have their homes in the atmosphere or the ether carry out his commands. The affairs of the earth below are governed. No less care is taken in the case of man, that the soul should govern in the head, the vital force established in his breast execute its orders, and the lower parts, down to the groin and those organs placed below them, submit to rule.

11. Thus Physis, skilled artist as she was, chose the brain as the future seat of the soul, the heart as the source of vitality, and the liver as the source of appetite. In this way she set about preparing a divine dwelling place for divine guests. For she gave a rounded shape to the head, which occupied the chief position, following the example of the firmament and the sphere of the heavens. She raised the head to the position of a citadel or Capitol for the body as a whole, making it stand erect and tall. It was fitting that she so exalt the region of the head, where the divine quality of pure reason was to dwell. She placed this noblest part of the body, charged with the duty of understanding, furthest away from the digestive system and the grosser organs, lest its perceptions be affected by that waste that comes from the digestion of food.

12. Following an inscrutable design, she encased the substance of the brain, which she had made soft and fluid, within a hard earthen casing, lest it be easily damaged. She

recreationem cerebri visa est delegisse, ut in liquido possent facilius rerum imagines insidere.

13. Totam igitur capitis continentiam tres secernens in thalamos, eos trinis animae efficientiis consecravit. In sincipite provisum est, phantasia rerum formas anticipet, et rationi renuntiet quae viderit universa; in occipitis reductiore thalamo memoria conquiescat, ne, si primo visionum iacuisset in limine, figurarum frequentissimis perturbaretur incursibus. Primam interiacet et ultimam ratio media, de rebus alterutrius certo iudicio provisura.

14. Sic igitur ibidem, erga regiam capitis, machinamenta collocat internuntia sentiendi, ut, de proximo sensibus interpellantibus, de proximo prodeat qui iudicet intellectus. Quia enim ad plurima deferuntur erronei, a loco sapientiae non oportuit elongari. Caput itaque, dispositissimam cum suis diversoriis domum, animae et vivacitati eius Physis accelerat, ut iam succederet apparatae.

15. Verum simplex simplicis, unaque unius, animae virtus est, sed non uniformis egreditur. Per oculos enim visus, per aures egrediens est auditus. Ad eundem modum deformatur in ceteris, secundum diversitatem membrorum quibus utitur instrumentis. Sensus igitur uno de fonte prodeunt, sed diversas expediunt actiones. Ille colores, ille sonos, alter gustus, alter odoramina persentescit. Membris communis

had decided to employ a soft and delicate material in creating the brain, so that the images of things might rest more easily upon its clear surface.

13. Dividing the whole cavity of the head into three chambers, she assigned these to the three functions of the soul. In the frontal chamber provision was made for imagination to receive the shapes of things, and transmit all that it beheld to the reason; memory would reside in a chamber at the very back of the head, for if it were situated at the threshold of perception, it would be troubled by a continual invasion of images. Reason dwelt between these two, to supervise their activities with firm judgment.

14. Physis also sets in the same region the instruments for transmitting sense perception, close about the palace of the head, so that the judging intellect, when the messenger senses are close at hand, may maintain close contact with them. For as the senses are prone to many sorts of error, it is not right that they should be far removed from the seat of wisdom. Physis hastened to make the head an abode ideally suited, with its several chambers, for the soul and its vital powers, that it might enter a well prepared home.

15. Now as the soul is simple and one, so its power is simple and one, but it does not issue forth uniformly. For sight issues through the eyes, and hearing through the ears. Similarly it assumes different forms in the other senses, according to the difference of the organs it employs as its instruments. Thus, though they stem from a single source, the senses perform a variety of functions. One perceives colors, another sound, one flavors, another odors. Touch, common

omnibus, tactus diffusior invenitur. Sensus unde suboriuntur, ad ea cognatam intelligentiam tenent. Sine igne nec visus, sine aere nec odoratio conficitur, nec formatur auditio. Gustus aquae, tactus terrae cognatior, in consubstantialibus operantur. Cuius enim elementi qualitate consistunt, eodem similique iudicio comprehendunt.

Microcosmus 14

Cuditur artifici circumspectoque politu
  fabrica Naturae primipotentis Homo.
Delegisse caput propriam sapientia sedem
  creditur et thalamis exsecuisse tribus.
In tribus est animae ternus vigor; expedit actum
  incommutato quisque tenore suum.
Quae meminit postrema loco, virtus speculatrix
  est prior, e medio vis rationis agit.
Assistunt omnes operi, cum quinque ministri,
  sensus, quae cernunt exteriora docent.
Nuntius ingreditur sensus, mentemque quietam
  evocat, ut certa res ratione probet.

Nervus enim qui luce sua collustrat ocellos
  contrahit ex cerebro quod radiosus agit.
Intima lux animaeque dies concurrit ad ignis
  solaris radios aethereumque iubar;

to all of them, is spread abroad. The senses possess a power of apprehension related to the element from which each is derived. Sight is not exercised without fire, nor smell and hearing without air. Taste, born of water, and touch, closely related to earth, function in kindred materials. To the quality of the element by which they subsist, they also owe their power to perceive, by an identical and similar power of discrimination.

Microcosmus 14

Man, the work of powerful Nature, is formed with masterly and prudent skill. One may believe that wisdom chose the head as its proper station, and divided it into three chambers. In these three are the three powers of the soul; each fulfills its function in an unalterable continuity. The faculty that remembers is at the rear, the speculative power is foremost, and reason exerts its power from the center. All share in the work when their five servants, the senses, inform them of what they perceive outwardly. A messenger of sense enters and arouses the tranquil mind to confirm the matter by sure judgment.

That nerve which illumines the eyes with its light draws from the brain the power that it radiates. An inner light, a daylight of the soul, goes forth to meet the rays of the sun's fire and the brilliance of the ether; from this encounter the

de quo concursu vis et natura videndi
essendi causam materiamque trahit.
Ad formas rerum se porrigit huius acumen
lucis, et examen iudiciale facit;
iudicioque tamen non omnia sentit eodem:
Illius interdum languet, abundat opus.
Purius alba capit propriaeque simillima formae,
ad res dissimiles segnis hebesque venit.
Splendor splendori, lucique domestica lux est;
in noctem et tenebras otia visus agit.
Plana superficies teretis circumque rotundi:
corporis: haec oculis commoda forma fuit.
In plano rerum simulacra fidelius haerent,
et tereti levior motus inesse solet.
Quodque oculos motus, oculos nitor ornat, utrumque
redditur in formae conditione suae.
Neve lacessiri queat ut libet, intus adacta
tegmine septeno lux tunicata latet.
Silva supercilii casu praemunit ab omni
quem sibi res mollis et male firma timet.
Non nihil est hos esse duos: si langueat alter,
ut vice participis suppleat alter opus.
Palpebrae thalamus fessis, cum mulcet ad horam
lumina pacificus officiosa sopor.

Sol, oculus mundi, quantum communibus astris
praeminet, et caelum vendicat usque suum,
non aliter sensus alios obscurat honore
visus, et in solo lumine, totus homo est.
Quaerenti Empedocles quid viveret, inquit: "ut astra
inspiciam; caelum subtrahe—nullus ero."

power and the organ of sight derive the principle and the material means of their existence. A beam of this inner light applies itself to the forms of things, and makes a careful judicial assessment of them; however, it does not perceive all things with the same discernment: its power is feeble at one moment, ample at another. It fixes most clearly upon things which are bright and most like itself in form, but applies only a dim and feeble light to things unlike. As splendor is at home with splendor, so is light with light; in shadow and darkness sight falls idle.

The even surface of a smooth and rounded body: this is the form best suited to the eyes. The images of things adhere most faithfully to a level surface, and motion is easier in one that is round. And because the eye is endowed with both motion and brightness, both are considered in establishing its form. And as it is best that the eye not suffer injury, its light covers itself, contained within a sevenfold jacket. The forest of the brow protects it from every danger that so delicate and infirm an organ might fear. It is not for nothing that there are two: if one should fail, the other may perform the work in place of its partner. The lids are a bed chamber for the weary, when peaceful sleep soothes the dutiful orbs for a while.

Just as the Sun, the world's eye, is superior to its companion stars and claims as its own all below the heavens, likewise the sight overshadows the other senses in glory, and in their light alone the whole man is expressed. To one who asked why he was alive, Empedocles replied, "That I may behold the stars; deny me the heavens—I will be nothing."

Caeca manus detractat opus, pes ebrius errat,
quando opus in tenebris et sine luce movent.

Auditus sede inferior, virtutibus impar,
tardior in sensu, commoditate minor.
Arteriis sonus egreditur, vacuumque repellit
aera; percussus, percutit ille alium,
donec ad extremos elanguit ultima fines
motio, per tractus extenuata suos.
Aer materiam, formam instrumenta resignant;
hinc illinc, speciem vocis et esse trahunt.
Lingua sonos ferit in formam vocisque monetam,
et suus huic operi malleus esse potest.
Officiis formata suis, substantia vocis
ad patulas aures articulata venit.
Auriculis quasi vestibulo suscepta priore,
vox sonat et trahitur interiore domo.
Sermonis numeros extraque sonantia verba
auris, sed ratio significata capit.
Quod foris auditus interpres, lingua quod intra est
monstrat, et alterius postulat alter opem.
Tortilis est auris, ne quando transeat aer
frigidus ad cerebrum liberiore via:
Natura invalido timuit, sinuosus ad ipsum
transitus obtorto limite ducit iter.
Quicquid Roma legit, quicquid studuistis, Athenae,
quicquid Chaldaei dogmatis Indus habet,
quicquid Aristoteles divino pectore sensit,
cumque Platonistis Pythagorea cohors,
quicquid ad elenchos arguto disputat ore

The unseeing hand spoils its work, the foot strays drunkenly, when they perform their tasks in darkness, without light.

Hearing has a lower position, is inferior in power, more sluggish in perception, and less useful. Sound emerges from the windpipe and drives back the empty air; the air, once struck, strikes other air, until, having grown thinner as it spreads to its farthest limit, the final wave of sound fades away. Air provides the material, and the vocal organs the form; from these two sound derives the shape and substance of speech. The tongue forges sounds to the form and coinage of speech and serves as its hammer for this work. Once shaped for its purpose, the articulate substance of speech travels to the open ears. Having first been admitted as it were to the outer vestibule of the ear, the voice calls out and is drawn indoors. The ear grasps the rhythm and external resonance of the words, but reason recognizes what is signified. Hearing interprets what is external, the tongue reveals what is within, and each requires the aid of the other. The channel of the ear is twisted, lest cold air should ever pass by too open a path to the brain; Nature feared for its frail condition, and so a winding path leads to the brain along a twisting route.

All that Rome read, all that you studied, O Athens, whatever the Indus possessed of Chaldean wisdom, whatever Aristotle harbored in his inspired breast, the Platonists, the Pythagorean band, whatever the Gaul debates in syllogism

Gallus, et in medica iactitat arte Ligus,
cessit ad auditum: docilis prudensque periret
littera, si surdis auribus esset homo.

Quae tamen exprompsit et nudas prodidit artes,
cognita multiplici lingua nocere malo.
Nam male discreta quotiens insibilat aure
livida mordaces vipereosque sonos,
separat unanimos fratres, inimicat amicos,
abrumpitque fidem, dissociatque thoros,
turbat agros praedis, fora litibus, oppida bellis,
detegit arcanum, depositumque negat.

Gustus aquae cognatior est, propiorque liquori.
Constat ab humecto quicquid in ore sapit.
Sic mollem sensum molli Natura palato
et simili studuit conciliare suo.
Pauper in hoc sensu vellem defectior esset;
mente quidem saperet amplius, ore minus!
Quaerit ut exspoliet venatibus, alite, pisce,
gustus humum, gustus aera, gustus aquas.
Deliciosa fames, si quando recessit ab aula,
personae tenui perniciosa venit.
Prodigit aes, male conflat opes et avita ligurrit
quem bonus illexit detinuitque sapor.

Inter Pangaeum vel olentem naris odorem
dividit: hic cerebrum subruit, hic recreat.
Rebus odorandis causam corruptior aer
praestat, et in puro est debile naris opus.

with subtle speech, or the Ligurian pronounces in the art of medicine, all this is due to hearing; the wise and learned letter would perish if man existed with deaf ears.

Yet the tongue which gave voice to the needy arts and transmitted them, is known for doing harm in many evil ways. For whenever it carelessly whispers in the jealous ear backbiting and poisonous words, it separates loving brothers, unfriends friends, breaks bonds of trust, divides marriages, makes the land teem with robbery, the forum with quarrels, the city with war; it reveals secrets, and denies deposits.

Taste is closely related to water, and its affinity is with liquids. Whatever imparts a taste to the mouth is certainly derived from moisture. Thus Nature assigned this delicate sense to the delicate palate, and strove to please it with agreeable food. Would that poor man were more deficient in this sense, that he might taste more with his mind, less with his mouth! Taste seeks to strip the earth of game, the air of fowl, the sea of fish. Luxurious hunger, if it should ever leave the court, is ruinous to those of slender means. The man whom the taste of fine food has enticed and captured squanders money, is reckless with his resources, and eagerly laps up his inheritance.

The nose distinguishes between a Panchaian and an unpleasant odor; one unsettles the brain, the other restores it. Tainted air is the cause of the odors of things, and the working of this sense is impaired in pure air.

Tardior est tactus quam qui diiudicat escas,
quam qui captato sensus odore venit.
Militat in thalamis, tenero quoque servit amori
tactus, et argute saepe probare solet
aut castigato planum sub pectore ventrem,
aut in virgineo corpore molle femur.

Dignaque post cerebrum sequitur substantia cordis,
quamvis et cerebro conferat unde viget.
Corporis ignitus fomes, vitalis alumnus,
causa creans sensus conciliansque fidem,
humanae nodus conpaginis, ancora venis,
fundamen nervis, arteriisque tenor,
naturae columen, rex et dictator et auctor,
patricius tota corporis urbe sui.
Visitat ex medio partes sensusque ministros,
in sibi praescripto munere quemque tenet;
cui pectus penetrale sacrum, dignumque coloxum,
regnandi sedes imperiique thronus.
Forma sibi qualem germanus commodat ignis,
cuius in erecta cuspide surgit apex.
Fortius igne suo res fervida possit abuti;
ferventi madidus pulmo reportat opem.
Mollis et aerius, secus et lateraliter ambit,
humecta calidum frigiditate iuvans.
Ira sub ignito corde est, genialibus usa
sedibus, ut multum morigerante domo.
Cor tangat vel causa levis; transfertur ad omnes
corporis articulos particulata lues.
Nec laesum languere solet, sed paene doloris
anticipat sensum praemoriturque malo.

Touch is more sluggish than the sense which judges food, or that which is aroused when an odor is caught. Touch campaigns in bed, serves the cause of tender love, and is fond of slyly exploring the smooth belly below the modest breast, or the soft thigh of a virginal body.

The substance of the heart is second in dignity to the brain, though it imparts to the brain the source of its vitality. It is the animating spark of the body, nurse of its life, the creative principle of the senses and the cause of agreement among them; the central link in the human structure, the anchor of the veins, root of the sinews, and stabilizer of the arteries, mainstay of our nature, king, governor, creator, a noble lord amid the great city of his body. From the center he reaches out to the limbs and the senses, his ministers, each of which he maintains in the function assigned to it. The breast is his sacred shrine, his fitting habitation, his royal palace and imperial throne. Its form is such as its kindred element, fire, provides, whose flame rises in the shape of an upright spear.

A thing too intensely hot can be injured by its own fire; when the heart burns, the moist lungs bring their aid. Soft and airy, they closely surround the heart, ministering to its heat with their cool moisture. For wrath dwells in the fiery heart, finding there its natural dwelling, a home that indulges its habits. Let even a trivial matter irritate the heart; the fever is spread abroad into all parts of the body. Nor is it wont to languish only when stricken; it almost anticipates the pain it is to suffer, and succumbs to the evil in advance.

Humida vis cerebrum, cor ignea, mixtus utroque
aerius sanguis molle creavit epar.
Gibbosum formaque cavum, diaphragmate dextro,
hinc illinc spleni limitat et stomacho.
Quod manus ingessit, quod detrivere molares,
quod stomachus coxit, denique sumit epar.
Convertit mutatque cibos, specieque colorat
sanguinis, et chymos corporis esse facit.
Inde recursantes variato limite, venae
consimiles partes ad sua membra ferunt.
Deque repurgato defaecatoque liquore
deligit et damnat pro meliore bonum.
Commodat hanc operam spleni: mundare cruorem,
et vitia et sordes extenuare suas,
Ut veris succis et tantum sanguine puro
pascatur domini deliciosa fames.
Talibus ad summum rationibus, olla ciborum
est stomachus, stomachi fel cocus, auctor epar.
Insidet has epatis partes innata voluptas,
et gravis in nostra carne tyrannus amor.

Corporis extremum lascivum terminat inguen,
pressa sub occidua parte pudenda latent.
Iocundusque tamen et eorum commodus usus,
si quando, qualis, quantus oportet, erit.
Saecula ne pereant, descisaque cesset origo,
et repetat primum massa soluta chaos,
Ad Genios fetura duos concessit (et olim
commissum geminis fratribus) illud opus.
Cum morte invicti pugnant, genialibus armis,
naturam reparant, perpetuantque genus.

A property of moisture created the brain, a fiery one the heart, and an aerial blood compounded of the two the tender liver. Bulging and hollow in form, it is bordered by the diaphragm on the right, and by the spleen and the stomach on either side. What the hand thrusts into the mouth, what the teeth grind up, what the stomach digests, the liver receives at last. It adapts and transmutes the food, imbuing it with the color of blood, and produces from it nourishing juices for the body. Then, circulating along diverse paths the veins bear to their assigned members the portions conformed to them. Then when the fluids have again been cleansed and purged the liver chooses among them and rejects the good in favor of better. It assigns to the spleen the task of cleansing the blood, and reducing its flaws and impurities, so that the sensual hunger of the lordly body feeds only on healthy fluids and pure blood. For these reasons, though the stomach, in the highest position, is the pot for food, and the stomach's gall is its cook, the liver initiates the process. Natural desire dwells in the region of the liver, and love is a fell tyrant over our flesh.

The wanton loins terminate the lower body, and the private parts lie confined in this dark region. Their exercise will be pleasant and profitable, so long as the time, the manner, and the extent are fitting. Lest earthly life pass away, and generation be cut off, and material existence, dissolved, return to primordial chaos, propagation was made the charge of two Genii (as it was once entrusted to twin brothers). They fight unconquered against death with their life-giving weapons, renew our nature, and perpetuate our kind. They

Non mortale mori, non quod cadit esse caducum,
   non a stirpe hominem deperiisse sinunt.
Militat adversus Lachesim sollersque renodat
   mentula, Parcarum fila resecta manu.
Defluit ad renes, cerebri regione remissus,
   sanguis, et albentis spermatis instar habet.
Format et effingit sollers Natura liquorem,
   ut simili genesis ore reducat avos.

Influit ipsa sibi Mundi Natura; superstes,
   permanet et fluxu pascitur usque suo.
Scilicet ad summam rerum iactura recurrit,
   nec semel, ut possit saepe perire, perit.

Longe disparibus causis mutandus in horas,
   effluit occiduo corpore totus Homo.
Sic sibi deficiens, peregrinis indiget escis,
   sudat in hoc vitam denihilatque dies.

Membra quibus mundus non indiget, illa necesse est
   Physis in humana conditione daret:
excubias capitis oculos, modulaminis aures,
   ductoresque pedes omnificasque manus.

do not allow mortality to perish, nor what dies to be wholly owed to death, the human race to be cut off at the root. The phallus wars against Lachesis, to rejoin the vital threads severed by the hands of the Fates. Blood sent forth from the seat of the brain flows down to the loins, bearing the image of the shining sperm. Artful Nature imbues the fluid with form and likeness, that conception may reproduce the forms of ancestors.

The life of the Universe flows back into itself; it survives itself and is nourished by its very flowing away. For whatever is lost only merges again with the sum of things, and that it may die perpetually, never dies wholly.

But Man, subject at all times to the effects of dissimilar forces, wholly passes away with the failure of his body. Unable to sustain himself, and wanting nourishment from without, he exhausts his life, and a day nullifies his existence.

In creating man it was necessary that Physis bestow limbs of which the universe has no need: eyes to keep watch in the head, ears for varying sound, sure feet to bear him, and all-capable hands.

THE ASTROLOGER

Mathematicus

Semper ut ex aliqua felices parte querantur,
  leges humanae conditionis habent.
Miles erat Romae probus armis, rebus abundans,
  urbe potens, felix coniuge, clarus avis;
voce manu facie facundus largus honestus;
  vir sapiens stabilis tempore mente fide.
Sponsa viro non stirpe minor, non moribus impar,
  non aevo senior dissimilisve fide;
prompta, modesta, timens, non, ut solet esse frequenter,
  imperiosa suo femina pulcra viro.
Luxus opum nocuos quamvis declivis ad actus,
  non fecit mores degenerare bonos.
Cum soleat levitas iuvenilibus esse sub annis,
  non leve gessit opus femina pulchra potens.
pulchraque casta fuit, quae virtus rara venustis
  in fragili sexu rarior esse solet.
Femineae vitium naturae mobilitatem
  cavit et ingenitae crimina nequitiae;
affectusque leves quadam sub mole refixit
  et potuit sexus immemor esse sui.
Sic igitur proba iuncta probo, formosa decoro,
  callida sensato, religiosa pio.
Sors arrisit eis, favit Natura, beati
  omnibus excepto munere prolis erant,

The Astrologer

The laws that govern the human condition ensure that even fortunate people always find some grounds for complaint. In Rome there was a knight, valiant in war, rich in worldly goods, prominent in the city, blessed in his wife, of distinguished ancestry, fluent in speech, openhanded, noble in bearing; a wise man, mature and trustworthy. His wife was no less nobly born than her husband, not inferior in character, no older in years, no less trustworthy; direct, modest, unassuming, not overbearing with her husband, as a beautiful woman is often apt to be. Although abundant wealth is prone to damaging behavior, it did not cause her good character to incur dishonor. While frivolity is wont to be present during the years of youth, this beautiful, capable woman performed no frivolous acts. She was beautiful and also chaste, a virtue which, rare among people of beauty, is apt to be more rare among the tender sex. She rejected that failing of the female nature, fickleness, and crimes born of innate moral weakness; she banished wanton impulses with some effort, and was able to be unmindful of her sex.

Thus a worthy woman was united with a worthy man, beauty with dignity, prudence with intelligence, reverence with piety. Luck smiled on them, Nature favored them, they were blessed in every respect save the gift of a child,

perfecti minus hoc uno, si prole carere
  est a perfecta prosperitate minus.
Spes igitur sobolis multos damnata per annos
  cetera Naturae dona placere vetat;
successus alios, alios obscurat honores
  Fortunamque facit omnibus esse ream.
Flentque dolentque magis, nec enim Natura repugnat:
  nec gravitas aevi languidioris obest,
nec senis haec gelidos causari coniugis annos,
  ille nec uxoris frigida membra potest.
Aetati confisa suae superumque favori
  spem gerit in voto femina sola suo.
Spemque super dubiam Fati quid volveret ordo,
  certior esse volens consulit astrologum,
qui poterat stellis superum deprendere curas,
  Parcarum mentem consiliumque Iovis,
Naturae causas secretaque scire latentis
  et quae Fata quibus legibus ire velint.
Ille mathematicae studiis exercitus artis
  praetemptat numeros (astra movent numeri),
exquiritque vagos numeri ratione planetas,
  quorum sollicitus puncta gradusque notat;
et qua consulitur, momentum colligit horae
  et perpendit in his esse modumque rei.
"Est," ait, "est, video, tibi filius; ecce maritus
  implebit steriles fertilitate sinus.
et Paridem geret in facie, geret intus Achillem,
  nec probitas fastum nec sibi forma dabunt.
Pauperior Croesus, minus illo doctus Ulixes,
  Frena dabit ratio rebus et ingenio.

perfectly happy but for this one thing, if to lack children is to fall short of perfect prosperity. Their hope of offspring, disappointed for so many years, prevented the rest of Nature's gifts from giving them pleasure; it cast a shadow over other achievements, other honors, and made Fortune seem blameworthy in every way. They weep and lament the more, Since Nature presents no obstacle: no burden of enfeebling age hinders them; she cannot complain of the frosty age of an elderly husband, nor he of the chilled limbs of his wife.

Trusting in her youth and the favor of the gods, the wife alone retained hope of attaining what she longed for. Wishing to know more surely what the order of Fate might unfold regarding her uncertain hope, she consulted an astrologer, one who from the stars could discover the concerns of the gods, the plan of the Fates and the deliberations of Jove, who could know the hidden principles and inner depths of Nature, and what the Fates will to occur, and by what laws.

Well versed in the study of the astrological art, he first examines numbers (for numbers govern the stars), then studies the wandering planets on the basis of number, carefully noting their points and degrees; determines the precise moment of the hour in which his calculation is made; and in studying these things discovers the existence and nature of what he seeks. "There is," he says, "there is a son for you, I see him; lo, your husband will bring fertility to your sterile womb. And the child will be a Paris in beauty, inwardly an Achilles, but neither his valor nor his beauty will make him arrogant. Though Croesus be poorer, Ulysses less resourceful than he, reason will govern his wealth and his ready mind.

Inter felicis fatalia commoda vitae
  Romuleae dominus et pater urbis erit.
Patrem—sed taceo, nisi quod premis, arguis, instas—
  occidet Fato sic agitante suum.
Sic erit, adde fidem; Iovis est sic fixa voluntas.
  Quicquid praecinui nil habet ambigui.
Fata tibi spondent, dii spondent, sidera spondent;
  res rata, quam spondent sidera, Fata, dei."
Gaudeat his Fatis doleatve revertitur anceps
  femina caelestis conscia consilii.
Roma, tibi regem, mortem paritura marito
  tristitiam gaudens, gaudia tristis habet.
Sollicitam sensit vigili marcescere cura
  Vir suus et causas hic rogat. Illa docet.
Audit et attenta tristique recolligit aure
  miles Fata suae prodigiosa necis.
"Hoc," ait, "in voto superos piget esse secundos;
  inde mihi malus est Iupiter, unde bonus.
Quaesivi subolem, datus est mihi filius hostis;
  damna fero voti prosperitate mei.
Unde precor, meus uxor amor, mea sola voluptas,
  altera pars animae dimidiumque meae:
cum fuerit soboles genio concepta sinistro
  et tua maturum fuderit alvus honus,
affectus oblita pios oblitaque matrem
  ne dubites puerum mortificare tuum.
Si patiaris eum superesse, mihi morituro
  haec pietas species impietatis erit."
Finierat. Flevere simul, mora nulla sequenti
  nocte iacent pariter, concipit illa, tumet.

Among the fated successes of his fortunate life he will become the lord and father of the city of Romulus.

"His father—but here I would say nothing, except that you press, urge, insist—he will kill, for his fate demands it. So it will be, rest assured; the will of Jove is set. There is no ambiguity in what I have prophesied. The fates, the gods, the stars promise you this; and what the stars, the fates, the gods promise is unalterable."

Mindful of the heavens' determination, the wife returns home, uncertain whether she should rejoice or grieve at this fatal news. Destined to bear a king for thee, O Rome, but death for her husband, she feels sorrow as she rejoices, joy in her sadness. Her husband realizes that his troubled wife is wearied by unceasing worry, and asks the reason. She explains. The knight listens, and receives with attentive and sorrowful ear the prophecy of his unnaturally fated death.

"It is shameful," he says, "that the gods were favorable to our wish; Jupiter is cruel to me in being kind. I asked for a son, and the son given me is my enemy; I suffer destruction through the fulfillment of my prayer. Thus I pray, my wife, my love, my sole delight, sharer of my soul and half of my being: When the child has been conceived by this evil genius, and your womb has given forth its timely burden, do not hesitate, forgetting tender feelings, forgetting motherhood, to put your son to death. If you should allow him to survive, such compassion will show a lack of compassion for me who must die."

He had spoken. They both wept, but with no ensuing delay that night they lay together. She conceived and grew

Maternos menses Naturae legibus implens
  edidit ad numeri tempora certa sui.
In nascente fuit tantae deitatis imago,
  vix potuit credi materialis homo.
Nupta virum, mater puerum dum diligit, haeret
  et dubitat puero parcere sive viro.
Formosus niveusque puer se cogit amari
  et matrem mollit et vetat esse feram.
Pulcher et iratae visus ridere parenti
  oranti similis, ne moreretur, erat.
Ad speciem periere preces, discussit amatum
  formosae sobolis gratia mente virum.
Quae nunc esse suae soboli Medea parabat,
  coepit maternus scire quid esset amor.
Parcit ei pietate ferox maioraque vitae
  tempora dat nato, dum breviora viro;
et mentita necem procul inde remittit alendum
  et tacita miserum decipit arte patrem.
Exilio felix puer est alienaque lactens
  ubera nutritur sedulitate pia.
Crevit honor formae, cum florida cresceret aetas;
  laudari potuit tantus ab hoste decor.
Nomen in ambiguo, sed Patricida vocetur
  imperat arcana calliditate parens,
ut iuvenis tantumque nefas tantumque furorem
  horreat audito nomine saepe suo.
Ut rudis accepit primos infantia sensus
  traxit et interior vim rationis homo,
emicuit tam mente capax, velut esset adultus
  maturos pleni temporis usque dies;

large. Completing the months assigned to mothers by the laws of Nature, she gave birth at the time determined by their number. In the newborn child appeared the image of such divinity that he could scarcely be believed of human substance. Since the wife loved the husband, the mother the boy, she hesitated, in doubt whether to spare the boy or the man. The boy, fair and white, compelled her to love him, softened the mother and forbade her to be cruel. Beautiful, and seeming to smile at his angry parent, he was like one praying not to die. At the sight of him the prayers of her beloved husband lost their power, and the charm of the lovely child drove him from her mind. She who only now had been prepared to be a Medea to her offspring began to know a mother's love. She spared him, cruel in her tenderness, and gave a greater span of life to her son, but a shorter one to her husband; feigning his death, she sent him far away to be raised, and with artful silence deceived the unfortunate father.

The boy was fortunate in his exile; taking milk at a foreign breast he was nurtured with attentive tenderness. His bodily grace increased as his flourishing years advanced; such beauty might have been praised by an enemy. His name was puzzling, but his parent, with secret shrewdness, ordered that he be called Patricida, that the youth might tremble at the thought of so great a crime, such great madness, as often as he heard his name.

As his rude infancy gained its first understanding, and the inner man drew upon the power of reason, he displayed as much mental aptitude as if he had grown to the ripe days of

ascendensque gradus docilis promptaeque iuventae,
philosophis studuit proximus esse comes.
Novit enim quam sideribus, quam primitus orbi
sementem dederit materiamque Deus;
quae fuit in rebus ratio, quae causa creandis;
quos habeant nexus, quas elementa vices;
et numeri quo fonte fluant, qua lege ligentur,
quo sibi conveniant schemate dispositi;
musica quo numero vel qua sibi proximitate
dissimiles iungat consocietque sonos;
astra quibus spatiis distent septena planetae;
mensus utrosque polos, mensus utrumque mare
astrorumque vias humanaque fata sub astris,
et fesso caelos Hercule sustinuit.
Rhetoricosque volens non ignorare colores
succincte didicit perspicuumque loqui.
Naturas generum lima graviore revolvens
pectore divinum clausit Aristotelem;
et quicumque potest humana lacessere membra
aut dolor aut morbus, pellere novit eum.
Sic fecit pectusque capax mentemque profundam
amplum septenis artibus hospitium.
In Venerem suspecta quies vitiisque propinqua
otia iam iuveni causa timoris erant,
tranquillosque timens lascivi temporis annos
transit ad armatae pondera militiae.
Institit assiduus bellis meruitque favorem,
armaque successu non caruere suo.
Caesareos titulos transgressus et Herculis actus
unica Romuleae gloria gentis erat;

full maturity; ascending the stages of youthful docility and aptitude, he sought eagerly to be the close companion of philosophers. For he knew what seminal substance God had given to the stars, to the earth at their origin; what order existed among created things, and what was the cause of procreation; what bond the elements preserve, what changes they undergo; from what source numbers flow, by what law they are connected, by what system of arrangement they agree among themselves; by what proportion or what intervals music joins and harmonizes different tones; by what distances the seven planetary stars are separated; he measured both of the poles and each sea, the paths of the stars and the fates of human beings subject to the stars, and when Hercules grew weary he supported the heavens. While not wishing to be ignorant of the colors of rhetoric, he learned to speak succinctly and clearly. Pondering the natures of the categories with serious subtlety, he enclosed the divine Aristotle within his breast. And he knew how to expel any affliction or disease that can assail the human body. Thus he made his capacious breast and profound mind an ample dwelling for the seven Arts.

Leisure, suspect as leading to lechery, and idleness, prone to vice, were a cause of fear to the young man, and fearful of spending the years of wanton youth at his ease, he took on the weighty duties of armed knighthood. He was steadfast and aggressive in battle, and won favor, and his feats of arms were not denied reward. Surpassing the renown of Caesar and the feats of Hercules he was the sole glory of the people

quem probitas adeo virtusque levavit in altum,
esset ut Ausonii signifer imperii.
Sed super orbis opes supremaque culmina rerum
certat vis superum ponere posse virum.
Pugnat ad hoc Lachesis, super hoc Fortuna laborat,
comprobat hic vires Iupiter ipse suas.
Et quia sic fieri fatalis postulat ordo,
hanc sibi regnandi Fata dedere viam.
Aemula Romani Carthago nominis arma
forte sub Ausoniis finibus intulerat.
Ergo movent aquilas infaustaque signa Quirites,
conscriptosque patres hora sinistra trahit.
Occultarat enim sub opacis vallibus agmen
Poenus in excidium, regia Roma, tuum.
Sic super insidias inopinaque tela senatus
incidit et potuit tunc sine Marte capi.
Rex captivatur captivaturque tribunus,
nec deprensa potest turba referre pedem.
Ducuntur genus Aeneadum Latiaeque potestas
gentis et Albanae nobilitatis honor.
Non alibi potuit melius cognoscere Roma,
quam dubias dubius mundus haberet opes.
At Patricidam cum signifera legione
ducebat melior sors meliore via.
Qui procul aspecto confusi pulvere belli
protinus intendit succubuisse suos.
Occurens igitur venientem praevenit hostem
obiectoque sibi milite claudit iter;
hostilesque globos Fatis melioribus intrans
devincit Poenos, liberat Ausonios.

of Romulus; his valor and strength exalted him so far that he became the standard-bearer of the Ausonian empire.

But the might of the gods is working to place this man above all earthly powers, at the very summit of the world. Lachesis fights to this end, Fortune strives for this, here Jupiter himself proves his power. And because the order of fate required that this come to pass, the fates granted him this path to kingship.

It happened that Carthage, envious of the renown of Rome, had brought an army into Ausonian territory. Therefore the Quirites brought forward the eagles, ill-omened insignia, and an evil hour mustered the Senate. The Carthaginian had hidden his forces in a dark valley for your destruction, royal Rome. Thus the Senate encountered ambushes and unexpected missiles, and could then be captured without battle. The king was captured, the tribune was captured, and the rank and file, entrapped, were unable to retreat. The race of Aeneas, the might of the Latian people, the glory of the Alban nobility, were taken captive. In no other way could Rome better recognize how uncertain is the power which the uncertain world possesses.

But better fortune guided Patricida, with the standard-bearing legion, on a better path. When the dust of the confusion of battle could be seen far off, he at once understood that his people had been overcome. Therefore making haste he anticipated the oncoming enemy and blocked the road with his troops as a barrier; charging into the enemy horde, through the favor of the fates he defeated the Carthaginians and liberated the Ausonians.

Ridiculos hominum versat sors caeca labores,
saecula nostra iocus ludibriumque deis.
Conversis vicibus iacet Africa, Roma triumphat,
victores victos extimuere suos;
et tanquam timeat Romam sacer ordo deorum
protinus et celeri damna levavit ope.
Sic igitur potuit veniam Fortuna mereri,
dum dedit eventus post mala Fata bonos.
Sors audita mali luctu confecerat urbem,
magnaque maioris damna pudoris erant.
Laeta superveniens praemisso fama dolori
ex ipsis potuit gratior esse malis.
Primum narratur, qua valle quibusque latebris
Poenorum steterit insidiosa cohors
et quantus Latios belli caecaverit ardor,
ne tacitos possent ante videre dolos;
qualiter augustos Romanaque viscera patres
traxerit in laqueos Africa dira suos;
quam parva Patricida manu contriverit hostes
et tibi, Roma, tuos reddiderit populos.
Sic Patricida suis famosus et inclitus actis
creber et in vulgi plurimus ore sonat.
Rex ubi collegit, quas fert victoria, praedas
(nam lucri dominus, non tamen auctor erat),
Romam vertit iter patribusque legenda verendis
littera dirigitur. Littera talis erat:
ut sibi pro victa Carthagine debita laurus
et meritus Latio more daretur honor.
Romani super his bene quid statuatur, acuto
consilio versant exagitantque diu.

Blind chance overturns the ridiculous labors of men, and to the gods our life is a joke, a mockery. By a reversal of fortune Africa is laid low, Rome triumphs, the victors dread those they had conquered; and as though the sacred order of the gods feared Rome, all at once and with swift aid they averted disaster. Thus might Fortune gain forgiveness, when after cruel fates she granted a happy outcome.

News of the misfortune reduced the city to mourning, and the great disaster was a cause of greater shame. Happy tidings, following close on the previous sorrow, could be more welcome because of those very evils. First was reported in what valley and with what subterfuges the treacherous Carthaginian cohort had taken their stand, and how great an eagerness for battle blinded the Latins, so that they could not see the secret deceptions before them; how cruel Africa drew into its snares the noble fathers and manhood of Rome; and then how Patricida with a small company laid waste the enemy and restored your people to you, O Rome. Thus Patricida, famous and glorious for his deeds, was the name most frequently heard in the talk of the people.

When the king gathered the spoils that victory brings (for he was the master of this booty, though he had not acquired it), he turned toward Rome, and a letter was dispatched, to be read by the venerable fathers. The letter was to this effect: that the laurel due to him for the conquest of Carthage and the honor he had earned should be granted according to Latian custom. The Romans ponder and argue for a long time, considering carefully what judgment might

Undique pensatis rationis acumine rebus
  nil meriti factis regis inesse vident,
qui male fuscata Romani laude decoris
  victus et in bello praeda fuisset iners.
Neve tamen posset turpi doluisse repulsa
  (nam male contemptum fert gravis ira ducum),
pagina signatur, cuius dare sive negare
  ambiguus sensus significare queat:
"Nullius obsistit meritis servire parata
  semper victori regia Roma suo;
nam cui laurigeros meruit victoria currus,
  non illi meritos Roma negabit eos.
Qui populos vicit Carthaginis, ille, fatemur,
  ille triumphales scandere debet equos."
Spem mentita bonam fallaci littera vultu
  imprimis potuit laetificare ducem.
Mox ubi consuluit mentem totumque cucurrit
  et tulit ad sensum singula verba suum,
sicut homo discretus erat, non motus in iram
  "Ambagem dubiae sentio vocis," ait.
Ergo Patricidam—nec enim laudes alienas
  regia mens aegre sustinet—alloquitur:
"O iuvenis, quem, si quis inest vigor insitus astris,
  nascentem vidit sideris hora boni;
cui Fortuna favens, ne postmodo caeca vocetur,
  excusat vitii crimen onusque sui,
in cuius facie Naturae cuncta potentis
  argumenta patent (laus tua forma deae),
per quem—nec pudor est—ereptus ab hoste revertor
  redditus uxori deliciisque meis;

best be given on this case. When the affair had been examined from every angle and acutely judged, they found that there was no merit in the deeds of the king, who once conquered in war had been a passive prisoner, while the fair name of glorious Rome had been badly tarnished. However, lest he should have cause to complain of a demeaning rejection (for the stern anger of rulers cannot endure disdain), a document was issued, whose ambiguous message might indicate granting or withholding: "Royal Rome, always prepared to show respect to a victor, stands opposed to no man's just deserts; to him whose victory has earned a chariot decked with laurel, to him Rome will not deny these rewards. He who conquered the people of Carthage, he, we declare, should ascend the triumphal chariot."

At first this letter, feigning encouragement on its false surface, enabled the ruler to rejoice. But when he reflected, went over the whole document and considered the meaning of each word, being a man of discretion, not given to anger, he said, "I understand the windings of this ambiguous voice." Accordingly—since a royal mind does not feel displeasure when another is praised—he spoke to Patricida: "O youth, on whose birth, if any power inheres in the stars, a star in a favorable hour looked down; whom Fortune, lest she be called blind forever after, favors, and exempts from the guilt and burden of her vices; in whose face all the resources of powerful Nature are manifested (for your beauty is a tribute to the goddess); through whom—nor is it shameful to say—I have been snatched away from the enemy and restored to my wife and my life of pleasure;

ecce dies, qui progrediens ex ordine fati
  reddet virtuti praemia digna tuae.
Sceptra tuus, fateor, meruit labor; accipe sceptra
  et meritum regimen urbis et orbis habe.
Vicisti Poenos; et quos tibi Roma paravit
  curribus et pompis utere pace mea.
Iuste Roma videt servataque linea recti
  est in contemptu plus mihi grata meo.
Nec meus iste potest pudor aut iniuria dici,
  iustitiae melius nomen habere potest.
Ergo (nec invideo) venturi praescia laurus
  crinibus accedet digna corona tuis;
ergo (nec invideo) curru fulgente veheris
  laetaque Roma tuum nomen ad astra feret.
Grande voco meritum, quem dat tibi Roma, triumphum;
  quod tibi do, munus grandius esse puto:
Romanis hucusque meis te praefero regnis;
  estque fretum munus lataque terra meum."
Obstupuit iuvenis et—quae rarissima virtus—
  de sibi collato tristis honore fuit.
Dum parere negat, venientes ordine pompas
  aspiciunt, illinc vulgus et inde patres;
rex capitis diadema sui, licet ille repugnet,
  collocat in iuvenis vertice, sceptra manu.
Sic tectum trabea, sic omnia regis habentem
  obtulit. Oblatum Roma recepit eum,
et niveos super altus equos plaudente senatu
  ad Capitolinum ducitur usque Iovem.

behold the day which, advancing according to the design of fate, will grant rewards worthy of your valor. Your effort, I confess, has deserved the scepter; take the scepter, and assume deservedly the governance of the city and the world. You have conquered the Carthaginians; enjoy with my blessing the chariot and the procession which Rome has prepared for you. Rome sees justly, and it is the more pleasing to me that the standard of rectitude is maintained without regard for me. This cannot be considered shame or injury to me; it may better possess the name of justice. Thus (and I feel no envy) the laurel, prescient of things to come, will be brought as a worthy crown for your head; thus (and I feel no envy) you will be borne in a gleaming chariot, and a rejoicing Rome will raise your name to the stars. I call the triumph which Rome gives you a great reward; I consider that what I give you is a greater gift: I present to you the realms of the Romans, hitherto mine; my gift is the sea and the wide world."

The youth was astonished and—rarest of virtues—unhappy at the honor offered to him. While he is refusing to accept, they see the procession approaching in due order, from this side the common people, from that the senators; the king places his own diadem on the head of the youth, though he resists, and puts the scepter in his hand. Thus he presents him adorned with the royal trappings, and all the marks of a king. Rome receives him thus presented, and raised aloft behind snow white horses, while the Senate applauds, he is borne to the temple of Capitoline Jove.

Audierat—nec enim gestorum deficit index—
imperium nati mater amica sui.
Movit ad hoc pietas amor et natura parentem;
laetitia potuit paene perire sua.
In lacrimas tamen erumpunt pia gaudia matris,
quas dolor et potius dampna parare solent.
Ut satis applausit cognato mater honori,
legitimo risus fine repressa suos,
pectoris arcanum velut in penetrale recepta
et silet et, quid agat, consulit ingenium.
Astrologi super augurio, super ordine Fati
astupet et stellis sensit inesse fidem.
Iam de praeterito trahit argumenta futuri,
cetera praedicto credit itura modo.
Ergo re faciente fidem pro morte mariti
cogitur ad veros sponsa venire metus.
Ad sobolis decus aspiciens obitumque mariti
laeta per alternas fitque molesta vices.
Quando virum vel dulce viri quodcumque fuisset
praesens ante suae lumina mentis habet,
pectora iocundis successibus exhilarata
vindicat hospitium cura dolorque sibi.
Cum Patricida redit, qualem quantumque videri
dat maternus amor, non habet ira locum.
Cumque subit socialis amor foedusque mariti,
integritas vitae nec violata fides,
non peperisse velit, natus natique potestas
displicet, et prorsus desinit esse parens.
Interdum mitescit atrox blandamque parentem
induit, et vincit filius ipse virum.

Since news of these events was not wanting, the loving mother had heard that her son was now ruler. At this news natural affection and love stir the parent; she could almost have perished in her happiness. Yet the joyful devotion of the mother bursts forth into such tears as sorrow, or indeed disaster, normally bring. When the mother has duly applauded the honoring of her child, confining her joy within appropriate bounds, she falls silent, as if withdrawn into the secret inner chamber of her breast, and seeks to understand what she should do. She is amazed by the astrologer's prophecy and the design of fate, and she realizes that there is truth in the stars. Now from the past she draws indications of the future, and believes that the rest will proceed in the manner foretold. Thus, with circumstance creating credence, the wife is forced to entertain real fear concerning the death of her husband. Contemplating the glory of her child and her husband's death, she becomes alternately happy and troubled. When she has present her husband before the eyes of her mind, or whatever in her husband had been dear to her, care and sorrow claim as their dwelling the breast that had been made joyful by happy events. When Patricida returns to her mind, a mother's love allows him to appear such that there is no place for anger. And when loving companionship, the marital bond, blameless life and inviolate trust enter her mind, she wishes she had not given birth, her son and her son's high rank displease her, and she abruptly ceases to be a parent. Then for a while this harshness softens and she becomes the sweet parent, and that same son overcomes his

Alternis dolet et gaudet misereque beata
ponderat ad casus dulcia Fata malos.
Anxia distrahitur dubioque miserrima voto
fluctuat, et bellum mater et uxor agit.
Si queat aeterno Parcas praevertere cursu,
vellet pro domino Fata subire suo;
sed tristis Lachesis, sed inexorabile Fatum
nonnisi praescriptas ius habet ire vias.
Vir suus interea curis superoccupat aegram
tumque super fatis pervigil eius erat;
intuitoque viro, cuius prope fata videbat,
ingemit affectu vera Sabina pio,
compressaeque diu tandem velut agmine facto
discursu lacrimae liberiore fluunt.
Obriguit dominus lacrimis violentius ortis,
nescio quid taciti sensit inesse mali.
Currit in amplexus et dulciter oscula carae
coniugis irrumpit et rogat, unde dolet.
Cui tamen illa nihil; premit importunus et haeret,
instat et incumbit multiplicatque preces.
Quo plus maesta silet, potuit suspectius esse,
quod dubitat tanta sub gravitate loqui.
Quaerit perque fidem thalamique sacros hymeneos,
quis, quibus ex causis fluxerit iste dolor.
Si res consilii, tutas descendet in aures;
si scelus, hoc poterit scire maritus amans.
Lege thori thalamique fide compulsa fateri
quae melius poterant utiliusque tegi,
"Est," ait, "unde querar de te, Natura creatrix,
quae nihil ad summam perficis usque manum.

father. She grieves and rejoices by turns, miserably happy, and weighs kind fate against cruel mischance. Anxious and miserable she is distraught, and fluctuates, uncertain what to hope for; mother and wife are at war. Were she able to forestall the Fates in their eternal advance, she would wish to submit herself to the fates in place of her husband; but grim Lachesis and inexorable Fate are permitted to travel only along foreordained paths.

Meanwhile anxiety for her husband consumes the suffering woman: now she lies awake over his fate, and at the sight of the man, whose imminent doom she foresees, she weeps, a very Sabine in her tender feeling, and tears long suppressed finally flow, running unrestrained, like an onrushing army. The husband is shocked at tears so violently brought forth, and senses some strange unspoken evil. He rushes to embrace and tenderly kiss his beloved wife, and asks her why she is sad. But she tells him nothing; he holds her roughly and clings to her, he is insistent and overbearing, and he entreats her endlessly. The more she remains sorrowful and silent, the more suspicious can it seem, since she hesitates to speak in the face of such pressure. He asks, invoking the trust of the marriage bed and the sacred rites of marriage, what her sorrow means, and from what cause it has arisen. If it is a matter for deliberation, it will enter trustworthy ears; if a crime, a loving husband can accept this.

Compelled by the law of marriage and the trust of the marriage bed to confess what might better and more advantageously have been hidden, she speaks: "I have reason to complain of you, Nature, creator who bring nothing to full

Multa licet dederis, minus est, quod femina nascor;
  defecitque tuus hac mihi parte favor.
Is meus est sexus, cui simplicitas inimica,
  cui pudor ignotus, cui peregrina fides.
Is meus est sexus, qui detestatur honestum,
  qui, quicquid scelus est, vindicat esse suum.
Si libeat superis, genus evertatur iniquum
  femina, vivat homo tum suus orbe suo.
Aura nocens, maris unda tumens irataque pugna
  non necat ad numerum, femina dira, tuum.
Planta vel arbor habet, quibus extendatur in aevum,
  semina; perpetuant continuantque genus.
Femina non aliter radicem criminis in se
  sementemque mali materiamque tenet.
Tempora si redeant antiquae simplicitatis
  argutique cadat spiritus ingenii,
femina sufficiet artes reparare nocendi
  perfidiaeque novum forsitan addet opus.
Tempore mitescunt posita feritate leones,
  tempore leniri tigris et ursa solent;
fixa pedem manet ad facinus numquamque malignam
  mutat naturam femina sola suam.
Si qua suum penitus descivit femina sexum,
  plus niveo corvo prodigiosa fuit.
Sed quid naturae vitio vel quid genuinis
  moribus ascribo criminis huius onus?
Quod mala, quod nequam, quod atrox, quod perdita feci,
  ad sexum refero turpiter ipsa meum.
Non bene causa nitet, qua se mea culpa colorat;
  seque meum facinus non habet unde tegat.

perfection. While you have granted much, the fact that I am born a woman diminishes it; your kindness to me is lacking in this respect. Mine is the sex to which simplicity is an enemy, to which shame is unknown, to which trust is foreign. Mine is the sex which detests integrity, which claims as its own any crime whatsoever. If it please the gods, let womankind, that wicked gender, be destroyed; then let man live for himself in a world of his own. A destructive wind, the swelling waves of the ocean, the fury of war do not result in murders to equal yours, fell woman. A plant or tree possesses seeds by which it can prolong life through the ages, which ensure the perpetuity and continuity of its kind. A woman likewise harbors the root of crime within herself, the seeds and substance of evil. If the olden days of open honesty should return, and the spirit of crafty ingenuity should perish, woman would be capable of restoring the destructive arts, and might well add some new form of treachery. In time lions grow tame, laying aside their fierceness, in time tiger and bear are wont to be pacified; woman alone remains fixedly set on crime, and never changes her perverse nature. Should any woman wholly free herself from her sex, she would be more of a marvel than a snow-white raven.

"But why do I ascribe the guilt of this crime to a natural failing or ingrained behavior? What I myself have done, evil, vile, monstrous, abandoned as I am, I basely impute to my sex. There is no elegant argument with which my guilt disguises itself; my crime has no way to hide itself.

O coniunx decepte diu! Tibi creditur uxor
quae tibi non uxor, sed magis hostis erat.
Forsitan obsequiis et blanda sedulitate
credebas animum promeruisse meum.
A primis aevi gradibus tuus unicus ardor,
unicus affectus, unica cura fui.
Sed benefacta tuis male respondentia votis
aequalis meriti non habuere vices.
Obsequium damnis, odiis pensamus amorem,
opprobrio laudem, proditione fidem.
Quaere, marite, novum poenae genus, exime ferrum,
viscera funde solo, distrahe membra rotis!
His ego digna malis, quae iudicio Rhadamanthi
Tartarea patitur noxia turba domo.
Sed quia suspensus dubio sermone teneris,
accipe quo tendant, quid mea verba velint.
Olim, si memini, peperi, quem sidera regem
spondebantque senis sceptra tenere Numae;
spondebant—sed flere magis quam dicere fas est,
pro dolor!—auctorem funeris esse tui.
Territus augurio contra sua viscera matrem
praecipis armari progeniemque premi.
Sed natura minis monituque potentior omni
non potuit partes destituisse suas.
Mentior extinctum; credis. Temerarie credis,
sed puer alterius lactis habebat opem.
Sic igitur—culpamve velis facinusve vocari—
nunc illi puero vivitur ista dies.
Filius ille tuus, cuius rationis acumen,
actus mirari, verba probare soles.

"O husband so long deceived! You believed her a wife who was no wife to you, but rather an enemy. Perhaps you believed that by obedience and tender attentions you had won my heart. From the earliest stage of our life your only desire, your only affection, your only care was for me. But your generous acts, responding poorly to your hopes, did not receive a return of equal merit. We repaid service with injury, love with hatred, praise with abuse, trust with betrayal. Husband, seek out a new form of punishment, draw your sword, scatter my entrails on the earth, tear apart my limbs on the wheel! I am deserving of those pains which, by the sentence of Rhadamanthus, the guilty throng suffers in their Tartarean home. But because you are held in suspense by this obscure speech, hear where my words are pointing, hear what they mean. Some time ago, if my memory is correct, I gave birth to one who the stars declared would wield as king the scepter of ancient Numa; one who, they declared —but one should weep rather than say this, alas!—, would be the agent of your death. Terrified by the augury, you ordered that the mother make war on her own flesh, and that her child be destroyed. But nature, more powerful than any threat or admonition, could not forsake a part of herself. I say falsely that the child has been destroyed; you believe it. You believe unthinkingly, but the boy was sustained by the milk of another.

"Therefore—you may call it a fault or a crime—this boy is alive this very day. It is your son whose keenness of mind, whose acts you often marvel at, whose words you commend.

Filius ille tuus, quem praedicat orbis et omnis
quae sub septeno climate terra iacet.
Filius ille tuus, de quo quoque livor et hostis,
de quo mentiri Fama vel ipsa timet.
Filius ille tuus, cui nec Natura decorem,
nec Fortuna superaddere possit opes.
Filius ille tuus, cuius Carthago triumphos
nec genus Hannibalis erubuisse potest.
Filius ille tuus, quem regni sede locatum
cernis honorata sceptra tenere manu.
Verba mathematici, nisi quod tua fata supersunt,
omnia decreto fine peracta vides,
currentesque suo fataliter ordine stellae
et tua defixo Fata tenore trahent."
Vir stupuit potuitque diu non credere rebus,
eventus quarum prodigiosus erat.
Sollicitus longumque silens se pectore toto
contulit ad mentis interiora suae.
Provida consulitur ratio vigilatque receptus
intus apud sese totus et omnis homo.
Singula discutiens gaudendum sensit et ipsam
perniciem proprii coepit amare mali.
Ergo decus generis et honores concipit altos
contemptorque suae perditionis ait:
"Cara comes, mihi sanctus amor, mihi gratia concors,
parce queri, lacrimas comprime, pone metus.
Non vitio tua facta dedi; pulchrisque marito
fraudibus et pulchra proditione places.
Non sub iudicibus timeas adducta severis;
tam sincera tuum causa tuetur opus.

It is your son whom the world extols, and every land that lies beneath the seven zones. It is your son of whom envy and hatred, too, and even Fame herself fear to speak falsely. It is your son to whose beauty Nature could add nothing, whose wealth Fortune could not increase. It is your son for whose triumphs Carthage and the people of Hannibal need feel no shame. It is your son whom you see established on the royal throne, holding in his hand the scepter of his office.

"You see that all the words of the astrologer have been fulfilled by the destined result, save that your fate remains; and the stars, impelled by a fatal design, will bring your fate, too, in their unvarying course."

The man was astonished, and for a while could not believe a story the circumstances of which were so unnatural. Troubled and silent for a long time, he retreated wholly to the inner recesses of his mind. Prudent reason is consulted, and the whole man, withdrawn within himself, is wholly alert. Examining each detail, he feels that there is cause for joy, and begins to feel love for the very agent of his own destruction. Therefore he keeps in mind the glory and the lofty honors of his family, contemptuous of his own ruin, and speaks: "Dear companion, my blessed love, my harmonious delight, cease to lament, restrain your tears, set aside your fear. I do not consider your acts a crime; your noble deception and betrayal are pleasing to your husband. Do not fear to be brought before severe judges; such sincerity of

Ipsa licet sileas, pro te Natura loquetur;
sunt oratores iusque piumque tui.
Non tibi rhetoricos opus induxisse colores;
ad regimen causae non leve robur habes.
Mater eras; maternus amor pietasque coegit.
Medeamque fugis aemula Penelopes.
Iure timere queam, quae pignora mortificassent,
has etiam promptas in mea Fata manus.
Sed redimendus erat dominator et urbis et orbis
unius ex facili perditione senis.
Ut vetus arbor ego, cuius de stirpe renascens
virgula servatur; ipsa recisa perit.
Virga suam matrem longum distendit in aevum
perpetuatque meus filius esse meum.
Mira quidem novitas: laetus dolor, utile damnum:
quae duo fortunae cernis inesse meae.
Obsequium praestasse putat Fortuna duobus,
surgat ut ex nostro sanguine sceptra regens.
Non decet ingratos divini muneris esse;
tangit munificos mens hilarata deos.
Non veniunt homini nisi magno magna labore,
partaque Phlegraeo sidera Marte Iovi.
Ut merear regisque pater dominusque vocari,
morte mea tanti nomen honoris emo.
Sed moriens ego non moriar, totusque superstes
totus et in tali prole renatus ero.
Quod de fatali descendit origine rerum,
ne dicas fieri fraude vel arte tua.;
Fatum me perimit, Fatum servavit eundem,
quem servasse putas: omnia lege meant.

purpose is your defense. Though you are silent, nature will speak for you; right and devotion are your orators. You need not have adopted the colors of rhetoric; there is no lack of force to put forward your case. You were a mother; a mother's love and devotion urged you on. You flee the role of Medea and emulate Penelope. I might well fear that the hands of her who had murdered her own child might also be ready to inflict my Fate. But by the insignificant death of a single old man the lord and master of the city and the world is preserved. I am like an old tree from whose stock a newborn shoot is preserved, while the tree itself is cut down and dies. The shoot extends the life of its mother tree into the distant future, and my son perpetuates my existence.

"A new wonder indeed: a happy sorrow, a useful ruin; you see that both of these exist in my fortune. Fortune assumes that she has shown herself the servant of us both, that from our blood might rise a sceptered king. It is improper to be ungrateful for a divine gift; a mind exhibiting joy pleases the generous gods. Great things do not come to a man without great labor; it was by the Phlegraean battle that heaven was gained for Jove. That I may be rewarded with the title of lord, and father of a king, I purchase this glorious name with my death. But in dying I will not die; I will fully survive, and in such a son I will be wholly reborn. Do not say that what descends from the fatal source of human affairs comes to pass by deceit or contrivance of yours: Fate destroys me, Fate has preserved him whom you suppose you have preserved. All things proceed according to law.

Dum patitur Lachesis, iamiamque minantia rumpi
nostra fatigato pollice fila trahit,
Praesentem placet affari propiusque videre,
quem superi rerum constituere caput.
Si semel amplexus iungam, semel oscula nato,
sufficiet vitae terminus ille meae.
Laetior Elysios veniam gentesque sepultas
et Chaos et Stygii pallida regna Iovis."
Ergo Palatinas Tarpeii culminis arces
per circumflexos scandit uterque gradus.
Illic cum patribus residens Patricida verendis
in commune suae consulit urbis opus,
ne pereant leges, ne decidat ordo senatus,
Romae maiestas imperiique decus.
Ingressi splendore domus potuere teneri,
si minor aut levior causa tulisset iter.
Ad regem graviter summisque laboribus itur,
nam circumstantum densius agmen erat.
Ut plebis rupere globos, penetratur ad ipsas
primatum cathedras imperiique thronum.
Matris ad occursus (nec enim pater agnitus illi)
assurgit solio rex Patricida suo,
Imperii fastu vel maiestate reiecta
totus maternis subditur officiis.
Subsequitur blandaque manu comportat euntem,
alloquitur blande, blandius audit eam;
naturaeque suae non immemor alta potestas
personam servae conditionis agit.
Cui genetrix: "Secede loco matrique benignus
condescende tuae; dicere pauca volo.

"While Lachesis permits it, drawing out with weary thumb my thread which threatens to break at any moment, it is my wish to converse with and see close at hand the one whom the gods have established as the master of worldly affairs. If I may once embrace and kiss my son, it will be a satisfying conclusion to my life. I will come more happily to Elysium, and the buried dead, and Chaos, and the pale realm of the Stygian Jove."

Accordingly the two ascend by the winding steps to the Palatine citadel atop the Tarpeian rock. There Patricida, seated with the venerable fathers, deliberates about the general welfare of his city, lest the laws be destroyed, lest the authority of the Senate, the majesty of Rome, the dignity of empire should fail. Entering, they might have been detained by the splendor of the building if a lesser or more trivial purpose had prompted their journey. They make their way to the king slowly and with the utmost difficulty, for the throng of those surrounding him was dense. Breaking through the crowd of common people, they reach the very seats of the nobles and the imperial throne.

At the approach of his mother (for his father was unknown to him) Patricida the king rose from his throne, imperial pomp and majesty cast aside, wholly concerned with his duty to his mother. He attends her closely and supports her with gentle hand as she walks, speaks to her tenderly and more tenderly listens; lofty power, not forgetful of its origin, assumes the character of servility.

The mother speaks: "Come away from this place, and kindly indulge your mother; I have a few things to tell you.

Redde parum te, nate, mihi, furare labori
  te quandoque gravi; iura senatus agat.
Cura tuae mentis moderando debita mundo
  ex aliqua saltem parte remittat onus.
Roma sibi vigilet, propriis quoque viribus usa;
  interdum discat rege carere suo.
Hoc precor, hoc iubeo, regem precor, impero nato;
  ius habet in partus mater amica suos.
Declines igitur turbam turbaeque tumultum;
  non bene consilium ducitur in medium.
Alta volunt propria sub maiestate latere
  nec tuto veniunt ad populare palam."
Ergo divertunt, ubi longa pace silebat
  deditus arcanis consiliisque locus.
Quod sancitur ibi tacitum, sublime, profundum,
  auribus eripitur, Fama maligna, tuis.
Res regum tacitique locus privata senatus
  audit et aeterna nocte sepulta premit.
Sedit uterque parens et filius inter utrumque.
  Dicendi primum femina fecit iter:
"Fili, cuius opes, sapientia, forma, potestas
  sunt mihi sidereis significata notis,
dum recolo meritumque tuum vitaeque nitorem,
  gaudeo, nate, tibi, gaudeo, nate, mihi.
Si qua parte mihi posset subrepere fastus,
  nempe futura fui laude superba tua.
Per te Romulidas libertas prisca revisit,
  ausa suum terris exeruisse caput.
Olim decretis aeterni legibus aevi
  debitus in regimen temporis huius eras;

Give a little of yourself to me, my son; draw yourself away from heavy labor once in a while; let the senate administer justice. Let your conscientious mind, dedicated to governing the world, give up at least some portion of its burden. Let Rome draw on her own powers and watch over herself; let her learn for a while to do without her king. This is my prayer, this my command, my prayer to my king, my command to my son; a loving mother has rights over her children. Withdraw from the crowd and the crowd's tumult; a council meeting cannot be conducted properly in public. High affairs must be veiled by the appropriate aura of majesty, and do not appear openly before the people without danger."

Therefore they withdraw to a place reserved for secret deliberations, where there had long been calm and silence. The secret, lofty, profound matters solemnized there are withheld from your hearing, malicious Rumor. This place hears the business of kings and the private affairs of a secret senate, and keeps them buried in eternal darkness.

The parents sit and the son sits between them. The woman is the first to enter into speech: "My son, whose valor, wisdom, beauty, power were revealed to me in the patterns of the stars, when I consider your worthiness and the splendor of your life, I rejoice, my son, for you and for myself. If ever a touch of pride should manage to catch me unawares, surely I will have been made proud by praise of you. Through you the liberty of old has come again to the people of Romulus, daring to lift its head from the earth. Long ago you were promised as ruler of this temporal world by laws eternally decreed; you bring justice to our time and return

nostraque iustificas priscumque reducis in aurum
saecula nec ferri nomen habere sinis.
Naturae praelarga manus te praetulit orbi
et dedit in solo munere cuncta semel;
utiliusque nihil in postera saecla reservans
prodiga donatrix paene remansit inops.
Iam neque miretur censorem Iustinianum;
iam neque se iactet Roma Catone suo.
Si populus felix Augustos vixit in annos,
nostra nec inferius tempora numen habent.
Astrorum cognosco fidem: Chaldaeaque cura
Assyriusque labor vim rationis habent.
Dictus eras sensu Graecos quoque vincere: vincis;
Marte valere: vales; sceptra tenere: tenes.
Sed quamvis sublime caput sub sidera condas
rex super humanum dispositorque genus,
unum deerat adhuc—non nosse tuum genitorem—
ad solidae plenas prosperitatis opes.
Sed votis astricta tuis Fortuna laborat,
ut tua sit nulla gloria parte minor.
Iste pater, pater iste tuus—cognosce, revise—
qui de carne sua contulit esse tibi!"
Filius exsurgit, surgit pater, oscula iungunt,
nec cohibet lacrimas iste vel iste suas.
Implicitis strictisque diu complexibus haerent,
et cognata sacer pectora mulcet amor.
At genitor vultu non exsatiatus amato
haeret et in iuvenem lumina fixa tenet.
Aspiciens igitur tantae miracula formae
aut stupefactus ad haec aut hilaratus ait:

us to the ancient age of gold, refusing to admit the name of iron. The bounteous hand of Nature presented you to the world, and in this one gift gave all things at once; retaining nothing to provide for later ages, our prodigal benefactress is left nearly destitute. Now let none marvel at the just strictures of Justinian, or Rome pride herself on her Cato. If our people lived a happy life in the years of Augustus, our own times possess a majesty in no way inferior.

"I acknowledge the truth of the stars: the watchfulness of the Chaldean, the Assyrian's study have the force of reason. It was said that you would surpass the Greeks in understanding: you surpass them; that you would be a mighty warrior: you are mighty; that you would attain the scepter: you have attained it. But though you hold supreme authority beneath the heavens, though you are king and governor of the human race, one thing has still been lacking to the full realization of true prosperity: you do not know your father. But Fortune is at work, bound by your wishes, that your glory may not be lacking in any respect. This, this is your father—know him, behold him—who from his own flesh conferred existence upon you!"

The son rises, the father rises, they exchange kisses, and neither restrains his tears. Long they cling together in a close embrace, and a blessed love soothes their kindred breasts. But the father, insatiable, is held by the beloved face, and keeps his eyes fixed on the youth. Stunned and overjoyed at beholding such miraculous beauty, he speaks:

"Militiae specialis honor, rationis et aequi
immotus limes perpetuusque tenor,
nate—sed usurpo nomen fortasse paternum;
qui saevus pater est, desinit esse pater.
Nate, fatebor enim, tua te gestabat in alvo
mater, eoque mori tempore iussus eras;
iussus eras, iussi perfecti roboris annos
maturosque volens anticipare dies.
Poena paratur ei quem non dampnaverat error,
et praeiudicium lingua paterna facit.
Ordo sed aeternus praefixaque nexio rerum
humanae vanum dissipat artis opus;
servaturque puer, placide qui temperet orbem
Romuleaque regat moenia facta manu.
Si durae feritatis homo Romana gubernet,
funditus ex imo vertere cuncta queat.
Ne pereat mundus, te simplicitatis amicum
imposuit Latio provida cura Jovis.
Imperii gladium libertatemque nocendi
in placidi mutas et miserantis opus,
qui mundum placidus, mentem regis imperiosus
et regis nomen rectius inde tenes.
Quem geris, expugnas hominem carnisque malignae
insistis motus lege tenere vagos.
Te cohibes, vivisque senex iuvenilibus annis,
nec te discincte, sed sapienter agis.
Intra Naturae voluisti vivere fines,
lora tamen freni liberioris habens.
Nec removes formave tumens opibusve solutus
proposita stabiles a ratione gradus.

"Special pride of our soldiery, immovable bulwark and enduring upholder of reason and justice, my son—but perhaps I usurp the name of father: a father who is cruel ceases to be a father. For I will confess, my son, at the time when your mother was carrying you in her womb you had been sentenced to die; you had been sentenced, I gave the order, wishing to forestall your years of full strength and maturity. Punishment was prepared for one whom no crime had condemned, and a father's tongue gave the premature judgment.

"But an eternal order and the foreordained interconnection of events destroys the vain effort of human skill; the boy survives, to rule the world in peace, and reign over walls built by the hands of Romulus. If a man of harsh cruelty governed Roman affairs he might utterly destroy everything. Lest the world should perish, the provident concern of Jove for Latium made you, a friend of simplicity, our ruler. You turn the sword of conquest and the freedom to do harm toward works of peace and compassion; you govern the world peacefully, and impose imperial power on your own spirit, and thus you justly possess the name of king.

"You conquer the man you bear within yourself, and you are vigorous in imposing law on the wayward movements of perverse carnality. You discipline yourself, and in your youthful years you live as a man of age, conducting yourself not carelessly but wisely. You have chosen to live within the bounds of Nature, though you have the power to loosen the reins. Neither vain in your beauty nor dissolute in your wealth, you do not divert your steady course from rational

Quo ius latius est votique licentia maior,
articulo vitam sub breviore trahis.
Unde fit, ut caeli curis pro parte relictis
pronius intendant ad tua vota dei.
Ipse pater superum, quotiens vel magna requiris,
quamvis accelerans tardior esse timet.
Cum tibi multimodi daret ornamenta decoris,
Iupiter in dando movit utrasque manus.
Dulce rubet facies, fecundum robore pectus,
lingua perita loqui, fortis ad arma manus.
Ne quid in humanis solidum consistere rebus
dicat et apponat credere stultus homo,
inter successus et gaudia prosperitatum
ater et infelix angulus unus erit:
Fili, me perimes, immotaque pensa Sororum
istud ab aeterno constituere scelus.
Olim dispositi lex et violentia Fati
utetur manibus in mea Fata tuis.
Dextram, non animum praebebis, nate, furori;
qui tua tela regat, spiritus alter erit.
Vi firmamenti divinorumque supernis
cursibus astrorum cogeris esse nocens.
Cogeris esse nocens manifestaque culpa deorum
est, ubi non possis mitior esse patri.
Parcarum seriesque tenax fixumque necesse
simpliciter nostrae crimina caedis habent.
Tu neque, nate, nocens, nec enim reor esse nocentem,
qui, quia non potuit non nocuisse, nocet.
Non sine respectu, sine re Patricida vocaris:
nominis attendas significata tui.

purpose. Though the scope of your authority is broad, and the freedom to indulge your wishes is great, you contain your life within modest limits. Hence it is that the gods, setting aside heavenly concerns for a time, give ready attention to your prayers. The very father of the gods, whenever you are in need of some great thing, though he acts swiftly, fears that he is too slow. When he would bestow upon you the adornments of manifold beauty, Jupiter, in giving, used both his hands. Your face has a ruddy charm, your breast swells with strength, your tongue is skillful in speech, your hand strong in arms.

"But lest foolish humanity should declare, and establish as its belief, that anything in human affairs is solid and enduring, amid our happy times and the joys of our prosperity there will be one dark and ill-omened corner: My son, you will slay me; the unalterable spinning of the Sisters has established this crime from the beginning. The law and the cruelty of a Fate determined long ago will employ your hands to impose my doom. But you will lend your hand, not your mind, to this mad act, my son; it will be an alien spirit that controls your weapon. You will be forced to act cruelly by the power of the firmament and the heavenly courses of the divine stars. You will be forced to act cruelly, and the guilt lies plainly with the gods, when you are made incapable of showing mercy to your father. The firm course of the Fates and fixed necessity plainly bear the guilt for my murder. You are not cruel, my son, for I do not consider him cruel who does harm because he is unable not to do harm. Not without consideration, not without reason are you called Patricida: give thought to the significance of your

Condono mea, nate, tibi . . ." Cum dicere vellet
"funera," vox linguam nulla secuta suam.
Imperfecta foret ruptae sententia vocis,
sed pia supplevit lacrima vocis opus.
Liquitur in lacrimas oculis superinsitus humor,
quasque potest, pietas blanda ministrat opes.
Cumque tamen scirent curas et pondera regni
arte Patricidae consilioque regi,
in Latii commune bonum peccare timentes
colloquii gratas corripuere moras.
Ergo recessuri natum super oscula lassant
alternantque vices participantque virum.
Ad delibandum complexandumque vicissim
praebet ad alternos se Patricida sinus.
Distrahitur, discedit ab hac, prensatur ab illo,
et venit ad dominos publica cura duos.
Cernere risus erat miserosque piosque parentes;
tam male vel sanctus se moderatur amor.
Attendens, quantoque probro quantoque pudore
fata velint vitam commaculare suam,
altius ingemuit Patricida suamque relabi
fortunam sensit comminuique decus.
Scit facilem rapidumque vagae vertiginis orbem
et caeci vultus numinis ambiguos,
quodque nequit certoque gradu fixoque tenore
quanta velis mundi gloria stare diu.
Maerorem post laeta timens, post blanda ruinam
secum sollicito pectore multa movet.
Fortunae legesque graves moresque maligni
ingeminant curas ingeminantque metum.

name. I pardon you, my son, for my . . ." When he would have said "death," no sound issued into speech. The meaning of the interrupted voice would have been incomplete, but loving tears take over the task of the voice. The moisture dwelling in his eyes dissolves into tears, and sweet devotion performs such work as it can.

But since the parents know that the cares and burdens of the kingdom are managed by the skill and judgment of Patricida, they are fearful of offending against the common good of Latium in having claimed this pleasant interval of conversation. Thus, preparing to leave, they weary their son with further kisses, perform this role by turns and share their son. Patricida offers himself to the bosom of each in turn, kissing and embracing them both. He is distracted, he withdraws from her, is seized by him, and affairs of state are now in the hands of two masters. It was comical to see the parents, at once unhappy and loving: so poorly does even blessed love contain itself.

Patricida, pondering the great disgrace and shame with which the Fates intended to stain his life, groaned inwardly, thinking that his fortune was declining and his glory would crumble. He knows the wheel, whirling at random, easily and swiftly, and the ambiguous face of the blind goddess, and he knows that no earthly glory whatever can long remain in a sure position, on a firm path. Fearing grief afterjoy, disaster after happy times, he considers many things within his troubled breast. The grim laws and malicious ways of Fortune compound his troubles and compound his fear.

Saepe suas metitur opes actusque decoros
 colligit in numerum cunctaque gesta probe.
Carthago deleta subit regesque subacti,
 et dolet aspiciens, quantus et unde cadat.
Longos successus, longos Fortuna favores
 punit et incestat deteriore malo:
damnator cari capitis vitaeque paternae
 ex rigida Fati lege futurus erat.
Mors patris et meritis et laudibus ingerit umbram;
 multiplici superest unica culpa bono.
Emptum morte velit, ut eodem limite posset
 finis principio concolor ire suo.
"Si fas sideribus, si fas illudere Parcis,
 Fata necemque patris praeveniemus," ait.
"Roma Patricidam dici, non esse videbit,
 et mendax sensus nominis huius erit.
Nostra quid aethereis mens est cognatior astris,
 si durae Lachesis triste necesse ferat?
Frustra particulam divinae mentis habemus,
 si nequeat ratio nostra cavere sibi.
Sic elementa Deus, sic ignea sidera fecit,
 ut neque sideribus subditus esset homo;
sed puri datur ingenii solertia maior,
 possit ut obiectis obvius ire malis."
Hinc Capitolinas, quibus influit Albula, sedes
 venit et imperii nobile pressit ebur.
Regali iubet edicto, sibi sistat ad unum
 collectus populus iunctaque turba senum,
iurisconsulti praetextatique Quirites,
 Albani, Fabii patriciumque genus

Repeatedly he assesses his wealth, counts over his glorious actions, and affirms all his noble deeds. Carthage destroyed comes to mind, and her captive rulers, and he grieves, reflecting on his greatness, and the great height from which he may fall. Fortune is punishing his long success, his long enjoyment of honor, and defiling him with the worst of evils: by the unbending decree of fate he is to be the destroyer of one dear to him, the life of his father. His father's death overshadows his rewards and acclaim; one guilty act outlives a great quantity of goodness. He wishes he were himself claimed by death, that his end, following the same path, might be worthy of his origin.

"If it it is right to repudiate the stars, the Fates," he said, "we will forestall the fates, and my father's death. Rome will see that I am not a parricide, though I am so named, and the significance of this name will become false. Why is our mind so closely akin to the heavenly stars, if it must suffer the grim necessity of harsh Lachesis? In vain do we possess a portion of divine understanding, if our reason is unable to provide for itself. God made the elements and the fiery stars such that man would not be subjected to the stars; instead he is endowed with the greater resource of pure intelligence, that he may confront opposing evil."

Thence he comes to the Capitoline palace, where the Albula flows, and takes his seat on the ruler's noble ivory throne. By royal edict he commands that the people, one and all, be gathered together before him, and the assembled body of elders, the lawyers, toga-wearing citizens, the Albans, the Fabians, those of patrician rank, the senators,

conscriptique patres, quorum moderamine mundus
stringitur et certis cogitur ire modis.
Ergo nobilitas et purpura venerat omnis
multaque congestae milia plebis erant.
Sic ubi dictator iussique sedere tribuni
et cum signifero consul uterque suo,
erigitur de sede throni monstratque silendum
maiestate manus. Denique verba facit:
"Sanguis Iuleus, soboles Gradiva, Quirites
(hinc olim vires ducitis, inde genus),
noscite, nec dubios suspensa mente tenebo,
quid moveat, vester quid Patricida velit:
postulat ambiguum sublato nomine munus.
Quicquid id est, regi porrige, Roma, tuo.
Suspectam timidamque licet se praebeat anceps
quaestio, nil anceps quaestio fraudis habet.
Per superum, per si qua manet reverentia nostri,
quicquid id est, regi porrige, Roma, tuo.
Non circumspecta neque consulta ratione,
sed quasi profuse dextera larga dabit.
Denigrat meritum dantis mora, factaque raptim
munera plus laudis plusque favoris habent.
Per superum, per siqua manet reverentia nostri,
quicquid id est, regi porrige, Roma, tuo.
Porrige, si merui, si mentis ad intima nostrae
nullus vel tenuis repperit error iter;
sincere si tota mihi mea vivitur aetas,
si nihil ex mundi colluvione tuli;
si, qui corda solet regum subvertere, fastus
nec Venus enervem praecipitemque dedit.

by whose direction the world is governed and forced to follow a steady course. Thus the nobility and all of high station had come, and the many thousands of common people were brought together. Then, when the chief magistrate, the tribunes, and the two consuls with their standard-bearers had been ordered to take their seats, Patricida rose from his throne and called for silence with a majestic gesture. Then he spoke:

"Descendants of Iulus, children of Mars—for from the one, citizens of Rome, your strength, from the other your race descends, I will not keep you in suspense with anxious minds; know what your Patricida proposes, what is his wish: he demands an ambiguous gift, concealing its name. Whatever it is, O Rome, grant it to your king. Though his cryptic request may present itself in a suspicious and uncertain manner, it harbors no deceit. By your reverence for the gods, by whatever reverence may be felt for me, whatever it is, O Rome, grant it to your king. The generous hand will give, not after reason has examined and pondered, but almost recklessly. Delay on the part of the giver demeans the worth of his gift, and gifts made in haste gain more praise and goodwill. By your reverence for the gods, by whatever reverence may be felt for me, whatever it is, O Rome, grant it to your king. Grant it if I have deserved it, if little or no sinfulness has found a path to my innermost thoughts; if my whole life is lived in truth to myself; if I have had no contact with worldly corruption; if neither scornful pride, which is wont to corrupt the hearts of kings, nor the lust of Venus has rendered me effeminate or reckless.

Nulla licet morum sit mentio nullaque vitae,
quae multos annos illabefacta manet,
saltem blanditiae nostrae crebrique rogatus
non poterunt populum non tetigisse pium.
Non ea Romuleam premit inclementia gentem,
supplicis ut surda respuat aure precem.
Rex ego dulce rogo; verbum, 'rogo,' regibus impar,
semper enim miserae vox ea sortis erit.
Per superum, per si qua manet reverentia nostri,
quicquid id est, regi porrige, Roma, tuo.
Crediderim munus magna pro parte coemptum,
cum color et vultus blandaque lingua rogat.
Turpe super donis dubitabitur inter amicos,
et mora donandi non leve crimen habet.
Occupet orantem placituri muneris auctor;
officio celeri gratia maior erit.
Profuit et Latio noster labor, et meritorum
non venit ad mores gratia surda bonos.
Promovi leges Latias coluique senatum,
nec meus in plebem perniciosus honor.
Quis Marius, quis Sulla potest, quis dicere Caesar:
'Nullus in imperio nullaque laesa meo.'?
Non meruit Patricida nihil Carthaginis altae
victor et Afrarum collabefactor opum.
Mentitos vox nostra sibi non arrogat actus;
cernite Poenorum moenia: fracta iacent.
Fracta iacent; captosque duces praedamque silebo,
ne videar laudes concelebrare meas.
Per superum, per si qua manet reverentia nostri,
quicquid id est, regi porrige, Roma, tuo."

Though nothing be said of my character, or of a life that remains inviolate after many years, at least our kindnesses and frequent audiences cannot fail to move a loyal people. The harshness that rejects a suppliant's prayer with deaf ear has not oppressed the people of Romulus.

"I the king appeal with gentle words, I appeal in a way not proper to kings; for the voice of misfortune will always be thus. By your reverence for the gods, by whatever reverence may be felt for me, whatever it is, grant it, O Rome, to your king. I would have believed my gift attained for the most part, since artful speech, a pleasing manner and a pleasant speech make the request. Hesitation over a gift between friends is a foul thing, and delay in giving incurs no small guilt. The grantor of a gift intended to please should anticipate the petitioner; there will be more gratitude for a service quickly rendered. Our labor has benefited Latium, and gratitude for virtuous conduct is not given with no thought of reward. I have strengthened Latin law, I have shown respect to the Senate, and my royal office has caused no hardship to the common people. What Marius, what Sulla, what Caesar could say, 'No man or woman has been injured under my rule'? Patricida, conqueror of lofty Carthage destroyer of the might of the Africans, has not been undeserving. Our voice does not arrogate to itself feigned achievements; look on the walls of Carthage: they lie in ruins. They lie in ruins—I will say nothing of captured leaders and plunder, lest I seem to proclaim my own praises. By your reverence for the gods, by whatever reverence may be felt for me, whatever it is, grant it, O Rome, to your king."

Deiectum vidisse ducem misereque loquentem
  erubuit populus, erubuere patres.
Proque bono bona fama viro meritumque perorat,
  nec patitur steriles principis ire preces.
Estque rogare ducum species violenta iubendi,
  et quasi nudato supplicat ense potens.
"Detur," ait populus, "detur," sacer ordo, tribuni
  "detur": vox cunctis unica "detur" erat.
Dant igitur, quodcumque petat, discrimine nullo,
  si Latiae totas postulet urbis opes.
Non tuus excipitur castus, Lucretia, lectus
  nec pyra sacrifici praecipitanda Numae.
Ut Patricida preces exauditum videt iri
  sensit et arbitrio cuncta venire suo,
"Cuius," ait, "fuerim spe muneris ambitiosus
  quidve mihi dederis, Romula turba, vide.
Nil equidem cupio nostris superaddere rebus;
  invenit finem copia nostra suum.
Nec dives Latium nec habet latissimus orbis,
  quo queat in maius crescere noster honor.
Non Phrygios lapides pigmentaque gentis Eoae,
  non quas Pactolus versat et Hermus opes,
non Tyrios cultus nec equos regionis Iberae,
  non ebur aut ebenum, discolor Inde, tuum,
non Mironis opus neque vivi marmoris artem.
  Sed peto, quod duro possit ab hoste dari:
ut liceat propriamque mihi consciscere mortem
  et miseram vitae praecipitare diem.
Est ea votorum species et summa meorum;
  his pro muneribus vox mea blanda fuit.

The people, the fathers blushed to see their ruler downcast and miserable as he spoke. Worthiness and good reputation pleaded for the good man, and did not allow his prayers to be fruitless. And the petition of a king is a forceful kind of command, and he supplicates as if with sword unsheathed. "Let it be granted," say the people, the senators, the tribunes; the single utterance of all was "let it be granted." They grant, then, whatever he asks, unconditionally, though he should demand all the wealth of the Latian city. Nor is your chaste bed exempted, Lucretia, nor the fiery gift that fell before sacrificing Numa.

As Patricida saw that his prayers would be heard, and realized that all was going according to his wishes, "Behold, tribe of Romulus," he said, "for what gift I have been ambitious, and what you have granted me. By no means did I wish to add to our wealth; our abundance has reached its limit. And neither wealthy Latium nor the wide world possesses anything whereby my eminence could be made greater. Not Phrygian jewels, or the dyes of the eastern peoples, not those riches which Pactolus and Hermus toss about, not Tyrian robes, or horses from the Iberian lands, not ivory, or your ebony, dark-skinned Indian; not the work of Miro, or the art that brings marble to life. Instead I seek what could be granted by a cruel enemy: that it be permitted me to inflict my own death, and hasten the last day of my wretched life. This is the shape and substance of my prayer; my gentle plea was for this reward.

Induperatorem quem tu tibi, Roma, crearas
  et dederas populi publica iura tui,
nonnisi vel populo vel concedente senatu
  vult libertatem mortis habere suae.
Munus, Roma, tuum mors est mea; nescia peccas,
  defenditque tuum nubilus error opus.
Simplicitas populi, pietas elusa senatus
  non poterit nostri sanguinis esse rea.
Sed neque blanditiis me sollicitate, Quirites,
  neve supervacuas multiplicate preces;
proposito descire suo coeptisque moveri
  nostra nequit ratio, sed sibi fixa manet.
Quaesivi; nec ego iam non quaesisse nociva
  munera nec populus non tribuisse potest.
Doctus et extensae mentis famaeque prioris
  astrologus nobis prodigiosa canit.
Dicit enim sic pensa trium fusosque sororum
  volvere, sic cursus sidera ferre suos,
ut perimat Patricida patrem carumque cruorem
  fundat et incipiat turpiter esse nocens.
Sive meam vidit natalem Scorpius horam
  sive Sagittiferi stella timenda senis;
aut gravis alterutro Saturnus inhaeserat astro,
  fuderat aut virus Martia stella suum;
dum puram puro licuit sub corpore mentem
  esse nec ad scelerum perniciosa trahi,
innocuae placuit vitae felicior usus.
  Illo crimen erat tempore velle mori;
nunc, quia compellor turpi sordescere culpa
  abstrahor et vitae simplicitate meae,

"He whom you, O Rome, established as your emperor, entrusting to him the governance of your people, does not wish to claim the freedom to effect his death unless the people and the senate give their assent. Your gift, O Rome, is my death. You sin unknowingly, cloudy ignorance excuses your act. The simplicity of the people, the mistaken devotion of the Senate cannot be deemed guilty of causing my death.

"But do not trouble me with tenderness, my citizens, nor keep repeating useless prayers; my mind cannot abandon its purpose or be diverted from what it has undertaken, but remains steadfast. I have made my request; I am now unable not to request this hurtful gift, nor can my people not grant it. A learned astrologer of far-ranging mind and superior reputation, prophesies monstrous things to us. For he says that the spinning of the three sisters so unrolls, the stars pursue their courses in such a way, that Patricida must kill his father, shed blood dear to him, and become a vile criminal. Whether Scorpio oversaw the hour of my birth, or the fearful star of the aged Archer; whether cruel Saturn clung to either sign, or the star of Mars poured forth its poison; while I was permitted a pure mind in a pure body, and was driven to no ruinous crimes, the blessed enjoyment of a blameless life was my pleasure. In those days to wish to die was a crime; now, because I am compelled to defile myself with foul guilt, and I am withdrawn from the simplicity of

aethereos haustus, animam, partemque caducam
corpus ab alterutro dissociare libet.
In latebras animae gladius penetrabit adactus,
profluet et vitae maxima causa cruor.
Discutiet ferrum carnis mentisque tenorem
concordesque vices complacitamque fidem.
"Discutiet," dico: nec enim mea mens habitabit
corpoream vitio participante domum.
Nam velut opposita contraria fronte repugnant,
sic meus in vitium spiritus arma movet,
et mea mens oriunda polo cognataque stellis
naturae memor est principiique sui.
Et quia primores puros intelligit ortus,
filia splendoris noctis abhorret opus.
Noctis abhorret opus, altaeque capax rationis
spiritus ad carnis fluxa venire timet.
Nec mea sic carni mens ancillatur iniquae
nec sic descivit depuduitque semel,
frangat ut incoctum generoso pectus honesto
vel rigidos sensus culpa resolvat iners.
Ergo dum sancto mens est in corpore sancta
nilque super carnis conditione gemit;
secedat luteaque domo carnisque tenebris
vivificusque fomes aethereumque iubar;
in terram terrena caro, mens ignis ad ignem:
ad speciem redeat portio quaeque suam.
Corporis invisi caecis excedere claustris
non trepidat meritis mens mea tuta suis;
carnis ab excessu superos migrabit ad axes
sideris in numerum restituenda sui.

my life, it is my wish to separate that ethereal spirit, my soul, and my perishable bodily portion from one another. The sword's thrust will penetrate the hidden seat of my soul, and blood, the main source of life, will pour forth. Steel will sever the bond of body and spirit, their harmonious interactions and mutual compact. 'Sever,' I say: for my mind will not abide in a bodily home where sin has a place. For just as opposites repel when confronted with their contraries, so my spirit takes up arms against sin, and my mind, sprung from high heaven, kindred to the stars, is mindful of its nature and its source. And because it understands its pure and noble origin, as the child of splendor it abhors the work of darkness. My spirit, capable of lofty thoughts, abhors the work of darkness, and fears to join the unstable life of the flesh. My mind is not so subservient to the hurtful flesh, has never been so abandoned or so shameless that enervating sin might assail a breast imbued with nobility and honor, or weaken my strength of mind. Thus while blessed mind exists in a pure body, and sheds no tears over its fleshly state; let this life-giving flame, this ethereal radiance withdraw from its muddy home, the darkness of the flesh; let each portion return to its kind, earthly flesh to earth, fiery mind to fire. My mind, secure in its merit, does not fear to go forth from the dark confines of the blind body; once departed from the flesh it will journey to the high heavens, to

Iocundum felixque mori cur abnegat, aut cur
  Roma mihi campos invidet Elysios?
Depositae post carnis onus cognata revisam
  sidera iam vita liberiore fruens,
rebus prospiciam Latiis urbique timebo
  maiorisque feram sedulitatis opem."
Argumenta movent perplexaque verba Quirites,
  non data, quae dederint, arte probare volunt.
"Non decet aut decuit rigidum sanctumque senatum
  argumentosa calliditate loqui,
Enthymema sonat, sonat hinc inductio. Varus
  verba per anfractus fertque refertque vagos.
Nescio quid magnum tacite concludere temptat
  et logica sensim me ratione ligat;
sed tamen argutis non est ea lingua sophistis,
  ut valeant coepto me removere meo.
Eloquitur vultumque sui sermonis inaurat
  Pollio facundi pectoris arma movens;
suadet, adornat, agit oratoremque figurat,
  alterat arte modos, alterat arte locos.
Non ea depictae venus est aut gratia voci,
  quae mea praevertat vota meumque mori.
Agrestis tam veste fuit quam voce Camillus,
  gratus apud superos rusticitate sua.
Non pictis nugis rigidi placuere Catones;
  sermo patens illis et sine veste fuit.
Agresti Latio monstravit Graecia blandum,
  Graecia perplexum, Graecia grande loqui.
O gravis illa dies, qua simplex et rude verum
  sorduit et picti plus placuere soni!

be restored to the place of its star. Why does Rome deny me a happy and fortunate death, why should she begrudge me the Elysian Fields? Once my fleshly burden is laid aside I will see my native stars again, and enjoy a freer life at last. Viewing Latin affairs from on high I will fear for the city, and I will be greatly concerned to protect her."

The citizens present arguments cunningly phrased, and seek to prove by this skill that what they have given was not given. "It is not proper and has never been proper for the stern and hallowed senate to speak with artful argumentation, here a resounding enthymeme, there a proof. Varus repeatedly brings forth ambiguous and rambling words. I know not what great conclusion he is secretly attempting to draw, as he binds me little by little with logical argument; however, not by the speech of clever sophists can they draw me back from what I have undertaken. Pollio is eloquent, and gilds the surface of his speech, wielding the weapons of his fluent mind; he persuades, elaborates, argues, plays the orator, artfully changes his style, artfully changes his proofs. But in a painted speech there is not the beauty or charm that might prevent the death I desire. Camillus was a farmer, in both dress and speech, but he was loved by the gods for his country ways. The stern Catos did not make themselves pleasing with painted trifles; their speech was clear and unadorned. Greece revealed smooth, ambiguous, grandiloquent speech to uncouth Latium. O unhappy day, when plain and simple truth became vile, and decorated tones

Aequor inaccessas utinam fecisset Athenas:
non foret eloquii Roma nitore nocens.
Quidve quibusve dabit, si nostras ipsius ibit
tam leve despectum Romula turba preces,
qui suus illorum dominus Latiique iacentis
captivas aquilas victor ab hoste tuli
aeternique probri maculas et crimina tersi,
rursus et induitur Roma colore suo?
Si nihil Ausonios exorans purpura tangit
personaeque meae gratia surda perit,
at mecum faciunt legum decreta meisque
vocibus assensum littera praebet anus:
ex olim meus est orator Iustinianus;
viventis causam mortua lingua facit.
Non auctore levi neque verbo paupere nitor,
arbiter in toto maximus orbe fuit:
'Dux populi victor munus, quod quaerit, habeto.'
Dux ego, victor ego, munera quaero: date.
Sed quia muneribus vestri fungatur honoris,
rex ideo vester desinit esse suus.
Pono citus trabeam, vestrum citus exuo regem
liber et explicitus ad mea vota, meus."

* * *

[The following lines are added at the end of the poem in Kraków, Biblioteka Jagiellońska, MS theol. oct. 94:]

Dixerat: hinc serpit murmur, tonat inde tumultus,
scinditur in varias turbida Roma vices.
Ipse caput dextram corpus diademate sceptro
purpureis privat rex sine rege manens.

were preferred! Would that the sea had made Athens inaccessible: Rome would not then be guilty of brilliant eloquence.

"What will the tribe of Romulus give, and to whom, if it will so readily show contempt for my prayers; I, their ruler, the victor who took back from the enemy the captured eagle-standards of defeated Latium, who wiped away the taint and guilt of eternal dishonor, so that Rome is once again decked with her proper color? If the plea of the purple touches the Ausonians not at all, and gratitude, deaf to the role I have played, falls away, yet the determinations of the law support me, and an ancient text offers approval for my appeal: my spokesman from of old is Justinian; the words of the dead plead the case of the living. I lean on no petty authority and no negligible words; he was the foremost judge in all the world: 'Let the leader of the people, the victor, be granted the gift he seeks.' I am the Leader, the victor, I seek a gift: grant it.

"But because he administers offices with which you have honored him, your king ceases to be his own man. I quickly lay aside my royal robes, quickly cease to be your king—my own man, set free to pursue my goal."

* * *

[Additional lines from Kraków, Biblioteka Jagiellońska, MS theol. oct. 94:]

He had spoken. A murmur gradually rises, then the sound becomes an uproar. A troubled Rome is divided into different factions. Patricida removes the crown from his head, the scepter from his hand, the purple robes from his body, and is left a king without kingship.

At pater in medio linguam sibi poscit; inaurat
castigata fides, vita probata loqui:

Pater

Patres, qui bella frenatis in otia, quorum
cervicosa pedi colla subacta iacent,
quorum discreta ratio, mens provida, quorum
dens sale conditus et sine dente sales,
advigilate viri votis: non danda requirit.
Qui repetenda petit; impetret absque tamen.

Patricida

Me nisi pro merito donent, nisi vota secundent,
si concessa mihi, si data turpe negent,
fortes e merita plangent virtute dabuntque,
qui bello dederant pectora, terga fugae.

Pater

Te nisi pro merito servent, nisi vota restringant,
ni non danda tibi iure neganda negent,
desperata ruet virtus; taedebit ephebos,
quod veniant meritis praemia surda suis.

Iudices

Vel dampni votum vel dampna suae probitatis
quis sapienter amat, quis patienter habet?

But his father amid the crowd demands the right to speak; his modest integrity and upright life enhance his words:

Father

Fathers, who reduce war to peace, beneath whose feet the necks of obstinate enemies lie subdued, whose judgment is discerning, whose minds are prudent, whose harshness is seasoned with wit, and whose wit is not harsh, be wary of the appeal of this man; he seeks what should not be given. Though he gain his request, he seeks what should be taken back from him.

Patricida

If they do not reward me as I deserve, if they do not grant my wishes, if they basely deny me what has been granted and given, brave men will mourn for virtue unrewarded, and those who had exposed their breasts in battle will turn their backs in flight.

Father

If they do not treat you as you deserve, if they do not check your wishes, if they do not withhold what should not be granted to you, being forbidden by law, virtue will fall into despair; young men will be disgusted that reward remains deaf to their merit.

Judges

Who that is wise can love, who that is patient can endure a vow of self-destruction or the destruction of a man's good

Munera pro meritis pensentur, nec probitatem
  improbet aut reprobos approbet ipse dator,
sed peccata cruce, sed fortia laude. Sed isti?
  Sed dentur meritis consona cuique suis.

character? Let gifts be weighed according to merit, and let
the giver neither discredit probity nor give credit to the rep-
robate, but let sins be punished, brave deeds praised. But 25a
as for him? Let each be granted what is appropriate to his
merits.

THE TWINS

De Gemellis

Roma duos habuit—res est, non fabula vana.
Auctores perhibent et pagina Quintiliana:
fuderat ut geminos labor unus parturiendi.
Sic fuerant similes forma specieque videndi,
et sic miscuerat color unus utrumque decorum,
quod vox una foret discretio sola duorum.
Quos ita Naturae manus ingeniosa potentis
finxerat ex anima vel corporeis elementis,
ut meminisse queat nihil in rerum genitura,
cui sit tantus honos vel tam speciosa figura.
Plurima cum desint felicibus ad sua vota,
fluxit ad hos solos rerum perfectio tota.
Quos tamen excoluit elementis sic moderatis,
ut nihil esset eis de labe superfluitatis.
In quibus expressit tanti moderaminis artem,
quod nullam voluit minus aut magis addere partem.
Fecit, et intuitis pede, mento, nare, capillis,
tunc magis artificem sese cognovit in illis.
Turpis ad hos, puer ante Iovem qui pocula ponis;
turpis eris, Memnon, et tu quoque turpis, Adonis.
  Felicique diu vixisset uterque iuventa,
ni foret ante diem sibi lux vitalis adempta.
Sed rota Fortunae, numquam rarove fidelis,
non sinit ut vivat homo longo tempore felix.
Cum velit humanae pacem turbare quietis,

The Twins

Rome possessed two—and this is fact, not mere fable. Ancient authors and the pages of Quintilian attest it: a single act of parturition brought forth twins. They were so similar to behold in form and appearance, and the same beautiful complexion had so imbued them both, that name alone was the sole means of distinguishing them. The inventive hand of powerful Nature had so fashioned them, from soul or from the physical elements, that she could recall nothing among her works that possessed such grace or so beautiful a form. Though many things might be lacking that would make her creations as well favored as she could wish, all creaturely perfection flowed into these two alone. Yet she had fashioned them from elements so carefully managed that there was no trace of excess in them. In them she had given expression to an art of such skill that she wished neither to increase nor reduce any part. She fashioned them, and looking upon foot, chin, nose, and hair, by these she knew herself to be a greater artist. Compared to them, O boy who sets the goblet before Jove, you will appear ugly; you will be ugly, Memnon, and you as well, Adonis.

Each would have lived out a happy youth, had not the light of life been taken from him untimely. But Fortune's wheel, never or rarely to be trusted, will not allow a man to live happy for a long time. When she wishes to disturb the peace of human tranquility, she inflicts on happy people the

invehit infirmi mala corporis, invida laetis.
Sic igitur, sicut similes parilesve fuere,
sic paribus fatis incepit utrerque dolere:
una mali species, eadem fortuna doloris,
isdem quippe modis et eisdem scilicet horis.
  Ut dolor incaluit morbique molestia crevit,
protinus et speciem formaeque notas abolevit.
Qui nunc ergo genas et nunc ornaverat ora,
et calor et sanguis secessit ad interiora;
quinque iacent sensus in corpore mortificati.
Cernere non possunt oculi languore gravati;
non valet escarum guttur sentire sapores;
non sentit tractanda manus, neque naris odores;
surdescunt aures et deficit usus earum.
Sic oblita iacet rerum natura suarum.
  Sed pater inde dolens implorat opem medicorum,
et venere duo: Graecus fuit alter eorum.
Ergo per urinas et venis saepe notatis
quaerunt unde fluant tantae mala debilitatis.
Sed nec in urinis vel pulsibus inspicientes
morborum causas potuerunt scire latentes.
Vincuntur medici; perit et sollertia Graeca;
saevit adhuc morbusque latens et passio caeca.
  "Quis modus his morbis? Quis finis ad hos cruciatus?"
Sic pater ad medicos. Respondit uterque rogatus:
"Cum simili morbo videamus utrumque gravari,
causa latet morbi, neuterque potest relevari,
ni prius alterius in visceribus videamus,
quis sit et unde fluat dolor, unde modo dubitamus.

hateful evils of bodily infirmity. Therefore, as the twins were similar or identical, so both began to suffer identical fates: a single type of illness, the same portion of suffering, of the same kind and at the same time.

As their suffering intensified and the effect of the illness increased, it quickly ruined their outward appearance and all traces of beauty. The warmth and blood which only now had brightened their faces and cheeks withdrew inward; the five bodily senses lay as if dead. The eyes, overcome by faintness, could not see; the throat was unable to perceive the flavors of food; the hand did not feel the things it must hold, nor could the nose sense odors; the ears grew deaf and ceased to function. Thus the nature of the world lay forgotten by them.

But the father in grief appealed to physicians for aid, and two appeared, one of whom was a Greek. They sought, through urine, and frequent study of the veins, whence an illness so debilitating might have arisen. But neither in urine nor through examining the pulses were they able to discern the hidden causes of the disease. The physicians are defeated; the subtle knowledge of Greece has failed; the lurking disease and its hidden fever still rage.

"What limit will there be to this disease? What end to this suffering?" The father asks the physicians. Each responds to his question: "Since we observe that both are afflicted by the same disease, and the cause is hidden, neither can be relieved unless we may first observe, in the entrails of one of them, what the illness is about which we are now in

Quilibet ut pereat, vitium redimet medicina;
si geminis parcas, germinos trahet una ruina."
  Sed pater, hoc fieri cernens opus atque necesse,
maluit unius quam nullius pater esse.
Ergo dedit medicis quemcumque magis voluerunt.
Membra secant, sedemque mali per viscera quaerunt.
(Scilicet in caeso medicorum cura notavit
quicquid in humanis membris Natura creavit.)
Inveniunt causamque mali morbumque latentem;
sic alium curant simili languore iacentem.
  Sed mater, gavisa nihil de sospite nato,
semper in alterius nati dolet anxia fato.
Ergo gemens alium velut a genitore necatum,
in ius, in causam patrem trahit ante senatum.
Femina, sicut erat magis ad lites animata,
sic prior inquit: "Eram geminorum prole beata;
hunc peto, qui minus est mihi de numero geminorum,
quem pater exstinxit et iniqua manus medicorum.
Ferro, non morbo periit puer ille peremptus,
cum sua fortassis curaret utrumque iuventus.
Aeger erat plane, tamen ex hoc non moreretur,
cum suus ex simili frater morbo relevetur."
  Responsurus ad haec surgit pater atque profatur,
seque parat verbis legalibus ut tueatur:
"Feminei sexus satis ostendens levitatem,
dum modo damna vides, neque cernis ad utilitatem.
Ni videat medicus prius unius interiora,
curaret neutrum, sed utrumque trahet gravis hora.

doubt, and whence it arises. That one of them must die is a difficulty which our medical art will make good; if you spare both twins, a single doom will bear both away."

But the father, recognizing that it was necessary and inevitable that this be done, preferred to be the father of one child rather than none. Thus he granted to the physicians whichever child they wished. They cut into the body and seek the source of the illness within. (Indeed the astuteness of physicians has observed through such incision whatever Nature has done in creating the human body.) They find the cause of the illness, the lurking disease, and thus cure the other child laid low by the same weakness.

But the mother, not at all happy because one son is cured, grieves continually, distressed by the fate of her other son. Thus in her grief, as though the other son had been killed by his father, she draws the father into a legal proceeding, a suit, before the Senate. As a woman, she is more inclined to quarrel; thus she speaks first: "I was blessed with the birth of twin sons; my plea concerns one who now has been subtracted from the number of the twins, whom his father and the hostile hands of the physicians have destroyed. This boy did not die of a disease, but was put to death with a knife, though perhaps their youth might have cured them both. He was ill to be sure, yet he might not have died from this, since his brother was delivered from the same disease."

The father rises to respond to this, and speaks; he is prepared with legal language to protect himself: "you make quite plain the shallow-mindedness of the feminine sex when you see only the death, and do not discern its useful purpose. If the physician had not first seen the innards of one of the boys, he would have cured neither, but a grim

Arguor unde magis potuit laus nostra venire,
nam minus est unum quam binos velle perire.
Si duo contingant aliquando pericula dura,
ex illis facimus minus et levius nocitura."
Res ut facta fuit et disceptatio talis,
diffinivit eam sententia iudicialis.

hour would have taken both. I am accused on grounds from which praise might rather come to us, for it is a lesser matter to will the death of one than of two. If at another time cruel danger befalls two persons, by this example we may reduce and alleviate the harm."

When an event and a dispute of this kind took place, the opinion of the judges made a determination.

THE UNGRATEFUL PAUPER

De paupere ingrato

Maesta parens miserae paupertas anxietatis
afflictis satis est dura superque satis.
Infelix quidam, sic ductus ad ultima rerum,
quod genus omne mali deprimeret miserum.
Exosus vitam, ne semper egeret egenus,
elegit laqueum mortis habere genus.
Collaque subiciens laqueo, quem sponte ligarat,
ut finire malum possit, obire parat.
Iam quodcumque potest homo morte doloris habere
senserat in laqueo mortuus ille fere,
cum celer accurrens quidam sibi vincula rupit
et facit ut vivat qui periisse cupit.
Ut tandem linguae vox reddita, spiritus ori,
quaerit et agnoscit cur velit ille mori.
Compatiens igitur miserandae pauperiei
mensibus undenis cuncta ministrat ei.
Cum satis afflicto dominus fecisse putaret,
destitit et placuit ne sibi plura daret.
Redditus antiquae miser anxius asperitati
flevit et incepit rursus amara pati;
et solitum referens ex paupertate dolorem,
"Utilius," dixit, "mortuus ante forem."
Ergo virum, furca qui solverat illaqueatum,
protrahit in causam iudicis ante statum,

The Ungrateful Pauper

Poverty, the grim parent of wretched anxiety, is harsh enough, more than enough, on those it afflicts.

A certain unfortunate man was driven to a state so extreme that every kind of evil burdened his wretchedness. He hated his life, and so that his neediness might not be endlessly in need, he decided to make a noose his means of death. That he might put an end to the ills of life he placed his neck in the noose, which he himself had strung up, and prepared to die. Nearly dead, he had already undergone in the noose whatever pain a man can feel in dying, when another man, running swiftly to him, broke his bonds, and caused to live one who had wished to perish. At length, as speech was restored to his tongue and breath to his mouth, the other sought to know why he wished to die. Then, out of compassion for his pitiable poverty, this man provided for all his needs for eleven months.

When this master considered that he had done enough for the unfortunate one, he ceased, and determined to give him no more. The wretched and unhappy man, returned to his harsh condition of old, wept and began again to suffer hardship; feeling again the familiar grief of poverty he said, "It would have been better for me to die before."

Therefore he draws into a lawsuit, before the judicial authority, the man who had released him from the gallows unhanged, and brings a charge against this man, who had

et causatur eum, qui mortis ruperat horam,
  cum nullam vitae vellet habere moram,
et quia sub laqueo iam senserat exitiali
  quicquid habere potest mors inimica mali.
Ergo sub adstricto legum discrimine quaerit
  iudicium, rursus cum moriturus erit,
cur vel egere sinat quem non sinit ut moriatur.
  Res haec iudicibus discutienda datur.

interrupted the hour of his death, when he wished to have not a moment more of life, and had already experienced in the fatal noose whatever evil is harbored by cruel death. Thus he seeks in strict legal terms a judgment as to why, when once again he shall be about to die, the man allows him to live in poverty though he does not allow him to die.

This matter is presented for consideration by the judges.

Note on the Texts

In twelfth-century orthography most manuscripts no longer distinguish *ae* or *oe,* using *e* for both. We have restored the diphthongs to their classical spelling. We distinguish consonantal *v* from vocalic *u.* We have replaced *michi* and *nichil* with *mihi* and *nihil,* replaced *j* with *i,* and words containing palatalized *ti-,* commonly spelled *ci-,* have been restored to classical spelling.

Cosmographia

The *Cosmographia* survives in at least fifty manuscripts.[1] A large number of these omit *Microcosmus* 8,[2] some contain only the verse portions of the work, some offer only selections of the verse. As noted in the Introduction, Florence, Biblioteca Medicea MS Laurentiana XXXIII 31 is written in the hand of Boccaccio.

The first edition, by Barach and Wrobel, is based on two manuscripts, which the editors themselves acknowledged to be inferior: Munich, Stadtbibliothek, Clm 23434, and Vienna, Österreichische Nationalbibliothek, MS 526. The text is carelessly edited, the choice of readings is often poor, and the apparatus is minimal.

The edition of Vernet, a dissertation that was never published, is excellent. It gives a full account of all the manuscripts known to the editor in 1937, but it is based mainly on four: Paris, Bibliothèque Nationale, MSS lat. 6752A and 14194; London, British Library, MS Sloane 2477; Rome, Biblioteca Vaticana, MS Pal. lat. 53. It includes a full apparatus criticus, extensive notes on sources, and a long and informative introduction on Bernardus and his intellectual milieu.

Dronke's *textus minor,* based on a single manuscript, Oxford, Bodleian Laud misc. 515 (13th century), but drawing on seven additional French and English manuscripts, accompanies the text with compact discussions of the structure, style, and language of the *Cosmographia,* and a selection of "testimonies," mainly from late Antique Neoplatonism that define the tradition in which Bernardus undoubtedly saw himself as working.

My text is that of Dronke, with a minimum of emendations, suggested by Vernet and by my own examination of twenty French and English manuscripts of the *Cosmographia.*

Mathematicus

There are seventeen known manuscripts of the *Mathematicus,* three of them florilegia containing only excerpts. In three manuscripts the poem is attributed to Bernardus, and in five it is juxtaposed with the *Cosmographia.* As Godman shows ("Ambiguity," 599–604), Bernardus's authorship was acknowledged in France for at least 150 years.

The *Mathematicus* was first edited, from what is now Paris, Bibliothèque Nationale, MS Lat. 5129, by Beaugendre in his edition of the *Opera* of Hildebert of Le Mans. This text was reprinted, with slight adjustments to orthography and punctuation, by J. J. Bourassé in PL 171. Hauréau in his edition of 1895 emended the text of Beaugendre using four of the eleven manuscripts known to him.

My text is based on the edition of Prelog, Heim, and Kiesslich, who examine and classify all the manuscripts. I have adopted a few readings from the edition of D'Alessandro, which offers a text close to theirs based on a similar classification of the manuscripts. The edition of Stone is based on a single twelfth-century manuscript, Tours, Bibliothèque Municipale, MS 300. The editor draws on the full tradition to emend her text but follows this manuscript too uncritically, and several of her readings are unacceptable on grammatical or metrical grounds.

In Kraków, Biblioteka Jagiellonska, MS theol. oct. 94 (the shelf-mark is that of its former home, the Preussische Staatsbibliothek, Berlin), a couplet is inserted after line 248, and twenty-six lines are added to the end of the poem. These were first printed by Wattenbach ("Beschreibung," 438), and in transcribing them I have adopted two of his emendations.

In 2007, Bertini, "Un nuovo manoscritto," announced his discovery of MS Metz, Bibliothèque Municipale 647, a fifteenth-century manuscript that contains lines 1 to 642 of the *Mathematicus,* with three lacunae totaling twenty-seven lines, and adds a conclusion of six somewhat awkward verses.

De Gemellis

The poem survives in eleven manuscripts, in two of which, Paris, Bibliothèque Nationale, MS latin 6415, and Rome,

Biblioteca Vaticana, MS Reg. lat. 370, it follows the *Mathematicus.* The edition of Fierville is based on St. Omer, Bibliothèque Municipale, MS 115, which presents the fullest version, with corrections from Paris, BN MS lat. 6415. The edition of Werner employs the St. Omer manuscript, with Vienna, Österreichische Nationalbibliothek, MS 609, and Zurich, Zentralbibliothek, MS C.58. My text, with one emendation, is that of Edwards, a critical edition based on Fierville's Paris manuscript.

De Paupere Ingrato

The poem follows *De gemellis* in four of the six manuscripts, including the two which also contain the *Mathematicus.* The manuscripts present the poem in versions varying from eighteen to thirty-two lines. The edition of du Méril is based on Paris, Bibliothèque Nationale lat. 6415, that of Auvray on Rome, Biblioteca Vaticana, MS Reg. lat. 370. Both manuscripts omit lines 23 to 26 of the text as printed here. Vernet presents the full text, based on these two manuscripts, St. Omer 115, and Angers, Bibliothèque Municipale, MS 241. The text of Edwards, which I offer here with two emendations, is based on Angers 241.

Notes

1 Dronke, ed. *Cosm.,* 64–66, lists forty-six manuscripts, and his "Bernardo Silvestre" adds four more.

2 Of the twenty-seven manuscripts known to Vernet that contain full versions of the *Cosmographia,* only six include *Microcosmus* 8. Vernet accepts the poem's authenticity and suggests that a leaf may have been lost from the archetype manuscript ("Bernardus Silvestris," 222–24).

Notes to the Texts

Cosmographia

BW = Barach Wrobel
Dr = Dronke
L = Oxford, Bodleian Library, MS Laud misc. 515
V = Vernet

Meg. 1.39 intra BW V: inter L Dr
Meg. 2.9 importare, ubi BW V: inportare, ut L Dr
Meg. 3.80 praeiacet BW V: postiacet L Dr
Meg. 3.168 humo BW V: humi L Dr
Meg. 3.292 coctana pallescunt, punica mala rubent BW V: coctaneus pallor, ceraseusque rubor L Dr
Meg. 3.351–52 *om.* V L Dr
Meg. 3.371 notis V: togis BW L Dr
post Meg. 3.440 *add.* V: Commendat Ligurim darsus, parilisque saporis, / stagna lacusque timens, longior umbra natat.
Micr. 1.1 num ad BW V: nunc ad L Dr
officiosa BW V: officio L Dr
Micr. 1.3 quem ratio BW V: quam ratio L Dr
duraret, si BW V: duraret, sed L Dr
Micr. 5.11 annuo Sol circumfertur V BW: annuo circumfertur L Dr
Micr. 5.18 Lunae mediantis BW V L: linee mediantis Dr
Micr. 6.27 relinquunt BW V: relinquit L Dr
Micr. 7.6 infimantur BW V: infirmantur L Dr
Micr. 7.11 illic Silvani BW V: illi Silvani L Dr
Micr. 8.29 cum sit mens ignea, cumque BW V: mens ignea, cumque repugnant L Dr

Micr. 10.24 curam BW V: causam L Dr
Micr. 11.3 dedero fuerit BW V: de deo fuerint L Dr
Micr. 11.5 ministra Mundo BW V L: ministra modo Dr
Micr. 11.10 provideri BW V: pervideri L Dr
Micr. 11.11 In tanta igitur V BW: Tanta igitur L Dr
Micr. 13.3 Obviam . . . execravit: *om.* L Dr
Micr. 13.9 qualitates: qualia *add.* L Dr
Micr. 14.40 sopor BW V L: sapor Dr
Micr. 14.49 sede BW V: sedet L Dr
Micr. 14.90 cibo V BW: suo L Dr
Micr. 14.95 deliciosa BW V: perniciosa L Dr
Micr. 14.118 munere BW V: nomine L Dr

The Astrologer

D = D'Alessandro
K = Kraków, Biblioteca Jagiellonska MS Theol. lat. oct. 94
M = Metz, Bibliotheque Municipale MS 647
PHK = Prelog, Heim, Kiesslich
S = Stone
Wa = Wattenbach

25–36 *om.* M
39–42 *om.* M
61–71 *om.* M
Post 248 *add.* K: Ergo—nec invideo—trabeati sceptra Quirini / accedent meritis gloria multa tuis.
257 ille D: ipse PHK S
287 mariti D S: maritum PHK
369 memini *scripsi:* meminit PHK D S
456 decus D S: decor PHK
463 occursum D: occursus PHK S
Post 642 *add.* M: Si sapimus, vel non, vel si ratione caremus / nil valet: ad fatum cuncta necesse fiunt. / At si fata regunt viventia cuncta sub astris, / cur homini ratio postea iuncta fuit? / Absitque fato vivamus non ratione: / vulgus iners credat, respuat hoc sapiens.

643–854	*om.* M
721	petat D S: petit PHK
763	fatalem D (771) S (821): natalem PHK
796	fomes D: comes PHK S (786)
12a	repetenda Wa PHK D: repetanda K S
19a	ruet Wa D: tuet K PHK S

The Twins

E = Edwards
W = Werner

6	vox sola W: vox una E

The Ungrateful Pauper

E = Edwards
V = Vernet

21	referens V: repetens E
30	cum V: cur E

Notes to the Translations

The numbering of notes to the prose chapters of the *Cosmographia* corresponds to that of the paragraphs to which they refer.

Cosmographia

On the term *cosmographia,* Stock, *Myth and Science,* 21. In Cassiodorus, *Institutiones* 1.25, it denotes a description of the world or geography. In Isidore, 6.2.1, and in the preface to Peter Comestor, *Historia Scholastica* (PL 198.1054A), it is used of the five scriptural books attributed to Moses.

Summary

Dronke, ed. *Cosm.,* 156, questions the authorship of the Summary, on the grounds that it contains several expressions that do not appear in the *Cosmographia* proper and does not exhibit Bernardus's characteristic use of the *cursus* (rhythmical endings to prose sentences). Its suggestive language, however, seems intended to evoke the character of Bernardus's prose.

2 *Speculatio* presumably refers to the three mirrors, or *specula,* that Noys presents to her three subordinates.

On the creation of man from "the remainder of the elements," *Timaeus* 41D, 42E.

feliciter is commonly used in the various formulae with which a scribe indicates the end of a text he has copied.

Megacosmus 1

4–5 On the punctuation and interpretation of these lines, see Dronke, ed. *Cosm.,* 163.

6 Silverstein, "Fabulous Cosmogony," 111, notes that the hymn to Pallas/Minerva that opens Martianus, Book 6, uses language very similar to lines 5 and 6 here, and line 6 of the hymn calls the goddess "the sacred Νοῦς of gods and men."

15 On the absence of envy in the divine as a factor in creation, *Timaeus* 29E.

22 Eriugena speaks of unformed matter as "desiring to be formed by the various numbers of sensible creatures," *Periphyseon* 2.549B. A gloss in MS Laud misc. 515, which contains a number of glosses not found in other manuscripts, explains *musica vincla* as "such consonance and convenience (*convenientia:* agreement, harmony) as the elements now possess."

57 Dronke, ed. *Cosm.,* 164, suggests that Silva, as well as Noys, is addressed here, but see Löfstedt, "Notizen," 203.

58 Bernardus mentions *carentia* only here and in *Meg.* 2.2. Calcidius, citing Aristotle, assigns *carentia* the status of a "principle." See *Meg.* 2.2n.

Megacosmus 2

1 On God as *Usia prima,* Apuleius, *De dogmate Platonis* 1.6.

de composito, "by agreement": Apuleius, *Apologia* 1.

efficientia, "power" or "influence" in Cicero, *Nat. D.* 2.37.95, and in early Christian theology, seems here to depend on *efficio* in the sense of "produce" or "effect."

2 *Silvestris* here has the double sense of "material" *(Silva)* and "rough" or "uncultivated."

Bernardus has altered the meaning of *discursio,* which in most earlier instances refers, like the more common *discursus,* to random, ungoverned movement.

With *vultibus incompositis* compare *Paradise Lost* 2.989: Milton's Chaos, too, appears "with visage incomposed."

Usiae . . . melius was apparently corrupted at an early stage, and my translation is tentative. The dissatisfaction Noys seems to express is heard again in *Micr.* 10.5–8.

Privation *(carentia),* Aristotle's στέρησις (*Phys.* 1.9.191b–92b), is cited by Calcidius, 288, as the source of the *malitia* in *silva,* though Aristotle states that the impulse to *malitia* must originate in matter itself (192a.15.25), for only matter can desire. *Comm.* 297–300 imputes evil to the perversity of Silva. *Comm.* 301 attributes to certain later Platonists the view that the evil in matter is *carentia virtutis,* "a lack of virtue," and *Comm.* 352 suggests that since Silva is in itself immobile, its chaotic movement (*Timaeus* 52D–53B) is not a symptom of evil, but a consequence of the intrusion of external "principles and elements." On inconsistencies in Calcidius's account, Whitman, *Allegory,* 172–75. On *carentia* in the *Cosmographia,* Asper, *"Silva Parens,"* 138–41.

4 My translation of *formarum prima subiectio* is based on Calcidius, 316, which asserts that Silva is none of the elements, but "the principal material and primal ground of a body *(corporis prima subiectionem).*"

5 In translating *essentiis* as "substances" rather than "essences," I follow the suggestion of Professor John Magee that Bernardus is recalling the discussion of substance, quality, and quantity in Aristotle, *Categories,* 4–6.

6 This paragraph is broadly based on *Timaeus* 31C–32A.

7 Calcidius, 290–93, discusses the Stoic distinction between *essentia* and *elementum.* Bronze, gold, iron are the *materia* of which things are made, but their *essentia* is "the primal *silva* or most ancient foundation of all things." See Winden, *Calcidius on Matter,* 96–100.

8 On the suggestive diction of this paragraph, in which the original unwieldy energy of Hyle "shows through" the descriptionof the newly ordered elements, Bezner, *Vela Veritatis,* 438–39.

Bernardus apparently takes *refixior* as equivalent to *fixior,* though its actual meaning is "more unfixed," "more unstable."

9 The opening sentence is based on *Timaeus* 31B–32C, where the Demiurge establishes a "friendly" relationship among the four elements by means of geometrical proportion.

ponderatio, in classical Latin "weighing" or "balancing," is used of the gravity of manner of Philosophy in Fulgentius, *Mitologiae* 1, and of gravity in the physical sense by Bernardus.

10 On the universe as a "full and consummate whole," *Timaeus* 32C–33B.

My rendering of *citra operis sortem* is speculative.

In translating I assume that *ut erat promptum* is Bernardus's misunderstood equivalent to *in promptu erat.*

11 The phrase *imbecilla hominum natio* is drawn from Calcidius, 181.

The "causes" mentioned in the final line are apparently the vestiges of the earlier turbulent state of matter.

12 I understand *necessariis* not as an adjective but as "consequences of necessity," the threats to order discussed in the previous paragraph, "necessity" being matter, and the potential intractability of matter (*Timaeus* 47B–48A; Calcidius, 269–70). For *necessarium* as a noun, Calcidius 155.

I take *desecutis* as a mistake for *desectis.*

13 The phrase *summi et exsuperantissimi dei* echoes Apuleius, *De Platone* 1.12, which has *deorum omnium* in place of *dei.*

Since *in qua vitae viventis imagines,* etc. seems to refer to the immediately preceding *natura,* though the attributes described are clearly those of Noys, it would seem that the *natura* in question might be Noys, considered as daughter of God. But both Lemoine and Maccagnolo understand *ex eius divinitate nata est Natura* as referring to Natura, the daughter of Noys. Lemoine persuasively cites *Asclepius* 20, where "the goodness of all things" is called "a nature born of [God's] divinity," ensuring the continuance of natural life. Thus the *Natura* phrase is apparently a rather awkward parenthesis.

13 As Bezner, *Vela Veritatis,* 445–47, observes, the mirror to which the mind of Noys is compared both is and is not the mind of God. In it are reflected "eternal notions" and "the intelligible universe," but the emphasis of the description is on "the fabric of time, the chain of destiny, the disposition of the ages": it resembles Nature's Table of Destiny more than Urania's Mirror of Providence (*Micr.* 11.3–9). Like Plato's Demiurge, Noys is a

divine but not an absolute power, engaged on behalf of *deus summus et exsuperantissimus* with necessity and mortality in the created universe.

14 *praeconfundere* is used by Calcidius, in a phrase added to his translation of *Timaeus* 49B, to denote the difficulty of defining elements as "qualities" rather than "things."

As the phrase *fomes vivificus* suggests, Endelechia is a principle of physical life. Bernardus apparently draws on Calcidius, 222–25, a discussion of Aristotle's definition of ἐντελέχεια as the "primary perfection" of a natural body capable of life (*De anima* 2.1.412a.27–28), as well as Martianus, 1.7, where Psyche, the human soul, is identified as "daughter of Endelechia and the Sun." The commentary on Martianus explains the union of Sun and Endelechia as having produced only the portion of the soul that is bodily and subject to the influence of the stars (*Commentary,* ed. Westra, 143–44.431–56).

I take *singulis* as ablative, and *refundo* in its usual meaning of "pour back" or "restore," so that *cum . . . refundatur* explains how Endelechia endures perpetually. One might take *singulis* as dative and *refundo* as "pour forth," in which case the phrase would explain why Endelechia's power to endure is beyond understanding.

15 With Lemoine and Maccagnolo, I take *quod hactenus approbatur* to mean that the "marriage" between Endelechia and the material universe has endured until the present time. It could perhaps be taken to mean that Noys, here as earlier, approves of what she has accomplished thus far.

16 Firmicus Maternus, *Mathesis* 3.1.9, discusses the periodic destruction of the universe by *pyrosis* and *cataclysmus.* Both Dronke (ed. *Cosm.,* 31; "Nature and Personification," 26) and Stock (*Myth and Science,* 67–68, 81–86) take creation in the *Cosmographia* as a stage in a cyclical process of creation, destruction, and renewal. But at the outset Silva is not *dis*integrated but still *un*integrated (*informis adhuc, Meg.* 1.1), and the idea of periodic destruction and renewal seems inconsistent with Bernardus's repeated assertion that the universe enjoys perpetual

life, that "by its eternal exemplar it is made to endure eternally."

Megacosmus 3

3 On this line, in which *in* governs both *caelo* and *ministris,* Dronke, ed. *Cosm.,* 164; Pfeiffer, *Contemplatio Caeli,* 275–76.

4 The verb *primitio* is almost certainly Bernardus's coinage, though Dronke notes a deponent, *primitior,* in the Itala translation of Prov. 3:9. Compare *denihilo* (*Micr.* 14.178), *extenebro* (*Meg.* 3.386), *siccito* (*Micr.* 10.40).

5 The reference to "purer fire" is apparently contradicted by *Micr.* 3.9, where the firmament is said to be composed of a fifth element, "neither fire nor derived from fire." Calcidius, who seems to accept the idea of a "fifth body" (in *Comm.* 84, a difficult chapter), speaks in *Comm.* 129 of Plato's view that the highest heaven consists of "serene" fire, distinct from the grosser ethereal fire. Bernardus may have seen this passage as defining serene fire as a separate, fifth element.

17–18 Dronke, ed. *Cosm.,* 165, has explained this puzzling couplet as indicating not the hierarchical position of Noys herself but an inherent property of the Thrones: "Just as, in the preceding verses, the Cherubim are said to behold the mysteries of God, and the Seraphim to burn with an ardour which is God himself, so the Thrones have an indwelling presence of divine providence."

26 The Virtues are embodiments of *virtus,* "power," in their case miraculous.

33 I am assuming that the *divina manus* of line 3 above is that of Noys, and that Noys is the subject of *scribit* here.

39 Phoroneus was the son of Inachus and king of Argos, reputedly the first ruler to gather people into cities, and for Isidore, 5.1.1, the first giver of laws to the Greeks.

47 "Milo" is the sculptor Myron of Eleuthera (fifth century BCE), mentioned also in *Math.* 737. He is a painter in Alan of Lille, *Anticlaudianus* 6.229–30.

55 On Eugenius, Introduction, vii, and n. 2.

59–60 See *Timaeus* 36E, 38BC, where the circular movement of the heavens in time is explained as the moving image of eternity; also Dronke, ed. *Cosm.*, 165.

61–63 On the zones, Virgil, *Geo.* 1.233–39; Claudian, *Rapt. Pros.* 1.259–65; Macrobius, *In Somn. Scip.* 2.5.

64 *collaterare,* "to admit on both sides," is apparently borrowed from Martianus, 3.249, where the letter *c* is said to admit a vowel on either side.

65–66 The colures intersect at the north pole and cross the Zodiac, one at the solstitial, the other at the equinoctial points. Martianus, 8.832–33. The belief that they do not extend to the south pole is reported by Macrobius, *In Somn. Scip.* 1.15.14.

73 *Arcturos* = *Arctos.*

77 The "Kneeler" is usually identified as Hercules; Cicero, *Nat. D.* 2.42.108, quoting his own translation of Aratus, does not identify him.

78 Helice and Cynosura are Greek names for the Greater and Lesser Bear: Cicero, *Nat. D.* 2.41.105, again quoting Aratus.

79 *Adriana* is a corruption of *Ariadna,* "Ariadne," whose crown is traditionally supposed to have become the constellation Corona: Ovid, *Met.* 8.176–82.

81 The swan is the constellation Cycnus, "Ledean," only in that Leda was ravished by Jove in the form of a swan. The constellation was originally the Ligurian king Cycnus: Ovid, *Met.* 2.367–80; Virgil, *Aen.* 10.189–93.

82–83 Cepheus and Cassiopeia were the parents of Andromeda and parents-in-law of Perseus: Ovid, *Met.* 4.665–764. A different version of their story is summarized by Hyginus, *Fabulae* 64.

83 The effulgence is presumably the Andromeda galaxy.

85 Heniochus ("rein-holder") is the constellation Auriga. The Kids, or *Haedi,* are two stars in his hand: Cicero, *Nat. D.* 2.43.110; Pliny, 18.278.

91 *Telum* is the constellation Sagitta.

92 The bird of Jove is the constellation Aquila.

94 The horse of Bellerophon is the winged horse Pegasus.

95 The Phrixean is Phrixus, and the "vessel" is the ram with golden fleece, which carried him from Thessaly to Colchis with his sister Helle, who was drowned during the journey and gave her name to the Hellespont.

96 The deltaic form is Deltoton, the Triangle.

97 The seven Hyades ("rainers": Cicero, *Nat. D.* 2.43.111) were daughters of Atlas and hence sisters of the Pleiades: Ovid, *Fast.* 3.105.

99–100 On Procyon and warm weather, Pliny, 18.268–72.

103 The Aselli are two small stars within Cancer, and the Manger is a small nebula between them: Pliny, 18.353.

104 The Herculean beasts are presumably Leo, identified with the Nemaean lion, and Hydra.

110 Haemonian = Thessalian: Sagittarius, originally the centaur Chiron.

113 As Bernardus will note in 259–60, Eridanus is the mythical river that received Phaethon, stricken by Jove's thunderbolt: Ovid, *Met.* 2.324. Its history as a constellation is obscure. As an earthly river it is commonly identified with the Po, though Bernardus will treat the two rivers separately in 255–56 and 259–60 below.

127 Capella, one of the brightest stars, is commonly seen as Amalthea, the Cretan nymph who is said to have nursed the infant Zeus/Jove with goat's milk, or, as here and in Ovid, *Fast.* 5.111–21, identified with the goat herself.

130 Aquarius. The vessel is borne by Ganymede, cupbearer to Zeus, recalled again in 453–54.

133–36 The point of this rather cryptic passage is perhaps that failure to make accurate distinctions among the stars would prevent human beings from learning astronomy and astrology. With these lines, compare the following from the *Qui celum* section of the *Experimentarius,* one of the portions tentatively attributed to Bernardus: "Our ancient ancestors . . . believed that the seven planets were gods, and in acknowledgment of their lordship they called the seven days [of the week] by their seven names in their honor, bestowing the name of a particular planet on each day. In memory of them this practice endures, continuing down to the present day"; *Experimentarius,* ed. Brini Savorelli, 313; Burnett, "Experimentarius," 116.

141–42 Lucan, 10.204.

172 On the climates, see Isidore, 3.42.4; Firmicus Maternus, *Mathesis* 2.11.2–9.

183 *Cithaera* is presumably Cithaeron, in Boeotia, sacred to the Muses and Bacchus and site of the deaths of Acteon and Pentheus.

186 Lipari is one of several small volcanic islands northeast of Sicily, known to Pliny as the "Aeolian" or "Volcanian" islands: Pliny, 3.92–94; Isidore, 14.6.37. It was traditionally the site of the smithy of Vulcan.

Bernardus here seems to speak of "terebinth" as a mountain, though in 314 below it reappears as a resin-bearing tree. Pliny, 16.73, notes that "terebinth loves mountains."

188 The ancient healer is Chiron or his pupil Aesculapius.

198 The Pyrenees, according to a gloss in Laud misc. 515.

205 *extruitur* suggests that tusks are the "ossa" referred to; but compare Job 40:18.

221–22 Male *onagri* are said to eat the testicles of newborn males; hence, mothers hide their offspring in deserted places: Isidore, 12.1.39.

225–26 The urine of the lynx crystallizes into a precious gem. He knows that men covet this gem and covers it over after urinating: Pliny, 8.137; Isidore, 12.2.20.

229–30 On the beaver's voluntary self-castration, Isidore, 12.2.21. Alexander Neckham, *De naturis rerum* 2.140, rebukes Bernardus for following "ridiculous popular opinion" here and notes that according to Solinus the beaver does not give up his testicles but swallows them: Solinus, 13.2.

231–33 Lines 231–32 and the last half of 233 are quoted by Petrus Cantor, *Verbum abbreviatum* 85 (*PL* 205.255A) as illustrating excessive "sumptuosity" in dress.

232 *martix = martrix.*

Bernardus seems to refer to two species of beaver, but *beber* or *bever* is simply the Germanic equivalent to *castor.* In the *Opus synonymorum* attributed to John of Garland (PL 150.1583A), the two terms are noted as synonyms.

233–34 Many manuscripts of the *Cosmographia* omit this couplet.

237 The great virago is Semiramis; Ovid, *Met.* 4.57–58.

241–42 Lucan, 8.595–608.

243 The Abana or Amana (now the Barada) was known to classical antiquity as the Chrysorroas; Pliny, 5.74. Bernardus is likely to have in mind 2 Kings 5:12, where Naaman speaks of the Abana as "better than all the waters of Israel."

251 The pairing of Alpheus and Arethusa recalls Ovid, *Met.* 5. 577–641: the nymph Arethusa, pursued by the river god Alpheus, escaped through metamorphosis, becoming a fountain. When Alpheus sought to mingle his waters with hers, the goddess Diana conveyed her underground to the island of Ortygia, close to Syracuse.

257–58 According to the fifth-century "Passion of the Martyrs of Agaune," the emperor Maximian led an army to Gaul that included a legion of Egyptian Christians from the Thebaïd, led by St. Maurice. When they repeatedly refused to perform sacrifices to the pagan gods, they were massacred at Agaunum in the Swiss Alps. The first cathedral of Tours, destroyed by fire in 1166, was dedicated to St. Maurice.

259–60 Ovid, *Met.* 2.324.

263 Martinopolis is Tours, Bernardus's native city. St. Martin ended his long and spiritually heroic life as bishop of Tours, where his grave became a much venerated pilgrimage site.

270 The tree of Pallas is the olive tree, an important symbol of Athens and Pallas Athena.

276 Virgil warns against exposing bees to yew—*Ecl.* 9.30, *Geo.* 4.47—and speaks with fondness of "Cecropian" (i.e., Athenian) bees, known for their honey: *Geo.* 4.177.

285 Alcinous, ruler of the Phaeacians, entertained Odysseus at his sumptuous court (Homer, *Odyssey* 7–12). His devotion to horticulture, especially the growing of fruit, was proverbial: Virgil, *Geo.* 2.87; Pliny, 19.49.

285–86 The source of this threefold classification is Virgil, *Geo.* 2.9–21.

289 Though *nux* is a generic term, Isidore, 17.7.21, applies it to the *iuglans,* or walnut. The plural *togis* may refer to the double covering noted as unique to the walnut by Pliny, 15.86.

290 This brief dismissal of the pear may be a joke. Bernardus would know the many varieties of pear and their elaborate and often multiple names; Pliny, 15.53–56. The joke is reversed by Johannes de Hauvilla, *Architrenius* 4.46–53.

291 Pliny, 23.141.

294 I assume that Bernardus refers to plums generally rather than the specific variety that Pliny, 15.41–42, calls *cerinum,* or "waxplum," and which, he says, keeps for a long time if properly stored, though most varieties, once ripe, are short-lived.

296 I take Phyllis here to be the Phyllis of pastoral (Virgil, *Ecl.* 5.10) rather than the lover of Demophoon, and I suppose that she, like the Amaryllis of *Ecl.* 2.52, ate chestnuts; Palmer, "Plant Names," 42, notes that Phyllis the lover of Demophoon was transformed to an almond tree but also that the almond is mentioned separately in line 300. Ratkowitsch, *Die Cosmographia,* 73, suggests almonds.

298 Pliny, 12.29.

299–300 Pliny, 16.103.

313 The Heliades were the sisters of Phaethon. Mourning his death, they were turned to trees and their tears became amber: Ovid, *Met.* 2.340–66.

317–36 Rubrics in the manuscripts identify these lines as describing a "far eastern place" *(locus orientalis)* or "sweet smelling glade" *(saepes odoratae),* and less often "paradise."

341 Bernardus may imagine the fountains choked with blood from the human sacrifices for which Diana's shrine at Aricia was well known. See *Aen.* 7.764, where Diana's altar is *pinguis,* which Servius, *ad loc.,* explains as alluding to the many sacrifices that have taken place upon it. Ratkowitsch, *Die Cosmographia,* 75, sees a reference to Ovid, *Met.* 15.487–551: the nymph Egeria, mourning the death of her husband, Numa, came to Aricia, where Diana, moved by her devotion, transformed her into a

fountain. As Ratkowitsch points out, the allusion would complement the pleasant associations of the Lycean grove in the second line of the couplet, for which she cites Virgil, *Ecl.* 10.15; *Geo.* 1.16, 3.2.

347–48 Grynia, a small town on the northwest coast of Asia Minor, had a temple of Apollo: Virgil, *Ecl.* 6.72–73.

351–52 Sila, in a mountainous area of the toe of Italy, could look on both the Tyrrhenian and the Ionian Sea: Pliny, 3.74.

This couplet, printed by both Dronke and Barach-Wrobel, appears in the margin of Munich Clm 23434, one of the manuscripts used by Barach and Wrobel. I have not found it elsewhere.

369 On sleep-inducing lettuce, see Pliny, 19.126.

371 For *notis* (from *Notus,* "the south wind") in place of *togis,* the reading of the Laud MS, see Palmer, "Plant Names," 56n57. Both Pliny, 20.42–43, and Odo, 1088–89, note as a matter of debate among physicians the view that onions cause flatulence. Dronke's *togis,* the reading of Laud misc. 515, is plausible (compare the walnut in 289), and the onion's many coats are a commonplace (see, e.g., *Metamorphosis Golye episcopi* 220, where Cistercians are "wrapped in three tunics, like onions"); but *repleta* makes better sense with *notis.*

373 As noted by Palmer, "Plant Names," 43, the unusual form *mentaster* (for *mentastrum*) appears in the specimen poetic description of a *locus amoenus* by Matthew of Vendôme, in which the influence of Bernardus is clear: *Ars Versificatoria,* 1.111.27. In the same poem Matthew also follows Bernardus in giving *purga* (for *spurga*) (45), *cinnamus* (for *cinnamomum*) (92), and perhaps also in his use of *coctana* (84a) and *amigdaleus* (99).

375 On the aphrodisiac properties of rocket, Pliny, 19.154, 20.19; on those of savory, Odo, 864–67. Ovid, *Ars Am.* 2.415–16, advises against savory as an aphrodisiac.

376 Pliny, 26.96, 26.99.

377–78 The heliotrope.

379–80 Pliny, 25.73.

386 Odo, 682–88.

387–88 On the snake's return to youth, Isidore, 12.4.46–47; on its use of fennel to restore its sight, Pliny, 8.99; Odo, 681–83. *Maratrus* is an alternative name for fennel, from the Greek μάραθρος.

390 Pliny, 20.245.

391–92 Odo, 600–601.

393 Odo, 650, 672.

395–96 On wild nard, Odo, 1535; on bugloss as a stimulus to hilarity, Pliny, 25.81; Isidore, 17.9.49.

397–98 On summer savory, Odo, 843–45; on plantain, *lanceolata,* Odo, 200–201, 232–33.

399 Pliny, 23.149, mentions rue as one ingredient of Mithridates's famous antidote to poison; at 19.136 he notes Cato's praise of cabbage.

400 Odo, 332–35. A crown of parsley was awarded to victors at the Isthmian and Nemean games. Odo suggests that Hercules originated the custom, though he confuses victory in the games with a Roman triumph. I retain the classical meaning of *apium,* though thirteenth-century glosses identify it as Old French *ache,* Middle English *merche* or *smalache,* "wild celery"; Hunt, *Plant Names,* 28.

401 *elna* = *enula* or *inula.* Odo, 1489–90, remarks that *elna* is the Greek name for the plant. On its use as a remedy for coughs (taken with a little honey), Pliny, 20.38; Odo, 1499–1500. On nettle and gout, Odo, 131–35.

For *facere* in the sense of "to be of use," "to be effective," Propertius, 3.1.20; Ovid, *Tristia* 3.8.23.

403–4 On dittany, Pliny, 26.142, 26.153; on panacea, Pliny, 20.169.

405–6 Odo, 409–10.

407 Pliny, 20.15, 27.46–48.

408 Pliny, 21.130; Odo, 1348–49. *caumata* recalls Job 30:30.

409 The seven varieties of Tithymal are described by Pliny, 26.62–71.

411 Pliny, 20.1–9.

413 On hemlock, Pliny, 25.151; Odo, 2029–34.

414 Neither Pliny nor Odo associates hellebore with death, though

Pliny, 25.59–61, notes that extreme care must be taken to avoid the violent side effects of applying it incorrectly.

420 Pliny, 18.361; Isidore, 12.6.11.

424 Pliny, 9.61.

425–26 Cicero, *Div.* 2.33; Horace, *Sat.* 2.4.30; Pliny, 2.41.109.

427–28 Probably the *torpeda,* or torpedo fish, capable of transmitting an electric shock that numbs or stupefies; mentioned briefly by Pliny, 9.67.143, and perhaps by Calcidius, 237.

429–30 The stickleback may be assigned aphrodisiac qualities, because its name, *stincus,* is also a common name for the herb satyrion; see line 376 above, and Isidore 17.9.43.

440 Ausonius, *Mosella* 120–23.

post 440 Here Vernet's edition inserts an additional couplet (see Notes to the Texts): "The carp lends distinction to the Loire, and there too swims the equally delicious maigre, a larger fish who shuns the lakes and marshes." This couplet appears in only two manuscripts of the *Cosmographia,* Paris, Bibliothèque Nationale, lat. 6752A, and Cambridge, Trinity College 0.7.40 (where it is added in the margin), and in two florilegia. Ratkowitsch, *Die Cosmographia,* 80, argues persuasively against attributing the couplet to Bernardus.

453 The boy is Ganymede.

457 Lucan, 5.711–16; Isidore, 12.7.14.

459 Juno's bird is the peacock.

460 Löfstedt, "Notizen," 205, argues persuasively that this line refers to the dove's very active sex life, aptly citing Ovid, *Ars Am.* 2.413.

461–62 Philomena and her sister are the nightingale and the swallow. Philomena was raped by Tereus, husband of her sister Procne, who cut out her tongue to prevent her revealing his action. Learning the truth, Procne killed her son, Itys, served his flesh to Tereus, and told him what he had eaten. When Tereus sought to kill the sisters, all three were turned to birds; Ovid, *Met.* 6.412–674.

464 The Phasis was a river in Medea's native Colchis: Ovid, *Met.* 7.298.

467 Perdix was the nephew of Daedalus, who trained him as an artisan. When the skill of Perdix threatened to exceed his own, Daedalus threw him from a high wall, but he was caught and turned to a partridge *(perdix)* by Pallas; Ovid, *Met.* 8.236–59.

469 On the crow's fabled longevity, Pliny, 7.48.153; on its prophetic powers, Isidore, 12.7.44.

470 The problematic coloring of the magpie is apparently proverbial. Jan Ziolkowski, ed., *Solomon and Marcolf* (Cambridge, Mass.: Harvard University Press, 2008), 208, quotes a brief *Streitgedicht* in which *Albedo* and *Nigredo* (Whiteness and Blackness) present rival claims to be the bird's defining color; Nature concludes that the bird's color is neither white nor black, but "unresolved" *(dubius)*.

475–76 The raven is "Delphic," because once the servant of Apollo. When she reported to the god the infidelity of his beloved Coronis, Apollo in his rage slew the girl and then turned on the bird, changing its color from white to black; Ovid, *Met.* 2.534–632. The bird's neglect of its young may recall Job 38:41.

Megacosmus 4

1 Thierry, *Tractatus* 5: "When the heaven was created, since it is extremely light and cannot remain still, and because it contains all things, . . . from the first moment of its creation it began to be turned in a circular path . . ."

With Maccagnolo I assume that "elements" in the first sentence refers both to the material elements *(partes),* which William of Conches calls *elementata,* and to the "pure" elements that compose them *(partes partium)*.

Asclepius 3: "The firmament, a god perceptible by sense, governs all bodies, whose growth and decline the sun and moon have in charge."

2 The opening sentence recalls Virgil, *Geo.* 2.325–26, and *Asclepius* 2: " . . . all that descends from on high is generative; and that which issues upward from below is nutritive. Earth . . . receives

all that is generative into itself, and renders back all that it has received."

3 On the birth of time, *Timaeus* 37C–38C. Bernardus can speak of the "substance" of time insofar as time is a created thing, composed of parts and endowed with motion.

4 Bernardus's language can make it difficult to distinguish *Usia* as God from *Usia* as matter (as in *Meg.* 4.4), but *Usia Primaeva* here *(pace* Stock, *Myth and Science,* 143) is clearly God. Noys in *Meg.* 2.1 refers to herself as having been generated by the *Usia prima.*

The final sentence recalls Seneca, *Quaestiones naturales* 2.45, on Jove, "to whom every name is appropriate: should you call him 'fate,' you will not be wrong; . . . should you call him 'providence,' you will speak rightly; . . . should you call him 'nature,' you will not be in error . . ." In *Asclepius* 20 God is said to have "no name, or rather every name, since he is one and all."

5 *luce inaccessibili* echoes 1 Timothy 6:16.

6 In *Asclepius* 20 the divine will is *bonitas omnis.*

The "prior knowledge" possessed by the Universe becomes the effect on the sublunar world of the influence exerted by the heavens.

7 On the terminology of the first sentence, see *Asclepius* 34: "Nature, imaging *(imaginans)* the world with species through the four elements, brings forth all things below the heavens that they may be found pleasing in the sight of God." The process is summarized in several manuscripts by Latin verses: *Yle prima fuit, quam pura elementa sequuntur; / tercia mixta manent quibus omnia constituuntur* ("First was Hyle, the pure elements were next; the third, mixed elements, from which all things are made, remain."); Jeauneau, "Notes sur l'École de Chartres," 835. On the distinction between the *elementum,* or pure element, and the *elementatum,* or physical element, William of Conches, *Philosophia* 1.20–22.

I read *conveniant* in the penultimate sentence as transitive, with *caelum* and *stellae* as its subjects and *elementa* as its object.

8 The emphasis on the preexistence and vitality of Hyle here and in the following paragraph recalls the account of the primary causes in *Asclepius* 14, and especially *Asclepius* 29–30: God is the eternal source of life for all living things, and "in the very vitality of eternity the world is given life *(agitata)* and the seat *(locus)* of the world is in this living eternity, and therefore it will never cease to move, nor be destroyed."

9 On the "perfect form" of the universe, *Timaeus* 33B.

On the relation of time to eternity, *Timaeus* 37C–38B; Calcidius, 105.

13 In *Asclepius* 20, God, conceived as bisexual, is "ever pregnant of his own will and ever giving birth to whatever he wishes to procreate."

Asclepius 39–40 treats εἱμαρμένη as divine law, whose subordinate powers, necessity and order, perform the role of Imarmene in the *Cosmographia.*

Microcosmus 1

3 On the colures, see *Meg.* 3.65–66n.

5 Amphitrite is the wife of Neptune, goddess of Ocean. Her introduction here seems to interrupt Noys's celebration of the riches of the earth, and a *fons humoris* is introduced later in the paragraph, suggesting that Bernardus might have read *Amphitrite* as genitive. But he would have known the name correctly from, for example, Ovid, *Met.* 1.14.

The *sectiones* are perhaps the smaller seas and gulfs that were known or supposed to exist in and around the great landmass of Europe, Africa, and Asia.

Microcosmus 2

1–6 I follow Dronke in assigning these lines to the narrator, prompted by the use of past tenses in the first six lines, which would seem to be out of place in the speech of Noys. But see Pabst, *Prosimetrum,* 475n501.

13–14 Since the sea has just been mentioned, I assume with Lemoine that *terra* denotes land, rather than the planet earth, though the language of 14 suggests the latter.

Microcosmus 3

1 This and subsequent celebrations of man's role and destiny are broadly based on *Asclepius* 10–12.

concertet means only "compete with" or "rival," but the sentence clearly indicates an intention to make man superior to all other creatures.

2 On creation as resulting from the overruling of necessity (ἀνάγκη), "the errant cause," by reason (νοῦς), *Timaeus* 47E–48A.

3 The "sowing" *(sementis)* of souls recalls *Timaeus* 42DE, where the Demiurge sows the immortal portions of the first generation of human souls on earth, and others among the planets, leaving it to the lesser gods to produce the mortal parts of the soul and the body.

5 *Anastros* is probably borrowed from Martianus, 8.814, where it is an adjective rather than a proper name. Nature's experience here is recalled by Alan of Lille, *Anticlaudianus* 4.332–40, describing the ascent of *Prudentia* from the atmosphere to the heavens.

6 The parallels, or zones, are discussed at length by Macrobius, *In Somn. Scip.* 2.5.

7 On Cancer as the "portal" for souls descending into earthly existence, Macrobius, *In Somn. Scip.* 1.12.1–4. In the rest of this chapter Macrobius discusses ancient beliefs about the soul's descent: Courcelle, "Tradition . . . du corps-prison"; Whitman, *Allegory,* 93–94.

8 The *Aplanes* (Greek, "unwandering") is the sphere of the fixed stars: Calcidius, 69; Macrobius, *In Somn. Scip.* 1.11.6, 2.4.8. In the *Aeneid* commentary (ed. Jones and Jones, 48) Martianus is said to have located the seat of Urania in the Aplanes, though the term does not appear in the *De nuptiis.*

9 Bernardus's characterization of the quintessence as "neither fire

nor derived from fire," closely echoes Apuleius, *De mundo* 1, which follows Aristotle, *De caelo* 1.3, in identifying the fifth element as "ether" and expressly distinguishing it from fire. This evidently contradicts *Meg.* 3.5, where the firmament is said to be "the purer essence of fire," and *Meg.* 3.134, where the stars in the firmament are called "heavenly fire." For a possible explanation, *Meg.* 3.5n.

Abu Ma'shar accepts the quintessential nature of the planets, for essentially the reason given by Bernardus here, *Introductorium* 1.3, ed. Lemay, vol. 5, 22, 733–41 (John of Seville); 1.2, vol. 8, 9, 275–86 (Hermann of Carinthia). William of Conches, *Dragmaticon* 3.5, opposes this view, on the grounds that nonelemental bodies could not transmit elemental qualities.

The use of *rapacitas* here resembles Calcidius's use of *raptatus,* which can refer to violent and irrational force, as in his rendering of *Timaeus* 43A (compare *Meg.* 1.27), but which in *Comm.* 73 denotes the driving impulse that causes the planets to produce the sounds of harmonious music.

10 In *Asclepius* 19 *Pantomorphos,* or *Omniformis,* is said to be chief of the planetary usiarchs. I read Bernardus as having transferred the term to his domain, though glosses on this passage understand *Pantomorpho* to refer, as in the *Asclepius,* to the Usiarch himself. Dronke (ed. *Cons.* 168) provides an excellent discussion of different possible interpretations.

Oyarses is a corruption of Greek οὐσιάρχης, "master of substance," which in *Asclepius* 19 denotes cosmic powers who regulate the life and activity of the stars and planets. The Usiarch of the region of the fixed stars is Παντόμορφος *vel omniformis,* whose office is to create "diverse forms for diverse creatures." Bernardus transfers the title to the place. On possible textual reasons for this shift, Dronke, ed. *Cosm.* 168. On the astrological background of this figure, Nitzsche, *Genius Figure,* 68–72.

In *Asclepius* 19 the Usiarchs of the seven planets exert control over the movements of the planets, so that they are seen by some as agents of fortune, or εἱμαρμένη. In *Microcosmus* 5 Bernardus identifies them with the planetary divinities themselves. (In the Scott text of the *Asclepius,* a single Usiarch governs the seven planets, but in the text known to Bernardus there were evidently seven.)

Microcosmus 4

The alternating hexameter and tetrameter lines of this poem imitate Boethius, *Cons.* 1.metr. 3.

49 Ovid, *Met.* 15.839, Jupiter's prophecy of the deification of Augustus.

Microcosmus 5

3 Bernardus probably drew the name Tugaton (τὸ ἀγαθόν, "the good") from Macrobius, *In Somn. Scip.* 1.2.14.

The lesser light of the eyes protects itself from the greater, divine light, and the result is darkness.

The three radiances, which clearly define the Trinity, also recall the head of *Arithmetica* in Martianus, 7.728, and perhaps the seven-rayed crown of Pallas Athena, 1.40. The final phrase echoes *Asclepius* 19, on the communication of divine knowledge, which, if not followed attentively, "will fly and flow away, or, better, flow back and remingle with the waters of its source."

4 On Bernardus's use of *cuidam* here, see Introduction, xxv.

6 *crudus* in the sense of "vigorous" recalls Virgil's description of Charon, *Aen.* 6.304.

Chronos, or Saturn, castrated his father Ouranos, or Caelus. When he cast the genitals into the sea, Aphrodite/Venus was born. Macrobius, *In Somn. Scip.* 1.2.11, cites this episode as the sort of myth philosophers reject as unworthy of serious analysis, but in *Saturnalia* 1.8.6–8 he offers a full interpretation, perhaps developing the partial reading in Cicero, *Nat. D.* 2.24–25.64. The castration occurs at the point when the universe is complete and represents the transferal of the powers of generation from heaven to earth, inaugurating the temporal order. The myth is transmitted by Servius, *In Aen.* 5.801, and by the Vatican Mythographers: Mythogr. I, 104 (a version in which Jove castrates Saturn); Mythogr. II, 40, 234.

7 On the etymology of the name of Jove, Cicero, *Nat. D.* 2.25.64.

Stock, *Myth and Science,* 183–84, notes that terms like *indulgentiarum* and *consistorium* (used also by Martianus, 1.64), and the characterization of Jupiter's court as an administrative center, make him a quasi-pope.

The likely source of the motif of the two vessels is Boethius, *Cons.* 2.pr.2.13–14; Ratkowitsch, *Die Cosmographia,* 90–92, suggests further sources.

8 On the office of Clotho, Calcidius, 144.

10 Pyriphlegethon, or more often Phlegethon, is the river of fire in the underworld: Virgil, *Aen.* 6.265, 551; Statius, *Theb.* 4.523. Martianus, 2.194, remarks that in the circle of Pyrois, Pyriphlegethon can be seen descending to the lower world.

On Pyrois as the planet or star of Mars, Cicero, *Nat. D.* 2.20.53; Apuleius, *De mundo,* 2, 29.

The use of *tabernaculum* is evidently intended to suggest the status of the sun as a "life-giving god" analogous to *Tugaton,* whose *tabernaculum* is defined in biblical terms in *Micr.* 7.5.

12 These attributes of the sun are concisely enumerated in Philology's prayer, Martianus, 2.185; also Macrobius, *In Somn. Scip.* 1.20.1–7; *Asclepius* 29.

From this point to the end of the chapter, the astronomical accounts of the planetary gods are augmented by conventional iconography that seems to have no clear bearing on the narrative.

13 Martianus mentions *Veris Fructus,* 1.52, and names *Celeritas* as a daughter of the Sun, 1.50. On the role of Celeritas, Lemoine, "La durée," 206. "Harmless Phaethon" is presumably still a child. Psyche is identified as "daughter of Entelechia and the Sun" by Martianus, 1.7. On her activity here, see Introduction, xxi.

14 The epithets of Lucifer and Cyllenius are taken from Apuleius, *De mundo* 29.

15 Bernardus, perhaps following William of Conches, *Philosophia* 2.23, gives a modern meaning to *intersectio,* which, as used by Vitruvius, 3.5.11, had referred to the space between two projecting dentils on the cornice of a building.

16 On the orbit of Mercury, Martianus, 8.857.

In Ovid's version of the story of Hermaphroditus, child of Hermes and Aphrodite, *Met.* 4.285–388, he becomes bisexual only when embraced by the nymph Salmacis, whose body unites with his. A brief reference in Martianus, 1.34, can be read as implying that he was bisexual from birth, and this assumption underlies Remigius's extended gloss on this passage (*In Mart. Cap.,* ed. Lutz, 1:107–8), in which Hermaphroditus stands for "a certain wantonness in speaking, when superfluous adornments of speech are sought, often to the neglect of truthful and rational discourse," a wantonness which Mercury's marriage with Philology will control. The Martianus commentary attributed to Bernardus includes an elaboration of this gloss (ed. Westra, 249.134–44).

17 Both Mercury and Venus were understood to orbit around the Sun. Since the orbit of Venus is wider than that of Mercury, it can be said to encompass those of both the others.

In ancient texts *subfumigo* refers to fumigation in the practical sense, but in the medieval instances I have found it refers to the use of incense or candles in liturgical contexts, whence its application to Venus' torch.

18 In the phrase that I have translated "by the interposition of the Moon as mediator," most manuscripts read *linee* for *lune.*

The final sentence recalls Macrobius, *In Somn. Scip.* 1.11.8.

20 The phrase *divinas . . . pascens* is borrowed from Apuleius, *De mundo* 2.293.

For the conjectural reading *ethin* in place of the *aethericon* of the earlier editions and the various readings of the manuscripts, Dronke, ed. *Cosm.,* 159, 169, and Maccagnolo, 518n27, whom I follow in translating the word as "property." *ethis* appears in the

Virgil commentary (ed. Jones and Jones, 31: *ethis mos vel consuetudo*), and in the *asccessus* (introduction) to William of Conches, *Glosae super Platonem: ethis enim est mos*.

The grammatical term *redditivus,* discussed by Priscian, *Inst. gramm.* 17.32, is applied to terms like *talis, tantus, tot,* through which a person or an object can be made to reflect or correspond to another person or object explicitly or implicitly identified.

Silverstein, "Fabulous Cosmogony," 96n27, traces *planeta Solis* as a name for the Moon to Abu Ma'shar, who in the *Introductorium* attributes it not to Ptolemy but to the author called by John of Seville "Hermes Aaidimon," and by Hermann of Carinthia, "Hermes post Abidemon" (John: 5.4.249–60, ed. Lemay, 5.182; Hermann: 5.4.130–37, ed. Lemay, 8.76). On this author, Lemay, *Abu Ma'shar,* 374–76.

Memphiticus as an epithet for Ptolemy is puzzling, since the astronomer apparently spent his entire life in Alexandria.

Microcosmus 6

13 *galaxe = galaxias.*

25–28 The first of these couplets breaks the sequence of couplets introduced by *quod,* which apparently resumes in line 27, though one must guess at the subject of *relinquunt.* Perhaps what is in question is the descent of the soul, as in *Micr.* 3.7. The passage may have been corrupted, and my translation is tentative.

Microcosmus 7

1 On Homer's Golden Chain (*Iliad* 8.19), Macrobius, *In Somn. Scip.* 1.14.15.

3 With the opening sentence, compare *Asclepius* 4; Apuleius, *De mundo* 24.343.

On the universe as manifesting God, Psalm 18:1; Romans 1:20.

5 The opening sentence recalls Psalm 18:6.

The "gleaming hosts" are the Seraphim.

Dronke, ed. *Cosm.* 169, points out that *plurimo* is an adjective ("most powerful") modifying *deo,* as with *plurimus . . . Sol* in Ovid, *Met.* 14.53. I have tried to convey this sense in simpler English.

in pace . . . superat echoes Philippians 4:7.

On *orthosphaera,* apparently coined by Bernardus to denote the firmament, Dronke, ed. *Cosm.,* 170. Dronke's textual notes, 159, show how the term puzzled copyists.

6–10 On these intermediary beings, Apuleius, *De deo Socratis* 6.132–9.141; Calcidius, 131–36.

6 The second sentence has no main verb. I translate as if *pervadens* were *pervadat.*

10 The reference of *Summa dei diligentia* is unclear. Lemoine reads it with *minus . . . malitia,* while Maccagnolo takes it with *angustissima . . . recesserunt.* Lemoine's reading seems to call the divine *diligentia* into question, but since the next sentence assigns a useful function to the *malitia* of the evil spirits, it is perhaps not implausible.

11 On these spirits, Martianus, 2.167; Ovid, Met. 1.192–95. In Martianus, 1.49, *Tellurus* appears among those invited to the wedding of Philology and Mercury between Ceres and *Terrae pater Vulcanus* ("Vulcan, Father of the Earth," perhaps a reference to the Stoic view of fire as creator of the other elements). Cristante, ed. *De nuptiis,* 149, reviews the various attempts to explain *Tellurus.* Bernardus has appropriated the name as a general term for the gods or spirits of the natural world.

12 On Summanus, Martianus, 2.161.

Microcosmus 8

This poem is omitted in the great majority of the manuscripts that preserve a full-length version of the *Cosmographia.* (See the Note on the Texts.)

9–10 Macrobius, *In Somn. Scip.*2.4.8, and above, *Micr.* 3.9.

15–16 This is essentially the justification of astrology offered by Firmicus Maternus, *Mathesis* 1.4.

19 Boreas and Favonius are the north and west winds, associated respectively with winter and spring.

21–22 Virgil, *Geo.* 2.325–27.

23–24 The lost daughter of Ceres is Proserpina, seized by Pluto and made queen of the underworld. In despair at her loss, Ceres caused the earth to become barren. When it was decreed that Proserpina would be restored to the world for half of the year, fertility was restored, and in the version of the myth adopted by Ovid, *Met.* 5.341–661, Ceres granted Triptolemus the secrets of agriculture. Proserpina's return to the world is commonly treated, as here, as representing the annual renewal of the earth. Augustine, *Civ. Dei* 7.20, 7.24, and Fulgentius, *Mitologiae* 1.10, cite the etymology that derives her name from *proserpere.*

32 *Timaeus* 35A.

35–36 *Timaeus* 42A–D; Calcidius, 199; Boethius, *Cons.* 2.pr.7.23.

38 I take *evolvens* in the sense of unrolling and reading a scroll.

Microcosmus 9

1 The Aeolian brothers are the winds, sons of Aeolus, the wind god.

On the *interstitia* of the four elements, Macrobius, *In Somn. Scip.* 1.6.36–40.

2 Most manuscripts read *Granusion,* derived from ὑγρὰν οὐσίαν, which in Calcidius, 129, denotes the lower atmosphere, but Dronke, ed. *Cosm.,* 171–72, argues persuasively for *Gramision,* pointing to Bernardus's own gloss, *graminum diversitatibus,* at the end of the paragraph. Dronke's argument is endorsed by Jolivet, "Les principes féminins," 304–5, and by Ratkowitsch, *Die Cosmographia,* 100–101.

Jolivet, "Les principes féminins," 275–78, detects an erotic note in terms like *compubescit* and references to Gramision as *sinus abditus* and *gremium.* He suggests that Gramision symbolizes the female genitalia, complementing the account of the work of the phallus in *Micr.* 14.158–66.

2–3 It is perhaps impossible to know whether Gramision is the *locus amoenus* of *Meg.* 3.317–38, though Kauntze, "Creation Grove," offers a theological reading of Gramision and the work of Physis that would support this view.

3 On *species* as "spice," the very full discussion in Du Cange, s. v., includes citations of John of Salisbury, *Policraticus* 5.10, and Johannes de Hauvilla, *Architrenius* 2.245.

4 The resin emitted by the Heliades (the sisters of Phaethon, who were turned to poplar trees as they mourned his death) is amber: *Meg.* 3.313n.

The Sabaeans of southwest Arabia were famous for their myrrh and frankincense.

Microcosmus 10

7–8 On the possible implication of these lines, see *Meg.* 2.2n.

13 The "primary universe" is the ideal universe, where man exists, in the mind of Noys.

27–32 Ovid, *Met.* 1.84–86; Macrobius, *In Somn. Scip.* 1.14.9–11.

37 *Dis,* originally an equivalent to *divus* or *deus,* later applied specifically to the god of the underworld and in poetry to the underworld itself.

53 This line suggestively echoes *Meg.* 3.336.

54 Ovid, *Met.* 15.839.

Microcosmus 11

3 I take *certitudo* as referring to knowledge "ascertained" by study or investigation.

4 As a gloss on the *intermina latitudo* of the Mirror, Laud misc. 515 offers a version of a "hermetic" maxim perhaps coined by Alan of Lille, defining God as "a circle of which the center is everywhere, but the periphery nowhere."

prospicuus introspectus defies translation; *prospicuus* can mean "visible at a distance," or "looking into the future," the vision gained by "looking into" the *speculum*.

I know of no precedent for Bernardus's use of *extortor* to characterize the power of the divine mind. In translating I have assumed that it is intended to balance *genitor*.

5 *complectibilis* was apparently coined by Boethius, *De hypothetico syllogismo* 2 (PL 64.863B), to denote what can be inferred or concluded in a syllogism.

The image of man is still "imaginary"; it has not yet been given actual embodiment.

7 Calcidius, 144.

9 My translation of the reference to the first Man is conjectural. The use of *ab* may indicate a description that begins with the head and proceeds downward, or *occipitis regio* may refer to the distinctive shape of the human head.

Microcosmus 12

The meter of this poem is the "Archilocheian" meter of Horace, *Odes* 4.7.

18 *commoderare,* "to set in order," a legal term.

23–24 Noys had seemed to indicate in *Micr.* 11.2 that the extraction of the elements from chaos had already been accomplished, as is suggested also by *Timaeus* 42E–43A, where the gods "borrow from the world" the elements required for the creation of man. From *Micr.* 13.1–2 we learn that the elements Physis inherits have in fact been refined and disciplined. That they are always on the point of reverting to their earlier state of mutual hostility is perhaps due to their being, for the moment, no longer subject to the discipline of the cosmic order , and not yet under the control of Physis.

53–54 Since Physis will encounter in 13.3 the same difficulties mentioned in lines 19 to 31 above, Urania's intervention will evidently control Silva only after soul and body have been joined.

Microcosmus 13

1 The terms *unitas* and *diversum* recall the creation of the world soul in *Timaeus* 35A–37B, and the account of *unitas* and *alteritas* in Thierry's *Tractatus,* 30–31; Häring, *Commentaries,* 568; the language of the paragraph echoes Calcidius, 27–28, 53. See Silverstein, "Fabulous Cosmogony," 101–2.

On the preparation of Hyle, Calcidius, 303–4.

2 Maccagnolo and Lemoine understand Physis as the subject of *Promiscuam . . . inconvulsis.* I think the subject is still "the diligence of God the creator," because of the continuing sequence of pluperfect verbs (assuming *revocarat,* the consistent reading of the manuscripts, to be a contraction of *revocaverat*) and the possible allusion (noted by Lemoine) to Boethius, *Cons.* 2.metr.8.10–15.

4 The opening sentence recalls *Timaeus* 42E–43A, where the "gods" who create the human body borrow from the already created universe portions of the elements (which are later to be restored).

7 On complexion, Timaeus 31B–32C; Macrobius, *In Somn. Scip.* 1.6.24–33. On complexion in human beings, Constantinus, *Pantegni* 1.6–9.

On the correspondence of temperament with elemental composition, Nemesius, *Premnon physicon* 4.3–5.

9 The verb *collibro* and also *commadeo* (*Meg.* 3.86) are attested only in Cato the Censor, *De agricultura,* a text to which Bernardus might have been led by the praises of agriculture that the old man is made to offer, in language as rich as that of Bernardus himself, in Cicero's *De senectute.*

10 *Timaeus* 44DE; Calcidius, 231–32.

11 *Timaeus* 44D; Calcidius, 233; Ratkowitsch, *Die Cosmographia,* 110.

13 On the three chambers and the three functions assigned to them, *Micr.* 14.3–8. On the history of the "internal senses," imagination, reason, and memory, Silverstein, "Fabulous Cosmogony," 97–98.

14 Calcidius, 231. The phrase *internuntia sentiendi* appears in Apuleius, *De dogmate Platonis* 1.16.

Microcosmus 14

2 That the epithet *primipotens,* used of God at *Micr.* 6.10, is used here of Nature suggests that what follows is to be understood wholly as a natural event and that the somber conclusion will be a comment on man's natural condition rather than on his ultimate destiny.

15–16 Calcidius, 246; William of Conches, *Philosophia* 4.23.40. Constantinus, *Pantegni* 4.11.

25–26 *Timaeus* 45B–D; Calcidius, 245.

27–28 *Timaeus* 45B.

34 William of Conches, *Philosophia* 4.22.39. Calcidius, 246, speaks of a fourfold covering, as does William, *Glosae super Platonem,* 138. But the number given in the manuscripts varies widely.

41–44 Calcidius, 247, citing Plato, *Republic* 508B.3–4. On the appropriation of Ovid, *Met.* 4.226–28, in these lines, Pfeiffer, *Contemplatio Caeli,* 261–62.

45–46 Calcidius, 266, apparently recalling Diogenes Laertius 2.10, credits a similar answer to Anaxagoras.

53–54 William of Conches, *Philosophia* 4.24.44; Boethius, *De institutione musica* 1.14.

75–76 Both Lemoine and Maccagnolo see here a reference to the *Sophistical Refutations* of Aristotle, said to have been rediscovered by Thierry of Chartres: Vernet, "Une épitaphe inédite," 665.

76 According to Lemoine, *Ligus* stands for Italy; according to Maccagnolo, for the school of Montpellier.

79 *nudas,* perhaps in the sense of lacking the adornment of eloquence: Philology without Mercury.

83 Virgil, *Aen.* 7.335. Bernardus may be recalling the exchange between Allecto and Juno in which this line occurs.

86 A *depositum* is money or material goods placed in trust with another, or the contract governing such a trust. In Leviticus 6:1–7

the Lord instructs Moses on dealing with the sin of one who denies a *depositum.*

91 *pauper,* man in general rather than a poor man. The thought is as in Cicero, *Nat. D.* 2.58.148.

99 Though the manuscripts give *Pangeum,* I take Bernardus to be referring here to Panchaia, a fabulous island supposed to be rich in incense and myrrh; Virgil, *Geo.* 2.139, 4.379. *Pangaea,* referring to a mountain in Thrace, also occurs in *Geo.* 4, at line 462.

107 *castigato:* Ovid, *Am.* 1.5.21.

110 Calcidius, 224, 232.

115–16 This sentence is an embellished version of Aristotle, *Parts of Animals* 3.4 and its commentary tradition, as summarized by Calcidius, 224. On the twelfth-century context of Bernardus's treatment of the heart, Ricklin, "Le coeur," 136–41.

119 *coloxum,* apparently found only here, is commonly glossed in the manuscripts as "a magnificent site at Rome" *(sedes Romae magnifica).* Professor Roger Wright has suggested to me that the original word may have been *colosseum,* which Bernardus, a Romance speaker, might have heard as trisyllabic, the *eu* a diphthong and the accent on the second syllable.

150 *cocus = coquus.*

159–60 Silverstein, "Fabulous Cosmogony," 109n118, sees these *genii* as the tutelary spirits of marriage; Stock, *Myth and Science,* 218, suggests that they are "the masculine and feminine aspects of creativity latent in matter." Both cite Censorinus, *De die natali* 3.3, for the belief that married households should honor a pair of *genii (binos genios).* But it seems clear that the *genii* of Bernardus are to be associated more directly with the physical nature of the male and the testicles, the *genialia arma* with which he fights against annihilation.

The reference to twin brothers perhaps alludes to an obscure myth related by Ovid. In *Met.* 13.681–99, the wandering Aeneas receives from the priest-king Anius a bowl inscribed with the story of how Thebes was saved from plague by the suicide of the daughters of Orion. When their bodies were burned, twin boys emerged from the fire, "lest the race should perish," and joined the funeral procession. They are commemorated as the *Coronae.*

165–66 Gervase of Melkley, *Ars poetica* 144, devotes one of his few passages of extended commentary to praise of this couplet.

170 Constantinus, *Pantegni* 3.34.

171–76 *Timaeus* 32C–33B; Calcidius, 24, 192.

179–82 *Timaeus* 33B–34A.

The Astrologer

20 Her character is so strong that she needs to make no allowance for feminine weakness.

97 On the significance of Medea in the poem (compare l. 418), Sivo, "Metamorfosi dell'animo," 97–103.

128 Hercules is said to have relieved Atlas in his task of supporting the heavens. Servius (*ad Aen.* 1.741) reads this as an allegory of Atlas's instruction of Hercules in astronomy, which becomes the standard gloss. See, e.g., William of Conches, *Glosae super Boetium,* 286, on *Cons.* 4.metr.7.29–31).

136 The seven Arts are the *trivium* and *quadrivium;* Introduction.

146 It is unclear what meaning Bernardus assigns to *signifer,* but he clearly imagines an office more prestigious than that of standard-bearer in a company led by a centurion, its common meaning in military contexts.

155 *Quirites* is a traditional name for citizens of Rome.

post 248 Two lines are inserted here in manuscript K (see Notes to the Text): "Thus (and I feel no envy) the scepter of royal Quirinus (i.e., Romulus) and much glory will reward your service."

304 Ovid mentions the proverbial virtue of Sabine women in *Am.* 1.8.39–40, 2.4.15, 3.8.61. Bernardus may also recall Hersilia, the Sabine wife of Romulus, whose grief at his death led Juno to transform her into the constellation Hora (Ovid, *Met.* 14.829–51).

365 Virgil, *Aen.* 6.566–69.

369 I have emended to *memini,* attested by two of the earliest manu-

scripts, because there seems to be no subject for *meminit.* The puzzling insertion of this verb is perhaps meant to suggest the reluctance of the wife and mother to recall what she must reveal.

384 On the "climates" or "zones," Macrobius, *In Somn. Scip.* 2.5, 7. The celestial climates correspond to earthly ones, represented as belts circling the earth in *Meg.* 3.61–62.

434 Phlegra was the site of the battle between the Olympian gods and the Giants (Virgil, *Geo.* 1.278–83; Ovid, *Met.* 10.150–51; Statius, *Theb.* 2.595–601).

642 Six lines are inserted after 642 in manuscript M, in which the poem breaks off at this point (see Notes to the Text): "If we are wise or not, or if we are deprived of reason, it makes no difference: all things occur necessarily according to fate. But if fate rules everything that lives beneath the starry heavens, why, then, was man equipped with reason? Far be it from us to live by fate and not by reason: the dull-witted vulgar may believe that, but the wise man repudiates it."

647 Albula was an ancient name for the Tiber (Virgil, *Aen.* 8.332; Ovid, *Fasti* 4.68), though Bernardus may have supposed it to be a separate river.

723 Lucretia was a national heroine. According to tradition her suicide, after being raped by the son of Tarquinius Superbus, the last king of Rome, led to the expulsion of the Tarquins and the founding of the Roman Republic.

724 A sacred shield, or *ancile,* said to have fallen from heaven as King Numa was performing a sacrifice (Lucan, 9.477–79), was preserved at Rome and believed to ensure the city's prosperity.

734 Both rivers were traditionally thought to bear gold.

735 Tyre was famous for a crimson dye produced from mollusks.

737 On Myron, *Meg.* 3.47n.

773 For *haustus* in the sense of "spirit," compare Virgil, *Geo.* 4.220.

849 This line seems to correspond to no "ancient text"; Justinian is apparently just a name to conjure with. But see Godman, "Ambiguity," 635–36.

The Twins

2 Quintilian was the supposed author of the Declamation on which the poem is based.

19 Ganymede.

20 Memnon, son of Aurora and king of the Ethiopians, was slain by Achilles at Troy; Ovid, *Met.* 13.576–82; Virgil, *Aen.* 1.489. He is not traditionally known for beauty.

70–76 The wife's irrational argument recalls the advocate in the ancient *declamatio,* who, on no apparent grounds, challenges the doctor's authority and the value of his autopsy.

The Ungrateful Pauper

11 Four manuscripts give *miles* in place of *quidam.*

16 As Edwards, "Poetic Invention," 216, suggests, terminating support before a year has elapsed may be intended to prevent the poor man from claiming the right to a continuing position in his benefactor's household.

Bibliography

Works by Bernardus Silvestris

Cosmographia

Bernard Silvestre: Cosmographie. Translated by Michel Lemoine. Paris: Editions du Cerf, 1998.

Bernardo Silvestre: Cosmografia. Translated by Enzo Maccagnolo. In Maccagnolo, *Il divino e il megacosmo. Testi filosofici e scientifici della scuola di Chartres,* 462–552. Milan: Rusconi, 1980.

Cosmographia. Edited by André Vernet. In Vernet, *Bernardus Silvestris: Recherches sur l'auteur suivies d'une édition critique de la "Cosmographia,"* 222–457. PhD diss., Paris, École Nationale des Chartes, 1938.

Cosmographia. Edited by Peter Dronke. Leiden: Brill, 1978.

The Cosmographia of Bernardus Silvestris. Translated by Winthrop Wetherbee. Records of Civilization: Sources and Studies 89. New York: Columbia University Press, 1973.

De Mundi universitate sive Megacosmus et Microcosmus. Edited by Carl Sigmund Barach and Johann Wrobel. Innsbruck: Wagner, 1876.

Über die allumfassende Einheit der Welt : Makrokosmos und Mikrokosmos. Bernardus Silvestris. Translated by Wilhelm Rath. Stuttgart: Mellinger, 1972.

Mathematicus

Mathematicus. In Hildebert of Le Mans, *Opera,* edited by Antoine Beaugendre, 1295–310. Paris, 1708. Repr. in PL 171.1365B–79D.

Mathematicus. Edited (with the *Passio sanctae Agnetis* of Peter Riga) by Barthélemy Hauréau. Paris, 1895.

Mathematicus. Edited and translated by Deirdre M. Stone. *Archives d'histoire doctrinale et littéraire du moyen âge* 63 (1996): 209–83.

Mathematicus. Edited and translated by Jan Prelog, Manfred Heim, and Michael Kiesslich. St. Ottilien: EOS, 1993.

Mathematicus. Edited and translated by Teresa d'Alessandro. In *Tragedie latine del XII e XIII secolo,* edited by Ferruccio Bertini, 9–159. Genoa: Dipartimento di Archeologia, Filologia Classica e loro Tradizioni, 1994.

Poems Attributed to Bernardus Silvestris

De gemellis. Edited by Charles Fierville, *Notices et extraits des manuscrits de la Bibliothèque Nationale et autres bibliothèques* 31.1 (1884) : 126–29.

De gemellis. Edited by Jakob Werner, *Beiträge zur Kunde der lateinischen Literatur des Mittelalters,* 55–58. Arrau: Sauerländer, 1905.

De gemellis. Edited by Robert R. Edwards, "Poetic Invention and the Medieval *Causae,*" *Mediaeval Studies* 55 (1993): 196–209.

De paupere ingrato. Edited by André Vernet. "Poésies latines des XIIe et XIIIe siècles." In *Melanges Felix Grat,* vol. 2, 256–57. Paris: En dépot chez Mme Pecquer-Grat, 1949.

De paupere ingrato. Edited by Robert R. Edwards, "Poetic Invention and the Medieval *Causae,*" *Mediaeval Studies* 55 (1993),:210–16.

Commentaries Attributed to Bernardus Silvestris

Commentario a Marziano Capella attribuito a Bernardo Silvestre, in *Scoto Eriugena, Remigio di Auxerre, Bernardo Silvestre e Anonimi. Tutti i commenti a Marziano Capella,* edited by Ilaria Ramelli, 1759–2077. Milan: Bompiani Il Pensiero Occidentale, 2006.

The Commentary on Martianus Capella's "De Nuptiis Philologiae et Mercurii" Attributed to Bernardus Silvestris. Edited by Haijo Jan Westra. Studies and Texts 80. Toronto: Pontifical Institute of Mediaeval Studies, 1986.

Commentary on the First Six Books of Virgil's Aeneid by Bernardus Silvestris. Translated by Earl G. Schreiber and Thomas E. Maresca. Lincoln: University of Nebraska Press, 1979.

Commentum quod dicitur Bernardi Silvestris super sex libros Eneidos Virgilii.

Edited by Julian W. and Elizabeth F. Jones. Lincoln: University of Nebraska Press, 1977.

Commentum super sex libros Eneidos Virgilii. Edited by Wilhelm Riedel. Greifswald: Abel, 1924.

Primary Sources

Abelard, Peter. *Opera Theologica.* 2 vols. Corpus Christianorum: Continuatio Mediaevalis 12, 13. Turnhout: Brepols, 1969, 1987.

Abu Ma'shar. *Liber Introductorii Maioris ad Scientiam Judiciorum Astrorum.* Edited by Richard Lemay. 9 vols. Naples: Istituto Universitario Orientale, 1996. Includes the Arabic text of the *Introductorium* (vols. 1–3), and the translations of John of Seville (vols. 4–6) and Hermann of Carinthia (vols. 7–8).

Adelard of Bath. *Conversations with His Nephew: On the Same and the Different, Questions on Natural Science,* and *On Birds.* Edited by Charles Burnett. Cambridge Medieval Classics 9. Cambridge: Cambridge University Press, 1998.

Alan of Lille. *Literary Works.* Edited and translated by Winthrop Wetherbee. Dumbarton Oaks Medieval Library 22. Cambridge, Mass.: Harvard University Press, 2013.

Albertus Magnus. *Speculum Astronomiae.* Edited by Paola Zambelli. In Zambelli, *The* Speculum Astronomiae *and Its Enigma. Astrology, Theology and Science in Albertus Magnus and His Contemporaries,* 203–306. Boston Studies in the Philosophy of Science 135. Dordrecht: Kluwer Academic Publishers, 1992.

Alfanus of Salerno. *See* Nemesius of Emesa.

Apuleius. *De philosophia libri.* Edited by Paul Thomas. Leipzig: Teubner, 1908.

Asclepius. In *Corpus Hermeticum,* edited by A. D. Nock, translated by A.-J. Festugière, 2:259–355. Paris: Belles Lettres, 1960.

Asclepius. In *Hermetica,* edited and translated by Walter Scott. Text and translation, 1:287–377; Commentary, 3:1–300. Oxford: Clarendon Press, 1924, 1926.

Bernard of Bologna. *Summa dictaminum.* Edited by Mirella Brini Savorelli,

"Il 'Dictamen' di Bernardo Silvestre," *Rivista critica di storia della filosofia* 20 (1965): 182–230.

Calcidius. *Commentaire au* Timée *de Platon.* Edited and translated by Béatrice Bakhouche, with Luc Brisson. 2 vols. Histoire des Doctrines de l'Antiquité Classique 42. Paris: J. Vrin, 2011.

——. *Timaeus a Calcidio translatus commentarioque instructus.* Edited by J. H. Waszink. Plato Latinus 4. London: Brill, 1962.

Constantinus Africanus. *L'Arte universale della medicina (Pantegni, Parte I - Libro I).* Edited and translated by Marco T. Malato and Umberto de Martini. Rome: Istituto di Storia della Medicina dell'Università di Roma, 1961.

Declamationes XIX maiores Quintiliano falso ascriptae. Edited by Lennart Haakanson. Stuttgart: Teubner, 1982. (*Declamatio* 4, 60–84; *Declamatio* 8, 153–69.)

Experimentarius. Edited by Mirella Brini Savorelli, "Un manuale di geomanzia presentato da Bernardo Silvestre da Tours: l'*Experimentarius,*" *Rivista critica di storia della filosofia* 14 (1959): 283–342.

Firmicus Maternus. *Mathesis.* Edited by W. Kroll, F. Skutsch, and K. Ziegler. 2 vols. Leipzig: Teubner, 1968.

Geoffrey of Vinsauf. *Poetria nova.* Edited by Ernest Gallo, *The* Poetria Nova *and Its Sources in Early Rhetorical Doctrine,* 14–129. The Hague, Paris: Mouton, 1971.

Gervase of Melkley. *Ars poetica.* Edited by Hans Jürgen Gräbener. Münster: Aschendorff, 1965.

Gervase of Tilbury. *Otia Imperialia.* Edited and translated by S. E. Banks and J. W. Binns. Oxford: Clarendon Press, 2002.

Godfrey of St. Victor. *Fons Philosophiae.* Analecta Medievalia Namurcensia 8. Namur: Editions Godenne, 1956.

Henri d'Andeli. *The Battle of the Seven Arts.* Edited and translated by L. J. Paetow. Memoirs of the University of California 1.1. Berkeley: University of California Press, 1914.

Hermann of Carinthia. *De Essentiis.* Edited by Charles Burnett. Studien und Texte zur Geistesgeschichte des Mittelalters 15. Leiden: Brill, 1982.

Hermetis Trismegisti de vi rerum principiis. Edited by Paolo Lucentini and

Mark D. Delp. Corpus Christianorum: Continuatio Mediaevalis 142. Turnhout: Brepols, 2006.

Honorius Augustodunensis. *Clavis Physicae.* Edited by Paolo Lucentini. Temi e Testi 21. Rome: Storia e Letteratura, 1974.

Johannes Scotus Eriugena. *Annotationes in Marcianum.* Edited by Cora E. Lutz. Cambridge, Mass.: Medieval Academy of America, 1939.

———. *Annotationes in Marcianum.* In *Scoto Eriugena, Remigio di Auxerre, Bernardo Silvestre e Anonimi. Tutti i commenti a Marziano Capella,* edited by Ilaria Ramelli, 93–580. Milan: Bompiani Il Pensiero Occidentale, 2006.

———. *Periphyseon.* Edited by Edouard Jeauneau. Corpus Christianorum: Continuatio Mediaevalis 161–64. Turnhout: Brepols, 1996–. Books 1–4 only.

John of Salisbury. *Metalogicon.* Edited by C. C. J. Webb. Oxford: Clarendon Press, 1929.

———. *Polycraticus.* Edited by C. C. J. Webb. 2 vols. Oxford: Clarendon Press, 1909.

Martianus Capella. *De nuptiis Philologiae et Mercurii.* Edited by James Willis. Leipzig: Teubner, 1983.

———. *De nuptiis Philologiae et Mercurii, Libri I–II.* Edited by Lucio Cristante, translated by Luciano Lenaz. Bibliotheca Weidmanniana 15. Hildesheim: Weidmann, 2011.

Matthew of Vendôme. *Opera.* Edited by Franco Munari. 3 vols. Rome: Storia e Letteratura, 1977–88.

Nemesius of Emesa. *Premnon physicon,* translated into Latin by Alfanus of Salerno. Edited by Karl Burkhard. Leipzig: Teubner, 1917.

Odo of Meung ("Macer Floridus"). *De viribus herbarum.* Edited by Ludwig Choulant. Leipzig, 1832. Reprinted with introduction, notes, and German translation by Johannes Gottfried Mayer and Konrad Goehl. *Höhepunkte der Klostermedizin: Der "Macer floridus" und das Herbarium des Vitus Auslasser.* Leipzig: Reprint, Verlag, 2001.

Peter of Blois. *Carmina.* Edited by Carsten Wollin. Corpus Christianorum: Continuatio Mediaevalis 128. Turnhout: Brepols, 1998.

Plato. *Timaeus.* Translated by Francis M. Cornford in Plato's *Cosmology.* New York: Liberal Arts Press, 1957.

Richard de Fournival, *Biblionomia*. Edited by H. J. de Vleeschauwer. *La Biblionomia de Richard de Founival du Manuscrit 636 de la Bibliothèque de la Sorbonne. Texte en facsimilé avec la transcription de Léopold Delisle.* Mousaion 62. Pretoria, 1965.

Scriptores rerum mythicarum Latini tres Rome nuper reperti (Vatican Mythographers). Edited by Georg Heinrich Bode. Celle, 1834.

Thierry of Chartres. *Commentaries on Boethius by Thierry of Chartres and His School.* Edited by Nicholas Häring. Toronto: Pontifical Institute of Mediaeval Studies, 1971.

——. *The Latin Rhetorical Commentaries by Thierry of Chartres.* Edited by Karin M. Fredborg. Studies and Texts 84. Toronto: Pontifical Institute of Mediaeval Studies, 1988.

——. *Prologus in Heptateuchon.* Edited by Edouard Jeauneau. *Mediaeval Studies* 16 (1954): 171–75.

William of Conches. *Dragmaticon.* Edited by Italo Ronca. Corpus Christianorum: Continuatio Mediaevalis 152. Turnhout: Brepols, 1997.

——. *Glosae super Boetium.* Edited by Lodi Nauta. Corpus Christianorum: Continuatio Mediaevalis 158. Turnhout: Brepols, 1999.

——. *Glosae super Platonem.* Edited by Edouard Jeauneau. Corpus Christianorum: Continuatio Mediaevalis 203. Turnhout: Brepols, 2006.

——. *Philosophia.* Edited by Gregor Maurach. Pretoria: University of South Africa, 1980.

William of St. Thierry. *De erroribus Guillelmi de Conchis.* PL 180.333A–340D.

Secondary Sources

Asper, Marcus. "*Silva Parens.* Zur allegorischen Technik des Bernardus Silvestris." In *FABRICA: Studien zur antiken Literatur und ihrer Rezeption,* edited by Thoms Baier and Frank Schimann, 129–47. Beiträge zur Altertumskunde 90. Stuttgart: 1997.

Balint, Bridget K. *Ordering Chaos: The Self and the Cosmos in Twelfth-Century Latin Prosimetrum.* Leiden: Brill, 2009.

Bertini, Ferruccio. "Un nuovo manoscritto del *Mathematicus* di Bernardo Silvestre." *Journal of Medieval Latin* 17 (2007): 174–88.

——. "Le tragedie latine del XII secolo." In *Mito e realtà del potere nel teatro: dall'Antichità classica al Rinascimento,* edited by Maria Chiabò and

Federico Doglio, 157–74. Rome: Centro Studi sul Teatro Medioevale e Rinascimentale, 1987.

Bezner, Frank. *Vela Veritatis: Hermeneutik, Wissen und Sprache in der Intellectual History des 12. Jahrhunderts.* Studien und Texte zur Geistgeschichte des Mittelalters 85. Leiden: Brill, 2005.

Bourgain, Pascale. "La conception de la poésie chez les Chartrains." In *Aristote, l'Ecole de Chartres et la Cathédrale,* edited by Monique Cazeaux, 165–79. Chartres: Association des Amis du Centre Médiéval Européen de Chartres, 1997.

——. "Le tournant littéraire du milieu du xiie siècle." In *Le XIIe Siècle. Mutations et renouveau en France dans la première moitié du xiie siècle,* edited by Françoise Gasparri, 303–23. Cahiers du Léopard d'Or 3. Paris: Le Léopard d'Or, 1994.

Brisson, Luc. "Le discours comme univers, et l'univers comme discours." In Luc Brisson, *Lectures de Platon,* 209–18. Paris: J. Vrin, 2000.

——. *Plato the Myth Maker.* Translated by Gerald Naddaf. Chicago: University of Chicago Press, 1998.

Burkert, Walter. *Greek Religion.* Cambridge, Mass.: Harvard University Press, 1985.

Burnett, Charles. "The Contents and Affiliation of the Scientific Manuscripts Written at or Brought to Chartres in the Time of John of Salisbury." In *The World of John of Salisbury,* edited by Michael Wilks. Oxford: Blackwell, 1984.

——. "Scientific Speculations." In *A History of Twelfth-Century Western Philosophy,* edited by Peter Dronke, 151–76. Cambridge: Cambridge University Press, 1988.

——. "What is the *Experimentarius* of Bernardus Silvestris? A Preliminary Survey of the Material." *Archives d'histoire doctrinale et littéraire du moyen âge* 44 (1977): 79–125.

Camargo, Martin. "The *Libellus de arte dictandi rhetorice* Attributed to Peter of Blois." *Speculum* (1984): 16–41.

——. *Medieval Rhetorics of Prose Composition: Five English* Artes Dictandi *and Their Tradition.* Binghamton, N.Y.: Medieval and Renaissance Texts and Studies, 1995.

——. "A Twelfth-Century Treatise on 'Dictamen' and Metaphor." *Traditio* 47 (1992): 161–213.

Chenu, M.-D. "Involucrum: le mythe selon les théologiens médiévaux." *Archives d'histoire doctrinale et littéraire du moyen âge* 30 (1955): 75–79.

———. *La théologie au douzième siècle.* Études de Philosophie Médiévale 45. Paris: J. Vrin, 1957.

Copeland, Rita. "Thierry of Chartres and the Causes of Rhetoric: From the *Heptateuchon* to Teaching the *Ars rhetorica.*" In *The Classics in the Medieval and Renaissance Classroom: The Role of Ancient Texts in the Arts Curriculum as Revealed by Surviving Manuscripts and Early Printed Books,* edited by Juanita Feros Ruys, John O. Ward, and Melanie Heyworth, 81–102. Turnhout: Brepols, 2013.

Courcelle, Pierre. *La Consolation de Philosophie dans la tradition littéraire: Antécédents et Posterité de Boèce.* Paris: Études Augustiniennes, 1967.

———. "Tradition platonicienne et traditions chrétiennes du corps-prison." *Revue des études latines* 43 (1965): 406–43.

Curtius, Ernst Robert. *European Literature and the Latin Middle Ages.* New York: Pantheon, 1953.

Daems, Willem F. *Nomina simplicium medicinarum ex synonymariis Medii Aevi collecta. Semantische Unterschungen zum Fachwortschatz hoch- und spätmittelalterlicher Drogenkunde.* Studies in Ancient Medicine 6. Leiden: Brill, 1993.

Dronke, Peter. "L'amor che move il sole el'altre stelle." *Studi medievali,* ser. 3, 6 (1965): 389–422.

———. "Bernard Silvestris, Natura and Personification." *Journal of the Warburg and Courtauld Institutes* 43 (1980): 53–73.

———. "Bernardo Silvestre." In *Enciclopedia Virgiliana,* 1:497–500. Rome: Istituto della Enciclopedia Italiana, 1984.

———. *Fabula. Explorations into the Uses of Myth in Medieval Platonism.* Mittellateinische Studien und Texte 9. Leiden: Brill, 1974.

———. *"Integumenta virgilii."* In *Lectures médiévales de Virgile,* 313–29. Collection de l'École Française de Rome 80. Rome: École française de Rome, 1985.

———. "New Approaches to the School of Chartres." *Anuario de estudios medievales* 6 (1969): 117–40.

———. *The Spell of Calcidius. Platonic Concepts and Images in the Medieval West.* SISMEL, Millenio Medievale 74. Florence: Edizioni del Galluzzo, 2008.

———. "Thierry of Chartres." In *A History of Twelfth-Century Western Philosophy,* edited by Peter Dronke, 358–85. Cambridge: Cambridge University Press, 1988.

———. *Verse with Prose from Petronius to Dante: The Art and Scope of the Mixed Form.* Cambridge, Mass.: Harvard University Press, 1994.

Economou, George. *The Goddess Natura in Medieval Literature.* Cambridge, Mass.: Harvard University Press, 1972.

Edwards, Robert R. "Poetic Invention and the Medieval *Causae.*" *Mediaeval Studies* 55 (1993): 183–218.

Elford, Dorothy. "William of Conches." In *A History of Twelfth-Century Western Philosophy,* edited by Peter Dronke, 308–27. Cambridge: Cambridge University Press, 1988.

Ferruolo, Stephen C. *The Origins of the University: The Schools of Paris and Their Critics, 1100–1215.* Stanford: Stanford University Press, 1985.

Finckh, Ruth. *Minor Mundus Homo: Studien zur Mikrokosmos-Idee in der mittelalterlichen Literatur.* Palaestra 306. Göttingen: Vandenhoeck & Ruprecht, 1999.

Gersh, Stephen. *Concord in Discourse: Harmonics and Semiotics in Late Classical and Early Medieval Platonism.* Approaches to Semiotics 125. Berlin: Mouton de Gruyter, 1996.

———. *Middle Platonism and Neoplatonism: The Latin Tradition.* 2 vols. Notre Dame: University of Notre Dame Press, 1986.

———. "Platonism—Neoplatonism—Aristotelianism. Thierry of Chartres' Metaphysical System and Its Sources." In *Renaissance and Renewal in the Twelfth Century,* edited by Robert L. Benson and Giles Constable with Carol D. Lanham, 512–34. Cambridge, Mass.: Harvard University Press, 1982.

———. "(Pseudo-?) Bernard Silvestris and the Revival of Neoplatonic Virgilian Exegesis." In Stephen Gersh, *Reading Plato, Tracing Plato: From Ancient Commentary to Medieval Reception,* XVII.573–93. Variorum Collected Studies Series. Aldershot: Ashgate, 2005.

Giacone, Roberto. "Masters, Books and Library at Chartres According to the Cartularies of Notre Dame and Saint-Père." *Vivarium* 12 (1974): 30–51.

Gilson, Etienne. "La cosmogonie de Bernardus Silvestris." *Archives d'histoire doctrinale et littéraire du moyen âge* 3 (1928): 5–24.

———. "Le platonisme de Bernard de Chartres." *Revue néoscolastique* 25 (1923): 5–19.

Godman, Peter. "Ambiguity in the *Mathematicus* of Bernardus Silvestris." *Studi medievali,* ser. 3, 31 (1990): 583–648.

———. "*OPUS CONSUMMATUM OMNIUM ARTIUM . . . IMAGO:* From Bernard of Chartres to John of Hauvilla." *Zeitschrift für deutsches Altertum und deutsche Literatur* 124 (1995): 26–71.

———. "The Search for Urania. Cosmological Myth in Bernardus Silvestris and Pontano." In *Innovation und Originalität,* edited by Walter Haug and Burghart Wachinger, 70–97. Tübingen: Max Niemeyer, 1997.

———. *The Silent Masters. Latin Literature and Its Censors in the High Middle Ages.* Princeton: Princeton University Press, 2000.

Gregory, Tullio. "Abélard et Platon." In *Peter Abelard,* edited by E. M. Buytaert. The Hague: Leuven University Press, 1974.

———. *Anima mundi: la filosofia di Guglielmo di Conches e la scuola di Chartres.* Florence: G. C. Sansoni, 1955.

———. "Cosmologia biblica a cosmologie cristiane." In Tullio Gregory, *Speculum naturale. Percorsi del pensiero medievale,* 197–221. Storia e Letteratura 235. Rome: Edizioni di Storia e Letteratura, 2007.

———. *Platonismo medievale: studi e ricerche.* Istituto storico italiano per il Medio Evo: Studi storici, fasc. 26–27. Rome: nella sede dell'Istituto, 1958.

Hauréau, Barthélemy. "Maître Bernard." *Bibliothèque de l'École des chartes* 54 (1893), 792–94.

Haye, Thomas. *Päpste und Poeten. Die mittelalterliche Kurie als Objekt und Förderer panegyrischer Dichtung.* Berlin: Walter de Gruyter, 2009.

Huber, Christoph. *Die Aufnahme und Verarbeitung des Alanus ab Insulis in mittelhochdeutschen Dichtungen: Untersuchungen zu Thomasin von Zerklaere, Gottfried von Strassburg, Frauenlob, Heinrich von Neustadt, Heinrich von St. Gallen, Heinrich von Mügeln und Johannes von Tepl.* Munich: Artemis, 1988.

Hunt, Tony. *Plant Names of Medieval England.* Woodbridge: D. S. Brewer, 1989.

Jaeger, C. Stephen. *Medieval Humanism in Gottfried von Strassburg's Tristan und Isolde.* Heidelberg: Carl Winter, 1977.

Janson, Tore. *Prose Rhythm in Medieval Latin from the 9th to the 13th Century.* Studia Latina Stockholmensia 20. Stockholm: Almquist and Wiksell International, 1975.

Jeauneau, Edouard. "Macrobe, source du platonisme chartrain." *Studi medievali,* ser. 3, 1 (1960): 3–24.

———. "Notes sur l'École de Chartres." *Studi medievali,* ser. 3, 5 (1964): 821–65.

———. "L'usage de la notion *d'integumentum* à travers les gloses de Guillaume de Conches." *Archives d'histoire doctrinale et littéraire du moyen âge* 32 (1957): 35–100.

Jolivet, Jean. "Les principes féminins selon la 'Cosmographie' de Bernard Silvestre." In Jean Jolivet, *Philosophie médiévale arabe et latine,* 269–78. Études de Philosophie Médiévale 73. Paris: J. Vrin, 1995.

———. "L'univers de Bernard Silvestre." In *Aristote, l'Ecole de Chartres et la Cathédrale,* edited by Monique Cazeaux, 65–72. Chartres: Association des Amis du Centre Médiéval Européen de Chartres, 1997.

Kauntze, Mark. *Authority and Imitation: A Study of the* Cosmographia *of Bernard Silvestris.* Mittellateinische Studien und Texte 47. Leiden: Brill, 2014.

———. "The Creation Grove in the *Cosmographia* of Bernard Silvestris." *Medium Aevum* 78 (2009): 16–34.

Kelly, Douglas. *The Arts of Poetry and Prose.* Typologie des Sources du Moyen Âge Occidental 59. Turnhout: Brepols, 1991.

Klaes, Monica. "Die 'Summa' des Magister Bernardus: Zu Überlieferung und Textgeschichte einer zentralen Ars dictandi des 12. Jahrhunderts." *Frühmittelalterliche Studien* 24 (1990): 198-234.

Köhn, Rolf. "Schulbildung und Trivium im lateinischen Hochmittelalter und ihr möglicher praktischer Nutzen." In *Schulen und Studium im sozialen Wandel des hohen und späten Mittelalters,* edited by Johannes Fried, 203–84. Vorträge und Forschungen 30. Sigmaringen: Jan Thorbecke Verlag, 1986.

Krayer, Rudolf. *Frauenlob und die Natur-allegorese; motivgeschichtliche Untersuchungen. Ein Beitrag zur Geschichte des antiken Traditionsgutes.* Heidelberg: Carl Winter, 1960.

Lapidge, Michael. "The Stoic Inheritance." In *A History of Twelfth-Century*

Western Philosophy, edited by Peter Dronke, 81–112. Cambridge: Cambridge University Press, 1988.

Lemay, Richard. *Abu Ma'shar and Latin Aristotelianism in the Twelfth Century. The Recovery Of Aristotle's Natural Philosophy through Arabic Astrology.* American University of Beirut. Publiction of the Faculty of Arts and Sciences. Oriental Series 38. Beirut: Catholic Press, 1962.

Lemoine, Michel. "La durée dans la 'Cosmographie' de Bernard Silvestre." In *Das Sein der Dauer,* edited by Andreas Speer and David Wirmer, 196–210. Miscellanea Medievalia 34. Berlin: Walter de Gruyter, 2008.

Lewis, C. S. *The Allegory of Love: A Study in Medieval Tradition.* Oxford: Oxford University Press, 1936.

Löfstedt, Bengt. "Notizen zur Cosmographia des Bernardus Silvestris." *Bulletin du Cange* 51 (1993): 203–8.

Lomperis, Linda. "From God's Book to the Play of the Text in the *Cosmographia.*" *Medievalia et Humanistica* 16 (1988): 51–71.

Lucentini, Paolo. "L'*Asclepius* ermetico nel secolo XII." In Paolo Lucentini, *Platonismo, Ermetismo, Eresia nel Medioevo,* 71–105. Louvain-la-Neuve: Féderation Internationale des Instituts d'Études Médiévales, 2009.

———. "Il corpo e l'anima nella tradizione ermetica medievale." In Paolo Lucentini, *Platonismo, Ermetismo, Eresia nel Medioevo,* 223–34. Louvain-la-Neuve: Féderation Internationale des Instituts d'Études Médiévales, 2009.

———. "Il problema del male nell'*Asclepius.*" In Paolo Lucentini, *Platonismo, Ermetismo, Eresia nel Medioevo,* 49–69. Louvain-la-Neuve: Féderation Internationale des Instituts d'Études Médiévales, 2009.

Luscombe, David E. "Dialectic and Rhetoric in the Ninth and Twelfth Centuries: Continuity and Change." In *Dialektik und Rhetorik im früheren und hohen Mittelalter,* edited by Johannes Fried, 1–20. Munich: R. Oldenbourg, 1997.

———. *The School of Peter Abelard. The Influence of Abelard's Thought in the Early Scholastic Period.* Cambridge: Cambridge University Press, 1969.

Meier, Christel. "Wendepunkt der Allegorie im Mittelalter: Von der Schrifthermeneutik zur Lebenspraktik." In *Neue Richtungen in der hoch- und spätmittelalterlichen Bibelexegese,* edited by Robert E. Lerner, 39–64.

Schriften des Historischen Kollegs: Kolloquien 32. Munich: R. Oldenbourg, 1996.

Millar, Eric G. *A Thirteenth-Century Bestiary in the Library of Alnwick Castle.* Oxford: Roxburghe Club, 1958.

Newell, John. "Rationalism at the School of Chartres." *Vivarium* 21 (1983): 108–26.

Newman, Barbara. *God and the Goddesses. Vision, Poetry, and Belief in the Middle Ages.* Philadelphia: University of Pennsylvania Press, 2003.

Nitzsche, Jane Chance. *The Genius Figure in Antiquity and the Middle Ages.* New York: Columbia University Press, 1975.

Pabst, Bernhard. "Ideallandschaft und Ursprung der Menschheit. Paradieskonzeptionen und -lokalisierungen des Mittelalters im Wandel." *Frühmittelalterliche Studien* 38 (2004): 17–53.

———. *Prosimetrum. Tradition und Wandel einer Literaturform zwischen Spätantike und Spätmittelalter.* Vol. 1. Ordo 4.1. Weimar: Böhlau, 1994.

Palmer, Nigel F. "Plant Names in the *Cosmographia* of Bernardus Silvestris." *Scientiarum Historia* 20 (1994): 39–56.

Pfeiffer, Jens. *Contemplatio Caeli. Unterschungen zum Motiv der Himmelsbetrachtung in lateinischen texten der Antike und des Mittelalters.* Spolia Berolinensia 21. Hildesheim: Weidmann, 2001.

Piehler, Paul H. T. *The Visionary Landscape: A Study in Medieval Allegory.* London: Edward Arnold, 1971.

Pollman, Leo. *Chrétien de Troyes und der Conte del Graal.* Beihefte zur Zeitschrift für romanische Philologie 110. Tübingen: Max Niemeyer, 1965.

———. *Das Epos in den romanischen Literaturen: Verlust und Wandlungen.* Stuttgart: W. Kohlhammer, 1966.

Poole, Reginald L. "The Masters of the Schools at Paris and Chartres in John of Salisbury's Time." *English Historical Review* 35 (1920): 321–42.

Ratkowitsch, Christine. "Astrologie und Selbstmord im Mathematicus. Zu einem Gedicht aus dem Umkreis des Bernardus Silvestris." *Wiener Studien* 112 (1999): 175–229.

———. *Die Cosmographia des Bernardus Silvestris: Eine Theodizee.* Ordo 6. Weimar: Böhlau, 1995.

———. "Die Gewebe in Claudians Epos De raptu Proserpinae—ein Bindeglied zwischen Antike und Mittelalter." In *Die poetische Ekphrasis von*

Kunstwerken: eine literarische Tradition der Grossdichtung in Antike, Mittelalter und früher Neuzeit, edited by Christine Ratkowitsch, 17–42. Vienna: Österreichische Akademie der Wissenschaften, 2006.

Ricklin, Thomas. "Le coeur, soleil du corps: une redécouverte symbolique du XIIe siècle." *Micrologus* 11 (2003): 123–44.

Silverstein, Theodore. "The Fabulous Cosmogony of Bernardus Silvestris." *Modern Philology* 46 (1948–49): 92.116.

Sivo, Francesca. "La metamorfosi dell'anima: da madri a 'novercae.'" *Micrologus* 17 (2009): 55-128.

Southern, R. W. "Humanism and the School of Chartres." In R. W. Southern, *Medieval Humanism and Other Studies,* 61–85. Oxford: Blackwell, 1970.

———. *Platonism, Scholastic Method, and the School of Chartres.* Reading: Stenton Lecture, 1979.

———. *Scholastic Humanism and the Unification of Europe.* 2 vols. Oxford: Blackwell, 1995, 2001.

Speer, Andreas. "The Discovery of Nature: The Contribution of the Chartrians to Twelfth-Century Attempts to Found a *Scientia Naturalis.*" *Traditio* 51 (1997): 135–51.

———. *Die entdeckte Natur. Untersuchungen zu Begründungsversuchen einer "scientia naturalis" im 12. Jahrhundert.* Studien und Texte zur Geistesgeschichte des Mittelalters 45. Leiden: Brill, 1995.

Steinen, Wolfram von den. "Les sujets d'inspiration chez les poètes latins du XIIe siècle." *Cahiers de civilisation médiévale* 9 (1966): 165–75, 363–83.

Steinmetz, Ralf-henning. *Liebe als universales Prinzip bei Frauenlob: ein volkssprachlicher Weltentwurf in der europäischen Dichtung um 1300.* Tübingen: M. Niemeyer, 1994.

Stock, Brian. *Myth and Science in the Twelfth Century: A Study of Bernard Silvester.* Princeton: Princeton University Press, 1972.

Tilliette, Jean-Yves. *Des mots à la parole: Une lecture de la Poetria nova de Geoffroy de Vinsauf.* Geneva: Droz, 2000.

Vernet, André. "Bernardus Silvestris et sa *Cosmographia.*" *École Nationale des Chartes. Positions des thèses 1937:* 167–74.

———. "Bernardus Silvestris: recherches sur l'auteur et l'oeuvre, suivies d'une édition critique de la *Cosmographia.*" Thesis, École Nationale des Chartes. Paris, 1938.

——. "Une épitaphe inédite de Thierry de Chartres." In *Recueil de Travaux offert à Clovis Brunel,* 2 :660–70. Paris: Société de l'École des Chartes, 1955.

Waddell, Helen. *The Wandering Scholars.* London: Constable, 1927.

Ward, John O. "The Date of the Commentary on Cicero's *De inventione* by Thierry of Chartres and the Cornifician Attack on the Liberal Arts." *Viator* 3 (1972): 219–73.

Wattenbach, Wilhelm. "Beschreibung einer Handschrift mittelalterlicher Gedichte (Berl. Cod. Theol. Oct. 94)." In Wattenbach, *Kleine Abhandlungen zur mittelalterlichen Geschichte,* 431–65. Leipzig: Zentralantiquariat der Deutschen Demokratischen Republik, 1970.

Wetherbee, Winthrop. "Philosophy, Cosmology and the Twelfth-Century Renaissance." In *A History of Twelfth-Century Western Philosophy,* edited by Peter Dronke, 21–53. Cambridge: Cambridge University Press, 1988.

——. *Platonism and Poetry in the Twelfth Century: The Literary Influence of the School of Chartres.* Princeton: Princeton University Press, 1972.

White, Hugh. *Nature, Sex, and Goodness in a Medieval Literary Tradition.* Oxford: Oxford University Press, 2000.

Whitman, Jon. *Allegory: The Dynamics of an Ancient and Medieval Technique.* Cambridge, Mass.: Harvard University Press, 1987.

——. "Twelfth-Century Allegory: Philosophy and Imagination." In *The Cambridge Companion to Allegory,* edited by Rita Copeland and Peter T. Struck, 101–15. Cambridge: Cambridge University Press, 2010.

Whittaker, John, "Plutarch, Platonism and Christianity." In *Neoplatonism and Early Christian Thought: Essays in Honour of A. H. Armstrong,* edited by H. J. Blumenthal and R. A. Markus, 50–63. London: Variorum, 1981.

Winden, J. C. M. van. *Calcidius on Matter: His Doctrine and Sources: A Chapter in the History of Platonism.* 2nd ed. Leiden: Brill, 1965

Witt, Ronald G. "The Arts of Letter-Writing." In *The Cambridge History of Literary Criticism.* Vol. 1. The Middle Ages, edited by Alastair Minnis and Ian Johnson, 68–83. Cambridge: Cambridge University Press, 2005.

Wollin, Carsten. "Das Epitaphium Bernardi Silvestris in der Handschrift Angers B. M. 303." *Sacris Erudiri* 42 (2003): 369–402.

——. "Der 'Floridus Aspectus' D des Petrus Riga: Erstausgabe nach der

Handschrift Douai 825 (Teil I)." *Mittellateinisches Jahrbuch* 43 (2008): 355–91.

Woods, Marjorie Curry. *Classroom Commentaries: Teaching the Poetria Nova across Medieval and Renaissance Europe.* Columbus: Ohio State University Press, 2010.

Woolsey, Robert B. "Bernard Silvester and the Hermetic Asclepius." *Traditio* 6 (1948): 340–44.

Worstbrock, Franz Josef, Monika Klaes, and Jutta Lütten. *Repertorium der Artes Dictandi des Mittelalters.* Vol. 1: Von den Anfängen bis um 1200. Munich: Wilhelm Fink Verlag, 1992.

Zingesser, Eliza. "The Genesis of Poetry: Guillaume de Machaut's *Prologue,* Boethius's *Consolation of Philosophy,* and Chartian Neoplatonism." *Viator* 42 (2011), 143–56.

Ziomkowski, Robert M. *Science, Theology, and Myth in Medieval Creationism: Cosmogony in the Twelfth Century.* PhD diss., Cornell University, 2000.

Index of Names

The spelling of proper names in the manuscripts varies widely. They are listed here in their classical forms. The texts are abbreviated as follows: *Meg.* *(Megacosmus)*, *Micr.* *(Microcosmus)*, *Math.* *(Mathematicus)*, *Gem.* *(De Gemellis)*.